U. C. Library MAY 04 87	DATE DUE		
GAYLORD			PRINTED IN U.S.A.

ACTIVITY AND EXPERIENCE
Sources of English
Informal Education

ACTIVITY AND EXPERIENCE
Sources of English Informal Education

by
Lydia Averell Hurd Smith

with Prefatory Notes by
Theodore R. Sizer and John Blackie

AGATHON PRESS, INC.
NEW YORK

372.942
Sm6la

© 1976 by Lydia Averell Hurd Smith

All rights reserved. No portion of this book may be reproduced, stored in a retrieval system, or transmitted, in any form or by any means, electronic, mechanical, photocopying, recording, or otherwise, except for purposes of brief quotation, without permission of the publisher:

AGATHON PRESS, INC.
150 Fifth Avenue
New York, N.Y. 10011

Library of Congress Cataloging in Publication Data

Smith, Lydia Averell Hurd.
   Activity and experience.

   Bibliography: p.
   1. Education, Elementary – Great Britain
2. Education – Experimental methods. I. Title.
LA633.S62   372.9'41   75-22313
ISBN 0-87586-047-8

Printed in the United States

TABLE OF CONTENTS

Prefatory Notes   *Theodore R. Sizer*   xi
                     John Blackie   xiii
Acknowledgments   xv

PART ONE
Chapter 1. The Search for Sources   3
Chapter 2. The Children and Their Schools   11
   Early Beginnings   12
   Attitudes Towards Children   18
   The Importance of Observation   24
   Standards   32
   The Life of the School   36
Chapter 3. The Teachers and Their Work   60
   The Good Teacher   61
   The Teaching Moment   66
   Freedom and Discipline   67
   Headship   70
   Community Relations   72
   Pre-Service Teacher Training   75
   In-Service Training   80
   HMI's   83
Chapter 4. Three Influential Books   86
   Sir Percy Nunn's *Education: Its Data and First Principles*   86
   A. L. Stone's *Story of a School*   92
   Primary Education   98

Chapter 5. The Journey Home — 107
Basic Attitudes 107
Play 110
The School Schedule 111
Individualization 112
Art and Movement 113
How the Schools Evolved 114
Junior Schools 115
Teachers' Freedom 115
Teaching Method 116
Aiding or Stifling Development 118
The Role of Women 122
America 124
Notes to Part One 127

PART TWO
Chapter 1. One Teacher Reports — 131
Early Influences 131
  Period Ending November 20, 1941
  Observations at the Park School 131
  Penny 144
  Nottingham College of Education
  Notes on Observing and Recording 146
Some Points to Remember About Creative Play 147
Number Experiences in an Infant School 152
The Infant School As It Might Be 156
  The Stimulating Environment 158
  The Free Day in Practice 159
  Greater Teaching Responsibilities 162
Appendix A. Detailed Accounts of Children's Activities 163
Appendix B. Suggested Materials and Equipment to Be
            Used in Infants' Schools 180
Appendix C. Experimental Work in Music 184

Chapter 2. Some Further Documents   **187**
    Yorkshire Art Work — *Ruth Scrivener Mock*   187
    The Importance of Movement in the Development of
    Children at the Primary Stage — *Ruth Foster*   189
    What Active Enquiry Means for the Child — *Nathan Isaacs*   190
Bibliography   **203**
List of Respondents   213

To Marnie, who has made so much possible.

PREFATORY NOTES

Theodore R. Sizer

Optimism is one of the rarest animals in the educational zoo, and it is a delight to find it alive and well and in profusion in this useful new book by Lydia A. H. Smith. When they concern themselves with education, modern Americans seem to rediscover their Calvinism: they all too often think and write about their schools and about children with foreboding. Furthermore, the American response to the recent recognition that our schools were not meeting the many objectives which the society has placed upon them has often, in official circles at least, been to turn to the methods of the industrial assembly line and to design "products" which can be "disseminated." When in doubt, it seems, we approach a problem technologically. We thus look upon our children with concern and despair, and we look upon their education as a programmable "system."

One can only chuckle, then, at envisioning the likely reaction of the stereotypical educational bureaucrat to this assertion: "(children) have in them a creative power which, if wisely encouraged and tolerantly guided, may so remould our best that, as the dark shadows pass, the 'life of the world may move forward into broad, sunny uplands' and become worthier than any we have yet seen." He might easily dismiss that as mere verbal sauce, but the statement that the most important aspect of teacher-training was "the power of love" of children would surely unhinge him.

As those who bother to reflect upon the history of education well know, ideas such as these were translated in the United Kingdom far beyond their romantic rhetoric and into a practice of elementary education which now touches at least a third and perhaps more of British school children. An optimistic Sir Percy Nunn published the first of the foregoing quoted statements in 1920, and protestations of the importance of the love of children appeared not only in the lectures of well-meaning former teachers but even in the staid publications of His Majesty's Stationer. The optimism and humanity of the early English elementary school reformers is their outstanding characteristic and carried them through exceedingly difficult times to achieve those major reforms for which they are now properly acclaimed. How simple it seems! how fundamental: as Dr. Smith says, "children come to value people who value them." When one values a child, one believes in him and acknowledges him with the trusting support which is at the root of love.

Dr. Smith's book draws from the reminiscences of an extraordinary group of men and women — principally women — who in their quiet, informal, but determined way reshaped British primary education. No child for them was a product of original sin nor was he only an annoying little itch who needed discipline. They saw children as instinctively inquisitive and positive people, deserving of careful observation and encouragement. Their premise was that children's instincts were *good,* and the extent to which one let them "get on with it," "beavering away" at what interested them, was enough. The belief was, of course, that what interested the children even at the simplest level would eventually develop into concerns which touched interests beyond them as individuals, to concerns which were the basis of any sensible school curriculum. Dr. Smith, who traveled widely in the United Kingdom taping the reminiscences of this extraordinary generation of educators, has captured in their own words that spark of optimism which is the basic explanation for such success that English primary education has had.

What does such a remarkably unremarkable finding say to those of us who are concerned with the improvement of American schools? It reminds us that we must go back to first principles, to eschew an easy reliance on "systems" and structures, and should remember that the fundamental task of education is humane. And as it is humane, its bedrock is love and trust. Simple notions, these — glowingly shining from Lydia Smith's aging veterans — but terribly threatening to the America whose ethics remain more of Babbitt than any of us like to admit. Somehow, some way, we must grow up ourselves and recognize unashamedly these simple but sound virtues. Dr. Smith's book, through the example of our predecessors across the Atlantic, can well help us in this task.

Theodore R. Sizer
September 1974

John Blackie

To anyone who has been in fairly close touch with both the English and American educational scenes, one of the most remarkable recent changes has been the large and rapid growth of American interest in English primary schools. When, as a young English teacher, I spent a year (1926-27) at an American school, Americans knew about Oxford and Cambridge and the public schools and that was about all. In books on primary education published in the United States up to the late 1960's you would have searched in vain for the name of any English educator or any reference to English practice. The Plowden Council, with whom I visited America in 1966, were received with the generous hospitality and kindness which English visitors have come to regard as inherited American characteristics, but it was clear that their hosts knew little or nothing of the schools on which the visitors were about to report.

Almost overnight the situation changed, the change being triggered off by J. Featherstone's articles in *The New Republic* and, in the past few years, books about English primary schools have appeared in numbers in America, and every summer a stream of teachers desirous of visiting "open" or "integrated" or "informal" primary schools has crossed the Atlantic. This, though gratifying, has been embarrassing in two ways. First, the sheer quantity of visitors has created problems for Local Education Authorities and for the schools, though efforts have always been made to solve them. Second, there have been, in some cases, over-sanguine expectations among the visitors, concerning the quality of what they were going to see, the extent of the change that had taken place and the depth of understanding that could be reached during a brief visit.

Lydia Smith's book will be valuable for American as well as for English readers. The former will obtain from it a balanced and informal view and assessment of what they are likely to find when they come to England, while both will learn much which has never, I think, been available before of how the changes from old to new came about and what it was like to be involved in them.

Dr. Smith has recorded on tape the remarks of 39 people who were active at the early period of informality and experiment. This method, I rather think, is more familiar to Americans than to ourselves. English readers will have to become accustomed to the constant to-and-fro jumps from Dr. Smith's lucid prose, with its refreshing lack of jargon or "educanto," to the imperfections of spoken English when it appears in print. Those who have made the recordings (and I speak with feeling) will have to endure the shock of seeing what they said, in many cases, unedited in all its crudity and repetitiveness. But the advantages of these firsthand, eyewitness accounts greatly outweigh the minor distresses of reading them, which will be, I believe, an interesting and illuminating experience for English and American readers alike.

I am honoured and delighted to have been given this opportunity of welcoming Dr. Smith's book and of commending it to the careful attention of admirers, as well as to denigrators of the kind of education it describes.

John Blackie
March 1974

ACKNOWLEDGMENTS

I was very fortunate to be able to go to England during my sabbatical leave from Simmons College in the fall of 1972, and I have many debts to acknowledge. My family let me go, for which I am ever grateful, and friends gave me good contacts to use when I arrived. For three months I traveled all over the country, and met with great kindness everywhere. People made time to meet with me; they passed me along from one colleague to others; they put up with my persistent questions and my tape recorder with very good grace; they gave me books, manuscripts, pictures, early school records, letters, and even children's work from their teaching days years ago. My debt to them all is more than I can express, and I only hope I will do their kindness justice here.

This study all began in a conversation with Theodore Sizer, an old friend from graduate school days, who was then Dean of the Harvard Graduate School of Education. When in England himself, he had met some quite elderly ladies in the Bristol area, pioneers in child-centered teaching methods, and he was concerned that no one had yet sat down to talk with them and find out what their reflections were now, at the end of their long careers. I immediately shared that concern, and it was the beginning of the plans I laid and carried through during my trip and subsequently in this work. So I must acknowledge my debt to its originator.

Also, I received much encouragement from Edward Yeomans, of the National Association of Independent Schools, and director of the Greater Boston Teachers' Center, an organization which provides both advisory help and workshop experiences for teachers who want to move toward open education. He gave me many contacts in England, and also hours of kind attention as I was talking through my own ideas. To him, also, I owe a special debt.

When I was in England, I not only talked with pioneer teachers. I felt that while I was there I should also visit schools, teacher-training institutions, and anyone else who would talk with me about my project. Accordingly, I have many individual debts of kindness to acknowledge, for I met

xvi / Acknowledgments

many more people than the list of 39 major sources (Respondents) would indicate. I went to Oxfordshire for about a week, and thanks to the helpfulness of John Coe and his associate Bill Asbridge I visited Philip Best's Tower Hill School, the Hill View School, and Leafield School, and I also looked in at the Oxford teachers' center and the Woodstock Museum. To all these places, their staff and helpers, I extend my thanks.

I went to Yorkshire also, and thanks to the kind offices of Sir Alec Clegg and Miss Milne, I went to the Rossington-Holmescarr Junior School and met Mr. Tattersall; I visited the Normantown Common Infants School and Miss Carleton and her staff; Mr. Pritchard and his staff showed me the Garforth-Ninelands J.M.I. school; and I even went to the famous Woolley Hall and met Mr. Marriott for a good talk there. Most fortunate of all, perhaps, was that I was invited to stay with Mr. and Mrs. Peter Teed in Goole, a pleasant change indeed from hotel rooms. To my Yorkshire friends, then, I am most grateful for their kindness to me.

I also went to Leicestershire and had the good fortune to talk at length with Roy Illsley. And I visited Mrs. Irons, the head of the Headlands Infants School, Mr. Ward at Headlands Junior School, and Mr. Garratt and Mr. Dodge at the nearby grammar school. To these helpful people, I must also say my thanks.

While visiting at Homerton College I was taken to a most interesting school, the Grantchester School, and met its head, Miss Taylor, to whom I am grateful for a fine visit. Lastly, within the city of London I was fortunate to visit several schools. Of particular interest was the Cobourg Junior School and its head, Mr. Nind. I also saw the St. John Fisher Primary School and met the head, Miss Southgate; the Wyborne Infants School and Miss Willis; the Kintore Way Nursery School and Miss Furneaux; and the Twyford Comprehensive High School and its head, Mr. Osen. In some of these visits, I had the guidance and friendly help of Mr. Charles Thurgood, whose kindness was a special treat.

I had not much time to visit independent schools, especially since my interest was in the state schools, the mainstream of English education. However, I did spend some time with Mr. Meyer, the founder and retired head of Millfield School, thanks to the good offices of Mr. Gerstenberg; I met Mrs. Archer at the King Alfred School and also talked with the former head, Mr. Montgomery; and I visited briefly at the St. Christopher School, thanks to Mr. Harris. All these visits, though brief, I found most helpful.

Acknowledgments / xvii

I was fortunate enough to find time to visit a total of nine teacher-training institutions, and at two in particular I was able to gain some view of their programs — namely, the Froebel Institute at Roehampton and Goldsmiths' College. I also visited the Rachel McMillan College and met Miss Puddephat there; I went to Homerton College in Cambridge and talked with Miss Davies and others of that very interesting staff; Miss Garvie at Furzedown College was especially gracious to me, as were Mrs. Hill and others on the staff there; I met Mr. Zoeftig and Mrs. Brown at Battersea College for a good talk; at Stockwell College I met and taped Mrs. Lorna Ridgway; at the Institute of Education, University of London, I met Mrs. Spencer, Mr. McLeod, and Miss Roberts at different times; at Dartington Hall I was given a grand tour by Miss Foster of that very beautiful place and also a chance to see an extraordinary film of a movement lesson done by Bessie Bullogh; at Goldsmiths' College I talked at some length with Mr. Marsh, Mr. Skinner, Miss Duncan, and Miss Steiner; and finally, at Roehampton I spent two days talking with Miss Rapaport, Miss Tamburrini, Miss Johnson, and once, to my great pleasure, with a group of students. To all these very kind people I have a sizable debt indeed.

Finally, I also talked with four people who are involved in the history of education, so as to get my bearings and talk over my ideas; to these I owe thanks for their time and concern: Prof. Kogan, Prof. McCann, Prof. Humphreys, and Prof. Niblett.

Personal gratitude goes most sincerely to Lady Plowden, in whose daughter's house I was lucky enough to find a room; to Penelope Plowden Roper for taking me in as a boarder almost sight unseen; to my housemate, Hermano Alves, for hours of friendly talk; and to my neighbors, Charles and Gwen Thurgood, for their kindly attentions. With these people, I found a true home away from home, and I am extremely grateful to them all.

I should also mention the many fascinating hours I spent digging out source material in the library of the Department of Education and Science. There, Miss Jepson and her staff were more than kind, always finding time to look things up for me when I met a dead end.

The very greatest debt is, of course, to my husband. He coped nobly with our four children during my absence, he has encouraged my work at every step, and he gave the entire manuscript his careful and very skilled editorial attention in its final stages. Without Alan's help, I surely could not have managed at all.

L. A. H. S.

PART ONE

TWO KEY QUOTATIONS

The curriculum is to be thought of in terms of activity and experience rather than of knowledge to be acquired and facts to be stored. Its aims should be to develop in a child the fundamental interests of civilised life so far as these powers and interests lie within the compass of childhood, to encourage him to attain gradually to that control and orderly management of his energies, impulses, and emotions, which is the essence of moral and intellectual discipline, and to help him to discover the idea of duty and to ensue it, and to open out his imagination and his sympathies in such a way that he may be prepared to understand and to follow in later years the highest examples of excellence in life and conduct.

Report of the Consultative Committee on the Primary School (The Hadow Report), 1931

The only uniformity of practice that the Board of Education desire to see in the teaching of Public Elementary Schools is that each teacher shall think for himself, and work out for himself such methods of teaching as may use his powers to the best advantage and be best suited to the particular needs and conditions of the school. Uniformity in details of practice (except in the mere routine of school management) is not desirable even if it were attainable. But freedom implies a corresponding responsibility in its use.

From the Prefatory Note, *Handbook of Suggestions for the Consideration of Teachers,* 1918

Chapter 1
THE SEARCH FOR SOURCES

I

Educational philosophy which centers on the growing child has a long history, and by now it has branched out to include the study of child development in all its aspects. One thinks of the humane essays of Montaigne, the influential writings of Rousseau, the works of Pestalozzi and Froebel, and more recently the ideas of John Dewey. In the psychology of human development, the works of Freud and of Piaget are critical.

Yet, although child-centered theory is well developed, actual instances of schools which make use of it are remarkably few. Tolstoy's attempt to teach peasant children at Yasnaya Polyana is well known, as is Pestalozzi's school at Yverdun. But until the so-called progressive era, they were isolated examples. Then, between the turn of this century and the advent of World War II, in England and in the United States, there appeared schools and teachers who placed the child and his all-around development at the center of their work. They put into day-to-day practice what the theorists had long been advocating. In England, these schools attracted official attention to such an extent that their practices were sanctioned as early as 1905 in official publications.[1] The two quotations which open this book date from 1918 and 1931, and both are from government publications: they are key passages in the development of English child-centered schools during this century.

Many Americans have by now made their pilgrimage to England to see these remarkable schools, which now comprise about a third of all primary schools maintained with public funds[2] and which were first reported widely in the United States by Joseph Featherstone in 1968.[3] Books and articles have flowed from the press, and descriptions of the children, the classrooms, the teachers, and the high quality of the work done are now commonly available.[4] The origins and growth of these schools have been less well reported, but it is clear that they are the contemporary result of a development which goes back many years in English educational history.

In the fall and early winter of 1972 I too made my pilgrimage, looking for some of the sources of the ideas and practices which made such schools possible. I found that there are people in England, some now retired, who had been leaders in the development of informal schools or classes in past years, who had held positions of major responsibility for children and education broadly, and who were, therefore, sources of information which would be extremely useful. My interest was to visit them and to listen as carefully and openly as I could. Their words, from letters and taped interviews, form the most important part of this book, which is chiefly a distillation of their thinking. Often they were themselves pioneers, though none would have said so at the time; some had begun their own work in the early years of this century, and some had had older head teachers[5] who taught similarly even earlier. I heard about their careers as teachers and heads, as HMI's and local advisers, as lecturers and tutors. They told me of books, lectures, and sources that had meant much to them and of acquaintances and colleagues whose ideas had broadened their perspectives on their own work. Taken all together, their oral testimony[6] to the long development in which they played so vital a part forms an important chapter in educational history.

From their words a complex picture emerged, part of which it is my hope to describe in what follows. But one point of caution must be borne in mind: I met almost exclusively with those people who could lead me to the sources of informal schools in England. I did not try to get a view of English education as a whole, nor would that have been possible in the three months I was there. The material which this book reports comes from that special group of people within the state system and the wider educational world of England who are interested in one particular kind of education for children. Yet they had a rich diversity of experience and reflections, as the quotations in later chapters will show.

I have sorted out the general themes which these people spoke about, and the variations on those themes which make each person's work and contribution unique. I asked no set list of questions, but rather open-ended ones, being curious to know where our discussions would lead, and what topics my interviewees would consider worth bringing up. I hoped they would reflect, each in his or her own way, on the careers they had had. It is not surprising, of course, that they often knew each other, and rather handed me from one to another in a very friendly way. They differed, of course, in the particular stress they laid on the various aspects of the work they did and of that of others. Just as children differ from one another, so do adults; the differences in emphasis reflected the different interests and gifts of those who held them. For one the TV camera, for another the one-teacher school, for a third the travels of an HMI, for a fourth the intellectual challenge of theory. Each contributed in his or her own way.

This book is not intended to be a complete history of English informal schools, however, but only a beginning. Much work needs to be done, both in this country and in England, to explore the sources of a much-neglected part of educational history, to study the successes and failures of child-centered schools, and to learn from them what we can for current practice. Little is known about the effects of such schools on the later lives of children, for instance, and even less is known about the kinds of adults who work well in these classrooms or how to prepare them for their work. This book can be only a start, by looking at some of the sources—namely, the people whose personal careers made such a difference.

II

"At the heart of the educational process lies the child." It is no accident that the Plowden Report opens with these words. The view of the child and the role of the school which it expresses have long animated the best English primary schools, especially those for children under age 7. These ideas emerge: a child's whole growth and development is the school's central concern; he has a natural curiosity and wants to make sense of the world he lives in; his environment should be organized to awaken and respond to that natural desire; he must master his developmental stages in unhurried sequence; the soundest preparation for the future is a rich life in the present; a child learns best and most permanently when he is asking his own questions and pursuing the lines of investigation which are of interest to him; and the teacher's work is to foster children's all-around growth by encouragement and challenge, bringing to bear her own resourcefulness, intuition, and willingness to learn from the children she teaches.

In the best contemporary English schools, the child is not the only one who receives encouragement and help. From everyone in the school, progress is expected and ways are found to make it possible. There is an atmosphere created by the trust and respect with which every person in it is

6 / ACTIVITY AND EXPERIENCE

treated, an atmosphere which provides the supportive climate for learning, and also the expectancy that it will happen. Thus the positive relationships which characterize these schools are the most basic ingredients in their success; experimentation, trial and error, change, and ventures of all kinds are possible, always with the aim of achieving an ever-higher standard of accomplishment.

III

In the United States, the Bureau of Educational Experiments[7] had been set up in 1917 with a commitment to an experimental approach to education and to reporting work going on in the field. Between 1932 and 1940 the celebrated Eight-Year Study[8] was carried on; its five-volume report was published in 1942, on the eve of World War II. These efforts are by now all but forgotten, but they demonstrate that in the period between the wars some exciting progressive work was well underway in schools in this country. Americans have short memories, however, and tend to think that the British have invented "the answer" to effective schooling. The question, then, is not "Why the English and not the Americans?" but rather "Why did Americans lose the momentum which had developed before the the war, and why did the English not lose it?"

Some contemporary observers have felt that World War II itself was the crucial factor in the development of informal classrooms in England, but there is ample evidence to the contrary. There were, in many parts of the country, people who had long been teaching in progressive ways; there was a solid and respected body of published work to encourage such practices; and the government's position had long tended to support them.

The effects of the war were not unimportant, however. The war produced dislocations and emergency conditions in every part of English society, especially the schools. Young people went into the services, leaving jobs of every kind, including teaching. Less experienced hands helped out as needed, often mothers who were untrained in any formal way but who knew something about children. Old, traditional procedures fell away. Materials of every kind were scarce, and scrounging for things became the only way to supply classrooms and make do. Evacuating city children into the country meant that teachers who went with their schools had as their first duty the care and well-being of the children, not simply instruction.

For the first time, too, many teachers saw their children all day long, not just in response to a set class lesson. Adjustments of all kinds had to be made, therefore, and a multitude of old ways and attitudes abandoned. When service men and women returned, some wanted to go into teaching. To train them rapidly, Emergency Training Colleges were set up, frequently staffed by teachers who were familiar with freer ways of working with children. Upon completion of these courses, being more mature than the typical probationer, these men and women often moved ahead more quickly when they began to teach.

Thus the war alone did not produce informal schools, since there were already people in positions of responsibility for children who had been developing their work and ideas for many years. Yet the dislocations which were caused by the war and the readiness for new and better ways of educating increased the momentum which had begun. Fortunately, at that point a body of sound theory and practice was ready for use.

One must pause, however, to say that all this begins to sound as if the whole of England galvanized into one great messianic push toward freer, more child-centered schools. That was by no means the case, and it never has been. Yet by the end of World War II, there were people in respected positions, in county education offices, training colleges, and the Inspectorate, as well as in classrooms, who had had years of solid and successful experience and were not to be dismissed lightly as faddists. Their leadership, together with the disruptions caused by the war and the subsequent wish to make changes in the schools, may have been largely responsible for the continued movement toward informal schools in England. All these factors were absent in the United States.

IV

As an American I had to learn how education in England is organized, since it is quite different from our American system. Some of the differences, I found, account in part for the spread of child-centered practices, since there is considerable delegation of authority and considerable freedom in the use of it.

English public education (in the American sense) is controlled by a Local Education Authority, which is a subcommittee of the larger County Council or Borough Council. The LEA oversees all the schools maintained

8 / ACTIVITY AND EXPERIENCE

wholly or in part at public expense; it employs an executive, the Education Officer, whose task is the overall administration, development, and encouragement of the schools and teachers in his area. In each school there is the head, most often a very experienced teacher whose leadership influences the work of all the other teachers. There is in England the tradition that the head teacher is exactly what the title implies, a leader or teacher-in-chief. Unlike the American principal, the head's work is not primarily administrative, but educational. Within the staff, there may be probationers, or first-year teachers, with whom the head works closely, since he (or more often, she) must approve the final qualification at the end of the year. The role of the head, I heard from many quarters, is really crucial, for he or she is given much freedom in the operation of the school. But, as I also heard often, this freedom means the freedom to have a very good school or a very bad one.

English schools for children aged 5 to 7 are called "infant schools," and date from an early period. Robert Owen's school for infants was founded in 1816, and there has been a long tradition of separate schools for this age group, places where children are expected to play and be happy. The next age group, 7 to 11, go to "junior schools," although since 1944 these two levels have been under the term "primary schools." In some areas, too, there are nursery classes for the under-fives. And all these levels may be combined in a variety of ways: some infant schools have a nursery class attached, and some schools are "JMI's," meaning "junior mixed and infant schools." In both these cases the rather freer methods of the teachers at the lower age level have had a leavening effect on the work at the next level above.

The end of primary education has been, since the 1926 Hadow Report on Adolescence, at the age of 11+. The famous "11+ exam" is much less used now than earlier, but it still persists in part of the country. It is a standard test of reading and achievement in English and arithmetic given to all children whose parents wish them to take it, at the age of eleven or above. On the basis of the score achieved a child may go to grammar school and ultimately to university, or else to a secondary modern school and possibly a technical school thereafter. Great weight has long been attached to the 11+ exam, which determined the future of the children to so great an extent. It has counterparts in France and Germany, where similar tests make it possible for children to go into the lycée or gymnasium, or deny them that opportunity. In England there is currently a plan to bring together all secondary education into a single comprehensive system, somewhat on the American high school model, providing children with opportunities to qualify for a university education at some more advanced stage, instead of at the rather young age of 11.

Teachers in England train at training colleges. Until ten years ago, the maintained (public) colleges offered two-year programs, while those which followed the ideas of Friedrich Froebel were private institutions of three years' duration, providing a longer training. The Froebel colleges were, in fact, leaders in the study of child development, and their students spent a major part of their time observing children and studying them in considerable depth. Consequently, many of the child-centered teachers whom I met said, "Of course, I was Froebel-trained," acknowledging that their training was centered on child development. Today, all training colleges have been expanded to three-year courses, and Froebelians are to be found heading many departments, especially the infant and nursery programs. Following graduation from a training college, a student normally teaches the probationary year, and then receives her final qualification. Later on she may decide to return to a training college or go to one of the Institutes of Education set up by the government and attached to a university, for a diploma course, the equivalent of the American master's degree.

Working with the schools are Her Majesty's Inspectors (HMI's), an independent group of advisers, each of whom reports on the schools in his or her district. Local advisers, too, are used by some authorities to help teachers and heads with their experience and counsel. Teachers' centers, traveling museum displays, and residential conference centers all have developed since World War II, to provide support for the teacher in the classroom.[9]

V

Having learned how the schools of England are organized, I found another problem dogging my footsteps, a result of my being an American. The people whom I visited were, as I have said, chiefly of one educational persuasion, and so when they spoke of "good" schools, they meant those which embodied their ideas about sound ways to educate children. However, there is no similarly accepted terminology (or body of ideas) in this country, and it is difficult to find terms to describe the kind of schooling

10 / ACTIVITY AND EXPERIENCE

I was interested in investigating. Indeed, there are by now so many terms that nearly all one can do is list them by way of information and then use the ones that seem congenial.

My own preference is either the word "informal," since it emphasizes nontraditional, nonformal methods, or else "child-centered," with its stress on the central concern for the whole child. Other terms I use occasionally, like "activity-based," to refer particularly to the work going on in the classroom. Another word that one hears is "open," but in England that is an architectural term, not descriptive of any particular method as in the United States. Then there is "the integrated day," to refer to a schedule which integrates all activities into one long block of time, or "family grouping," which means a classroom with children of various ages working within it. One will also hear "progressive," "the materials-rich environment," "the play way," "infant-school methods," "experimental learning," "environmental studies," and so on. All of these, however and wherever used, have this in common: the initiative for learning comes from the learner, and the work of the teacher is to help him develop interest into knowledge, using all the tools and resources of civilization along the way. The adult point of view is a crucial part of the school environment. There is trust in the child's developing nature and trust in the teacher to use his or her resources wisely. Thus terms vary, but the ideas expressed are fundamentally similar.

Chapter 2
THE CHILDREN AND THEIR SCHOOLS

After many discussions with teachers about children and their schools, I had the clear feeling that they spoke with one voice. In details or in emphasis they differed, but in their devotion to an education based on the child's activity and experience and in their understanding that the initiative for learning comes from the learner, they were as one. Some focused chiefly on the work of Piaget, refining and explicating his insights into the development of children's thinking. Others worked mostly on creative expression for children — play, movement, art, drama, writing — observing children and learning from them as they grew through these activities and then basing further plans on the insights into children's needs and interests which they, the teachers, had gained thereby. Still others spoke chiefly of their concern for children's all-around development — physical, emotional, intellectual, and social. The idea of "the power of love" would be crucial to such people, underlying a supportive yet challenging attitude toward the child, which helps him develop a positive self-image.

Another common denominator should be mentioned: all the people with whom I talked spoke with great emphasis about the primacy of experience with children over theory about them. Most of them had worked with children for years, trying out their own experimental ways of helping them learn and in turn learning from them and refining their own thinking. Often, after long experience of this kind they went to a lecture, attended a course, read a book, or met an understanding person with similar ideas, to find their own ideas articulated and supported. But for them all, the actual, day-to-day, practical work with children was always the basis of whatever came later. Theories may have been welcome when the time came, but that was the result of a period of work preparing the mind to receive them.

The themes around which our discussions tended to center are these. First, that informal ways of teaching children are by no means new but date from many years ago. Second, that what is important is one's attitude toward a child's sound growth and how to bring it about. Third, that the "life" of a school figures prominently — the way in which a whole school is used to educate, everything being planned to meet the needs of the children in it. Fourth, the role of adults, both teachers and heads, is crucial. There were comments about the responsibility for planning, for maintaining standards, and for developing good relations with the community, and about opportunities for further growth in one's teaching. There were clear evidences of community respect for and trust in the professional qualities of teachers and of head teachers in particular. Naturally all these themes blur into one another to some extent, but they serve as organizing points for discussion and quotation.

Early Beginnings

One of the most persistent current myths, as pointed out in Chapter One, is that informal schools in Britain are a recent phenomenon and chiefly a result of the dislocations of World War II. That is far from the case, and the myth does a great disservice to those whose lifework it ignores. Slowly and spasmodically perhaps, the development has been going on a long time. One correspondent likens progress in education to the motion of a worm: the head is far ahead of the tail, which gets there later, but the two are connected along the long body (29).*

It must be remembered that the official position about what schools should be doing and what teachers should be doing in them had for many years been child-centered. The two quotations which open this book are the key statements. The ideas they contain were given official sanction, but they were not, of course, put into practice everywhere or at an even pace. In the 1930's, especially after the publication of the Hadow Report of 1931, there were also some people who wanted to be educationally up-to-date, but who did not understand the principles underlying the practices they were attempting. This problem grew worse and more prevalent in the 1940's:

> ... it was the thing to do. It did become a sort of gospel and everybody more or less thought that we have got to do this thing and we have got to push in stacks of materials. Whatever happens they have

---

*Numbers in parentheses refer to the numbered list of respondents, p. 214.

got to be active and if anybody appeared to be doing nothing, you began to worry a bit. The activity got a bit out of proportion. . . . Folks went for it head first. (22)

Nonetheless, the official attitudes existed and were widely known; they strengthened the hands of those teachers who were trying to work along the new freer lines and of the HMI's who were traveling around inspecting and advising in schools.

During my stay in England, moreover, I heard repeated references to informal schooling in the early years of the century and even before. Some teachers I met had been doing such work themselves, and some referred to the head teachers whom they had had as probationers, whose experience in activity-based teaching would go back before 1900. One has written to me that when she was working in London in the 1920's, she asked a well-known infant-school head how she had been able to devise a system of individual children's work within the framework of centers of interest. She replied that she learnt it as a young teacher herself from her headmistress, somewhere in the 1890's. One now-famous head wrote to her associate about her own experience in 1914 as a first-year teacher:[10]

> When I left college and started my teaching life with a class of sixty five-year-olds, I felt fairly confident and happy, realising I had been well trained in the teaching of reading, writing and number. This was in 1914 — during my first week the head teacher asked me, "How have you been trained to teach reading and number?" After my explanations she answered, "We do not teach it that way here, our methods are quite different."
>
> I was not told what the methods were, I was left to discover for myself my own methods. Our work was based on the children's expression work, following stories, rhymes and poetry, using all materials. Projects based on stories and rhymes were developed, using many materials, especially waste materials of all kinds.
>
> In this free expression of work the children were interested and absorbed in a completely different way from when they worked formally. (30)

Though each teacher would naturally differ in the exact working out of the details of school operation, the central ideas remained remarkably the same:

14 / ACTIVITY AND EXPERIENCE

> What has struck me as I was thinking of my own experiences was that the core of what some of us were thinking about years ago is the core of what is being done now, for the very obvious reason that it was based on children and how they think and how they learn and what they react to; although I would imagine that outside influences, mass media, the extra money they have, and the more they go about, and so on, have changed children's experiences to a certain extent. Basically, they are the same as they were when I began in the twenties, and so whatever words one uses are neither here nor there. I think there have been a lot of smokescreens drawn across this development because people would argue about what was meant by integration, and what was meant by activities, and this kind of nonsense. (38)

This same teacher had a good friend who had earlier been her HMI, and from whom she learned a great deal. That lady's work went back even farther:

> She came to stay with me once, when I was in the Inspectorate in the North Riding, and she had retired. And I remember bringing her breakfast up to her in her bed before going off to work, and I can only imagine that I had heard something by post which had excited me. I came in with her tray and I said this, and she said to me, "Monica, this is the fifties, and what you are talking about now I was doing in 1916." Now, that would be on her own, without any backing, without all these books that have been written since, without other teachers being cajoled into trying. She did it because of her own gumption. (38)

Here is another teacher of a junior school, whose work goes back many years:

> Most of modern progressive education in England began in the late 1920's and early 1930's, . . . to develop a child's potential and to encourage him to think for himself. . . . (37)

She goes on to describe how she used their active interest in woodworking to teach them some history:

> Well, now, when I finished my Froebel training, I taught from 1922 onwards for three years in a boys' preparatory school in London, and it taught me a great deal. It was a very good preparatory school, but an extremely formal one, and I saw these boys interested in all sorts of things in their free time and concentrating on collecting stamps

and all kinds of things in a way that they didn't seem to be able to concentrate in school. I was given, for example, in history "The Normans in Britain." It even seemed to me at that stage rather remote from these boys' interests, but the method was reading around the class from a text book, taking turns reading a paragraph, . . . and then being questioned on it. All that seemed very boring, and I expected it to be rather boring to the boys. I couldn't seem to make it very interesting, but then I got an idea that these boys were taught woodwork but they never made anything as far as I could see. They learned how to plane and to saw and to meet joints, and so on, and I thought again, this seems very boring. But they liked doing woodwork, so I collected lots of materials and I organized them, and we got a book and pictures and maps and made a plan, and the things wouldn't fit into a half an hour, so I spread it over the next two lessons. There was terrible trouble with the headmaster. He came in and said I was teaching these boys nothing except to do woodwork and things of that design. He was going to question them. Well, he was a very nice chap, really, and when it came to it, he came into the classroom and looked about, and we were absolutely occupied, . . . which rather interested him, I think. And he turned to me and said, "I think you had better ask the questions." They really knew quite a lot about the Normans, and they were most enthusiastic about the Normans in Britain. They brought books, and they read for themselves, and he was extremely impressed and said, "Get on with it, Miss Warr, get on with it." (37)

Another area of progress in the 1920's was child art,[11] as witness the experiences of a teacher who was taking art classes at Goldsmiths' College, London, in the evenings and teaching art by day, just prior to 1928:

> Then London knew nothing about what we call child art, but I worked with a marvelous headmaster who let me do what I suppose you'd call wild things. We used to make our own powder-colors from cheap distemper and size, and I used to whitewash sheets of newspapers for the children to paint on. My poor little waifs in Deptford painted pictures before children were allowed to paint pictures. I remember a woman (Marion Richardson) writing to me. . . . She said, "Look, I've seen some of your children's work. Isn't this a marvelous thing what these children can do and nobody believes it." There were little pockets of this happening. (34)

What was going on in London was also going on in the country. In scattered, one-teacher schools, with children ranging very widely in age and ability, teachers with imagination had to try "wild things":

16 / ACTIVITY AND EXPERIENCE

> Well, of course, it began in country schools, in the one-teacher school as a matter of necessity. It developed naturally, as a means of using what you have got, as a means of using the space and the children to the best advantage. (26) (36)
> The fact that there was such a wide age range emphasized the differences between individuals. I had of necessity to break away from class teaching, though I have been trained in a training college of good repute from 1926 to '28 to teach in a formal way. I remember being in one school in which I had a very big class of 10- to 12-year-olds. The headmaster used to love to talk to me about his war experiences. Once he started it was difficult to stop him, and one day he talked about some episode right through playtime and I hadn't been able to make adequate preparation for my next lesson, which was nature study, and I was going to be faced with more than 50 children when the bell rang. So on the spur of the moment, I said to them, "We are going into the field to see how many different kinds of grasses you can find." This collecting, identifying, and mounting of the grasses proved to be one of the most thrilling lessons we had. It was incidents like this that helped me to realise that children who were uninterested in hearing me talk and who were unable to read fluently enough to find out for themselves could be really interested if they were involved in a practical learning situation. So in those early years, the thirties, through trial and error and experimenting in situations, I geared more and more learning to the exploration of the school environment because I found that this was a way through to children of all abilities. (24)

An HMI, now retired, recalls his early work in the 1930's as a young inspector:

> In 1936 there were several of the infant teachers in S—— who were far ahead of their time, and they were quite competent. Nobody was interfering with them, it was too far off. But the infant schools were quite free. I can think now of at least three splendid head teachers who were tremendous personalities and really doing great jobs in their schools. It was very exciting to see this happen. (2)

Another teacher reflects on the influence of good methods in nursery school teaching on the work in infant schools. She had a class of about 58 children, aged five to about nine, in the northeast part of the country:

> At that time not very much was happening beyond formal work. The school was in very, very poor condition. It had a gas tank across the

road and a pickle factory next to it. . . . That particular settlement had a woman in charge of the nursery who was very much in favor of the McMillans' approach and not the Montessori.[12] The children had sand and water, and this was 1926. I remember going to see it and doing some part-time help with them and thinking how it shouldn't stop there. Some of it should go on into the school. I had a head who knew nothing about younger children, and therefore I had every opportunity to really do as I liked. Of course, they were very fumbling beginnings. I heard the McMillans on several occasions. . . . A number of infant schools incorporated the idea of this learning through experience, through play, . . . moving it up from the nursery, continuing it on. (9)

So successful were these methods in infant schools, indeed, that one local county adviser reports that in her area at least, "after the war there was no criticism. The infant battle was won" (22). From then on, one simply referred to "infant methods," and people knew the type of teaching that was meant.

These are only a few of the references I heard to early practices in both city and country schools, north and south, ranging from nursery schools to infants to junior-aged children. The infant schools led the way, however, having a long tradition of freedom and a focus on children's happy growth. The nursery classes, especially those inspired by the McMillans, were few in number by comparison. But it also became clear to me that, contrary to my expectation, this kind of schooling was not limited to infant schools. It existed at the junior level as well, according to the reports of teachers who were working with that age group in the early years. The pressure of the 11+ exam was given as the reason for a good deal of formal work done in preparation for it in junior schools, but in one area at least the results of more free methods outshone those of formal schools:

Some people believe that the 11+ exam could be used to prevent change by those who did not want to change. But one teacher in the County went to extremes in her use of the kind of methods that we are talking about and she promptly secured nearly four times as many places in the 11+ examination as one would have expected from her group. One would have expected 8 from the 32 children in her class and 28 in fact secured admission to the grammar school. (7)

From these and similar reports, then, it does seem clear that schools whose work was based on the activity and experience of the children were experimenting and moving ahead during the first few decades of this century and even earlier. Such work was described by the Hadow Reports of the 1930's, officially approved, and widely encouraged by at least some HMI's. Again, however, one has to recall that this kind of work was happening in "pockets" only, in scattered schools here and there. One correspondent refers to the "diverse and spasmodic" nature of the development of English schools. But the importance of the existence of even a few informal schools is that they did develop and that gradually their teachers gained confidence, met and talked, spread their ideas, and were promoted to headships, to the Inspectorate, to training colleges, or elsewhere. So eventually people of this persuasion were holding major posts around the country, and their ideas had permeated many more schools. The Plowden Report's figure of "about a third" is witness to their effectiveness, and it describes and validates the sound work they had done decades earlier. "In this very conservative country, nothing really grows unless it has a fairly deep root"(29).

Attitudes Towards Children

And what of the child himself, the focus of this long and careful development? What have been the general attitudes held by the teachers in informal classrooms about the children whom they have taught over the years? What potential have the teachers seen in the children?

These questions found eloquent answers among the people with whom I talked. I came away with the clear understanding that child-centered teaching is not a "new method" or a particular curriculum design or any other easily packaged product. It proceeds from a deeply felt set of attitudes toward children. By now, ideas about the growth of children are based firmly on research done on child development. Earlier, however, they were only the result of intuition and observation about how children could be made happy, what would help them concentrate on a chosen task, and how they could be kept working at their best and most satisfying level.

Characteristic of teachers working along these lines is the capacity to be surprised and moved by a child's work. Since the curriculum was based on the interests and needs of the children, anything might happen next. "Children can reveal a quality of looking and seeing that adults so readily lose" (7). I often heard teachers say that they were "simply staggered" at the extraordinarily beautiful or thoughtful work children could produce, quite unexpectedly but clearly in response to the challenge of an environment that met and extended their interests. These teachers trust the children; they trust their curiosity and inventiveness, and they trust their good sense about themselves. They are willing to be led by children and to learn from them; they observe as carefully as possible what a child is saying about himself in the way he works with the materials provided, with the aim of taking him to the next step and the next and the next, to the highest standard he can achieve. They are concerned with the all-around growth of the child — physical, intellectual, social, and emotional — believing that good health in any one area helps all the rest. They are anxious to help children develop a sense of their own powers and a sense of mastery over their environment, which build a self-confident approach to all the tasks which life may offer.

There were many ways of articulating the basic principles or aims toward which all were working:

> You see, I think there are several sorts of main planks. Everybody was valued for what they could do, each one. That's one of the main planks. And one of them, I do think, is the business of believing that the initiative for learning comes from the children. (5)

For another teacher, a "main plank" was the aim "to develop a child's potential, and to encourage him to think for himself" (37). For a third, the key was that good teachers "respected the children's proper dignity" (33). Here is an anecdote which illustrates the self-possession of children who are accustomed to being treated with suitable respect:

> We had a rather officious kind of visitor one day who obviously didn't know very much about children of that [nursery] age, but she was very much impressed by the way in which the children were concentrating on their various activities; and then she looked up in the corner of the room and saw a little boy sitting on a chair with his feet up on another chair and his eyes closed. She went up to him and said, "Come along, little man, don't you think you ought to be working like all the rest of the children?" He slowly opened his eyes and said, "No, I don't. I have done quite a lot of work this morning and now I am rather tired. So before I do any more work I am just going to pretend for a little time that I have been a night watchman."

This was in a very slummy part of London, where his father must have

20 / ACTIVITY AND EXPERIENCE

been a night watchman, and one of the things he needed was a good rest after being on duty all night. (13)

Clearly this little boy knew when he had worked enough, and when he needed rest, and the school had been arranged so that his natural pace could be allowed for. An HMI, going around and observing the quality of many such schools, felt that:

> The whole atmosphere of the school was one in which you felt that this was a place where human beings could grow. I don't want to make it an earthly paradise, but . . . they radiated this kind of belief in the possibility of children's growth. They [the teachers] just happened to have that attitude towards children. (2)

A similar emphasis on all-around growth is expressed by another teacher whose own work goes back into the 1920's:

> I am afraid you are going to hear the same thing over and over again, because so many of us worked together. This idea of children growing was a new idea to many teachers, the growth, the all-around growth. Before, it was how children learn numbers, how children learn to read, but this all-around growth is something that the work was really based on. (9)

Still another teacher was moved to go into her profession by hearing an HMI talk about children in a way that excited her, a way she had never heard before (in the 1920's):

> He talked to us about education in a very enlightened way and a really progressive way, and it caught me like that. . . . It was the philosophy I got that one didn't just sit children in rows and lecture to them. They had to grow. (14)

Each child was seen as different, each with a unique contribution to make to the life of the school. "Every individual mattered, and the interest in the individual mattered, and the companionship in thinking mattered with the children" (8). Such feelings were common to teachers who were deeply "minding about children" (17) and helping them daily toward "enjoying life absolutely to the fullest" (9).

One head of a poor slum school achieved a very considerable measure of success because, as she put it, the children knew that "the biggest thing is that we were for them and everybody had been against them" (3). With the schools thus "centered on children" (34), teachers could take the long view of each child's development, not hurrying nature but letting the children develop at their natural pace. They made every effort to give the children what they needed to enable them to grow most effectively at their current age and stage of development.

Children's needs are many, and the school must meet them. Some children most needed a sense "that they were important people. These children wanted to be given self-confidence, wanted to be able to talk to other people, wanted to be able to show off the things they had been doing" (38). These were children in a rather barren housing development in the 1930's. Another teacher said of similar children who had been dislocated and moved about a great deal during the war, "You taught whatever children needed to be taught" (28). What children seem to need to know is that their work helps their own growth:

> You get the children to see that, to be involved in their own learning, to be involved in the acquisition of knowledge or the acquisition of a skill so that they themselves see that they in fact are benefiting by this, they are not doing it for the sake of the teacher. (28)

Basically, said one teacher who was evacuated with his school twice during the war, his work began with "affection to the children" and also with the belief in children "being actively involved in their learning" (39). Not all children learn in the same way, and only by the children's own active involvement can the teacher observe and plan for their needs. "You've got to remember that some children learn by looking, other children by hearing, others by feeling, others by none of it, but some you can't tell at all, and others don't seem they would learn at all" (17).

In trying to provide worthwhile activities for children, it was essential "that they ought to be able to choose what they did" (14). They should have the sense that within reasonable limits they have some control over what and how they learned. Further, "every child's question must be answered simply and truthfully. They must never be told a lie" (13). Their questions are "just a search after truth, because this is one of the characteristics of children during their formative years" (13). Some questions, however, can be handled differently but with equal seriousness:

22 / ACTIVITY AND EXPERIENCE

> Our good teachers are constantly putting back to the children the questions they ask, but in a different form, so that it is the children who find the answer and the teacher who puts before them the means of finding the answer. This technique is valuable in helping a child to think through and try and sort out how a thing works. It is this thinking and problem solving that is more important than the finished product. (7)

When children enter school, then, it must be a rich and satisfying place where their individual needs are met, where they can choose their activities and answer their own questions, and where they can enjoy their powers to the fullest. But it must also be a place of beauty, reflecting the civilized ideals of the teacher and of society at large:

> We did get somewhere there towards creating more civilized surroundings for children to work in. They had had ugly schools, and I told them they looked like public lavatories and I don't know what. . . . We got the schools looking lovely and that's a start, and somehow the children were different. Of course, it was centered on children. (34)

This teacher believed that "children are born artists" and therefore need surroundings which evoke this gift. It was not meant, however, that adults dictated entirely what went up on the walls or that the displays were simply put up and left there. What was intended was a concern for the aesthetic quality of the surroundings in which a child spent so many hours and for the way materials were handled, discussed, and displayed:

> It is difficult to say what the magic is. The teacher is, however, concerned that the materials that she puts before the children are properly ordered, that they are carefully selected. Furthermore her quality as a teacher is contagious. She has a feeling for the materials that she uses. The way she holds them and looks at them, she hardly needs to say "Isn't this a beautiful shape? Isn't this light? Isn't this delicate?" She expresses herself by the way she just sits and handles the material. Other teachers of course do it in other ways. There is a great deal of concern in the way she talks to the children about the quality of the work they are doing, about the pleasure they get from mixing the paints, the colours that they find, and of course the teacher is meticulously careful in the way she mounts the children's work and puts it on the wall and talks about it with the rest of the class. (7)

The adult point of view, the contagious feeling which adults can communicate for the work that is going on, is taken for granted as part of the school environment.

Another emphasis that should be mentioned, repeatedly made clear to me, is that one can trust children. They can be helped, by patience and good sense, to take very considerable responsibility for themselves and one another; they can be relied upon, when the work fits them well, to get on with it unsupervised, thus freeing the teacher to work with individuals or small groups who need her. They have an accurate sense of themselves and will set proper limits in physical activities as well:

> We had two climbing frames and steps with slides down. We had ropes with hoops hung from the rafters. The climbing frames were very adventurous, they could get very high. . . . I never had an accident. (35)

> Once when I was going to a school with one of Her Majesty's Inspectors, the teacher had got a narrow plank between two sets of steps, and the children were being encouraged to walk over this at quite a height. . . . He couldn't bear it and walked forward to help a child. She said, "Please, don't spoil the child's confidence." (7)

Children's inventiveness could be released to use apparatus in new and agile ways, and the observant teacher could see children expressing themselves in styles that were individually their own, when untrammelled by adult cautions or fears:

> Somebody had realized that kids could have great powers of agility and inventiveness. The idea that infant and junior schools should have climbing apparatus was quite a shock. We said, "Look, we will see that the kids are properly equipped. . . . You are not to teach them anything. You will see what will happen. Leave the children to invent."
> . . . There was this great freeing and revelation of what children could do. (11)

Many teachers had this sense of surprise, the willingness to step back and "leave the children to invent" in many ways and then to wonder at the results. All this builds confidence in the child; he "gets command over something that has eluded him perhaps, and it may come in any field, and this achievement is vitalizing. I can, therefore I am" (11). A sense of well-being and integrity results from this kind of mastery: "The physical security gained by sure control of the body results in a measure of mental security. The most important thing, we felt, was to provide opportunity for the fullest freedom of movement, and in the open air as much as possible" (8).

All these statements are, again, ways of saying basically the same thing: teachers who worked in child-centered schools held a common faith in the powers of children and a determination to bring them to their fullest fruition.

The Importance of Observation

The evolution of teaching methods based on the activity and experience of children thus dates from long ago, and the teachers who worked with them held certain beliefs in common about the children they taught and had common ideas or goals toward which they worked. How did they put those into practice? There was only one place to begin, and that was with the careful observation and study of children of many ages in many settings. Nothing substitutes for this close attention paid to children as they act and react in various ways natural to them, and only after such close observations should one introduce new plans. The informal classroom is, of course, a perfect laboratory for such observation and planning, for it encourages individual work and small-group interaction around centers of interest chosen by the children themselves from the materials planned by the teacher. It does not permit children to respond in a one-dimensional way to a preplanned lesson by the teacher with its set list of questions which some children will grasp and others will not. Thus the classroom arrangement of these innovative teachers is conducive to the observation which in their view is so essential to good teaching. Here the children show their uniqueness; here teachers can watch and learn and plan and perhaps intervene, as interests are shown, to help the child take the next step:

> All our development has come from work that is happening, rather than being told a theory, and trying to work it out in practice. It's come up from observation of children. (9)
>
> When a child goes into a new situation, he displays himself and his character, the unity of his character, with great clarity. That is the time to watch him. (4)

The watchful eye of the teacher can pick up problems or special needs easily in such a setting. In the work of movement, for instance, how a child reacts with his body can be very telling:

> There was one boy who was never absorbed, moved very little, was always on the very edge with his back to the wall. His arms never left his side, and I thought to myself, I wonder if that is a very dependent boy, and afterwards I asked [the teacher]. He was the only son and his mother does everything for him. He can't involve himself because he is not accustomed to it, but in English he is remarkable. In any form of action he is helpless. (11)

This brings up another way in which teachers trained their observant eye — in some schools they went with children on expeditions to different places or on camping trips to the country, and in such settings they saw the whole child, not just the school one:

> I started the Guide Company again which had fallen into a bit of disuse, and I used to take these children to camp, faithfully every holiday, and I really got to know children. And then I discovered at camp some of the ones who had been written off at school were in fact the best campers, that they were not naughty or any of these things, and they really had got something to do. I never had one minute's trouble with discipline in all those years, because I met the children as human beings. (4)

During evacuation, particularly, there was ample opportunity to know children as human beings. "You learned so much from living with these children night and day, It was such a wonderful time to see them develop in all ways — physically, mentally, spiritually" (13).

If possible, one should take notes as activity goes on, as one teacher did with excellent results:

> I never wanted to be a head. I always wanted to be a class teacher because I was interested in following through experiments that we were involved in. And from the outset, I kept very detailed records — documented it. So it wasn't a question of us saying we're going to have a free day, or an integrated day, or we're going to have vertical grouping, and so on. There was an evolution, there was a slow growth, and one thing grew out of another. (12)

However, "you have to learn how to watch. You have also got to learn how to get it down, with this business of the rate of human forgetting" (4). Or again, "you can't observe unless you know what you are to see" (22). Courses for infant school teachers often concentrated on developing a

26 / ACTIVITY AND EXPERIENCE

checklist with specific things to look at, such as how little children move, what they approach a teacher for, how they sit, how they use fine motor coordination, how they begin a conversation with another child, or how they use paint or clay. All these are useful in knowing children as people, and from them the wise teacher learns enough to plan a challenging environment for the children she has to work with. And since no child and no group of children is identical with any other, one could not be "wedded" to any one method as perfect for all children:

> I think that if you're teaching children, and if you are with them, you must know them, and you can see what they need and what seems to be going well with them. You can't stick to a method because it is a method. We worked in our own ways, and slightly different ways, and discussed those with one another, which I think is quite good. (37)

Because of the genuine freedom which teachers in England had, this working out one's own way and talking it over with colleagues was possible, and a fruitful way to proceed.

In such a watchful atmosphere,

> one could feel quite certain that if the children had ability, they were not missing the opportunities to develop it. You know the children so well in that sort of situation that you are aware of what their abilities are, what their interests are, and so develop them. (24)

For a teacher, it was a question of having resources always at the ready, whatever need might arise:

> That is where the skill of the teacher comes in, in observing and watching, directing the energies of children into the right channels. (13)

For many teachers, the study of child psychology, when they undertook it, deepened and illuminated much of their experience with children:

> It isn't just children come and sort of do any old thing. I think it is up to the teacher to see what a child is doing and lead him on by producing the books or something to stimulate him a bit. That is why the teacher must understand something about child development as well as emotional development and realize when this child is not forming

any new concepts. If the stimulation is there and the material, then the child can go ahead. (26) (36)

But no one school of thought was the last word, for with such teachers every idea had to be sifted and considered in the light of the particular group of children:

> I think everything depends on having teachers who are capable of absorbing the ideas that might come from all over the place. People go to courses, and they discuss, and then perhaps somebody has an idea and makes it very coherent, and some teachers are sufficiently inspired by it to try. When once they try, of course, they interpret it in their own way, and you get advances. . . . It all depends on what kind of creature you think the child is, what kind of adult you hope he is going to become, and if you think it is an organic thing that you are helping to grow. (20)

This brings us back to the basic attitude toward children on the part of successful teachers, and to the need to study them and use any sound idea that comes one's way in order to help them grow. This attitude was very practical; there were no fine theories in a vacuum for these people, since every idea had to be tested in the real classroom with real children, and only those ideas were kept which proved themselves in that setting.

It takes time to sit and watch children, time to absorb and try new ideas, time to plan the classroom to challenge the children, time to allow natural development to take place. These things cannot be rushed, and they should not be. When children were in the same school with the same teacher for three or more years, as occurred in rural areas especially, there was plenty of time to know them well and to allow for their natural pace. With all the teachers whom I met, there was the unhurried sense of taking the time one needed, the long, leisurely view of a child's development, because they knew children well.

One of the "main planks . . . is really this helping children to push what they're interested in a little bit wider or deeper so that it becomes knowledge as being distinct from just being interested in it" (5). And although the relationship with the teacher is absolutely essential for any good work in the school, that is not the end of the matter. Once the relationship is soundly established, then work can go forward:

28 / ACTIVITY AND EXPERIENCE

Relationships are the absolute essence of it, but how do you build good relationships? It's by having a common interest. It's having something to relate to, and some schools, I don't think, have enough content. They've been happy when the children were happy. They were busy doing this or that, but I do think there's something else, which is this extension of the children's interests by conversation. . . . So that's the relationship plus something to learn from that person. (5)

Thus basing the work of the school on the apparent or whimsical fancies of children was not enough. Children should come to school "to work out their own worthwhile interests" (6). There should be no interference in this process, except for the very careful

> preparation of the room, proper notices, proper materials, worthwhile materials and materials right for the age. . . . A grownup who knows children knows what is just a smattering, not a real interest, just a whim. (6)

This teacher, like others, felt that whim was not enough; the work of the teacher who understood and cared about children's growth would go far beyond. She must consider what is best for that growth, what will extend the children's powers and their sense of confidence. As another teacher put it:

> Now, I thought, if children learned so much when they are interested, why not find out their natural interests, around about that age, because probably all children of seven to eight have fairly similar interests. Let's find out what they really are. Why not then base the curriculum on this, and don't worry about fitting in all the subjects at once. They will learn that way, and will use writing, reading, and arithmetic to further these interests. Treat them as tools and perfect them as far as they can go. (37)

The 3 R's were not forgotten, but they were put into the perspective of children's working on their worthwhile interests. Then they were quickly seen as indispensable tools. To get needed information from a book, one must read; to cast up the accounts for the school store, one must do arithmetic; to report on one's project or investigation, one must write.

This way of working from children's centers of interest, which is basic to the philosophy of the informal school, proved to be successful at any age and in any setting. Perhaps the most striking success was achieved in places where children had been uprooted or in some way ignored or badly treated. Such children sensed when the teachers "were for them" and when their "main thing was to interest the children" (33). They could not adjust to the formal routine of class teaching and sitting still and listening. But they could take part in a classroom experience that was built around the natural interests of children, where they were encouraged and enabled to be fully themselves. For instance, one teacher in the 1930's had a group of children who lived in a housing development. The parents "were all feeling lost and miserable," and the children had been uprooted from whatever home they had known. They turned up at various times during the year, all having moved out from the slums of London to this new and very unfamiliar setting:

> I had this group of children who had to be treated differently, who had to be won 'round, and we began doing what we loosely called projects, forgetting all about subject barriers, finding an interest. (38)

Similarly, other teachers told me how vital it was to begin with a child's interest if the child had failed in school or was considered backward. It was soon found that such children often were not backward at all but simply could not comprehend or adjust to formal methods. "They couldn't possibly learn collectively" (14), but they could be taught individually and "brought up to scratch."

Children who had been evacuated had a very similar difficulty. They had been uprooted and sent off to strange places, usually without parents, and their greatest need was something to interest them and keep them happily occupied (39). And when those children came back to London schools, it was hard to know how to teach them. Some teachers with wartime experience never went back to formal methods, if indeed they had ever used them:

> In the middle of a devastation, a sea of waste and rubble of brick dust, we had a motley collection of children coming from all over the place. Some had been receiving teaching in evacuation, some had lived in shelters virtually throughout the war. They were at all levels of ability and attainment, because of the varied kinds of teaching they had received. Some of them had been backwards and forwards into the coun-

try a dozen times and not really settled down anywhere. So there was no way that you could really go back to the formal teaching. . . . we took the chains off the schools, and opened up our thinking, and stopped this formalized daily program, and so on. We taught whatever children needed to be taught. (28)

The result of this freeing up of schooling was perfectly clear:

The children became involved in their own standards. They were enjoying what they were doing; they couldn't get at their books and their clay and their woodworking and their model making and their personal investigations, their personal studies — they couldn't get at them fast enough and you couldn't get rid of the children at the end of the day. They didn't want to go home, and they didn't want to go out and play at playtime. . . . It was certainly something quite new to me. I had not seen this before, and it was the attitude of the teachers to children and then the attitude of the children to what they were doing that seemed to me so refreshing. And also, one saw, dimly, if you could harness this, you were harnessing 40 minds to work rather than the teacher driving 40 people . . . . They saw that you come to school to improve your various capacities, and the school will do this for you. (28)

Those are two examples of the value of basing the children's work on their natural interests, one from a housing project in the 1930's and another from post-evacuation days in London. A third comes from a country school in the 1930's, the school where the teacher said to the children, "Let's go out in the school field":

I remember that near the school was a stream in which I had paddled as a child. "Let's look and see what is in the stream," I said. We were astonished to find amongst other living things the larvae of the giant dytiscus beetle, fearsome-looking creatures which would certainly have put me off paddling had I known of their existence. Setting up an aquarium to house the creatures we found, observing the emergence of a may fly from the home they had created, and watching a dytiscus beetle climb over a glass division and attack a huge tadpole, added knowledge and interest, and so learning seemed to make sense.

Running parallel through the village were a railway, a river, and a road. Making a model of this, the children appreciated why this was so. They became interested in scale and map-making and loved using 25" and 6" survey maps on which they could identify their homes, school, post office, and other landmarks and trace the journeys they and their families made. It was not from applied theories or from reading, but from experiments and experiences such as these, from application of sheer common sense in given situations, that I found this was a way through, particularly for children who were not really academic. But I found also that the brighter children got on so much more quickly and were able to go ahead rather than be held back as they were when the class moved together at an average pace. Whilst they speeded ahead, with occasional guidance and encouragement, I was able to help others who needed it. (24)

Later these same children moved into their rural environment to study and investigate it in all its aspects. They kept a diary of one field and of one animal and made it all as scientific as possible. They took responsibility for the animal pets they kept and kept track of amounts of food and rates of growth. All this challenged them while it also interested them, for they were dealing with their own world and deepening their awareness of it. Brighter children could move ahead at their own pace, and less academic ones could also play their part in a noncompetitive group of youngsters, investigating their own interests and asking their own questions. These children soon took a pride in their country environment and felt they knew a good deal about it. Their rural schooling had not alienated them from their home but had enriched their appreciation of it. And the combination of field and stream observations had provided them with the skills of investigation needed in any setting.

The strategy, then, for observant teachers who knew their children well was to watch for and provide for the interests which children naturally have and then to be ready to take them further and deeper. They started where they found the children, and they planned for their natural development along the lines of their personal interests. Traditional subject matter was never forgotten, but it was turned around to make it relate to the child's experience, to make it useful in pursuing what he wanted to find out about. Thus instead of merely reading around the room several paragraphs about the Normans in Britain, that teacher involved the children in their learning so that they knew a great deal about the Normans and were deeply interested in them.

Stimulating an interest which one knows is typical of an age group is one approach, just as providing for full expression and then responding to interests that arise is another. The two are not at all in conflict, these

32 / ACTIVITY AND EXPERIENCE

teachers felt, for while each child is unique he is also a variation on a common theme. A wise teacher knows both sides. On the one hand she knows enough about children to know what their interests are likely to be at a given age — to know that saying "Let's look and see what is in the stream" is likely to get an enthusiastic response if only because it is an active idea. On the other hand, she also provides material and experiences such that the individual child can express his or her particular interest freely. The problem is not how to get children's interests out into the open; that is easy enough, because children do have interests and are eager enough to show them to a sympathetic adult. The problem is what to do with the interest once it is there. But if one holds the belief that school should enhance the child's all-around growth, there is no other way. The challenge is to help the children achieve the best standard of work they can at their age and stage of development.[13]

Standards

This brings us to the matter of standards. No teacher whom I talked with failed to say that beginning with the child's interest and involving him in his own education is far more difficult than traditional, curriculum-centered teaching. But also no teacher failed to mention the fact that in her experience, work that is based on the activity and experience of children results in a higher standard and a wider range of achievement than formal methods. Although such work was more time-consuming, more challenging, and more absorbing, it was also more rewarding, for the stakes were high. In the 1930's, Susan Isaacs was saying that maturation may set the ceiling of achievement, but it does not *produce* achievement (4). To produce the achievement possible at each level of maturation became the teacher's job. Obviously there is no guarantee that it will work:

> It's got to be well done. . . . It's much harder, and if it goes wrong, the results are worse than the other system going wrong, and they're more obvious. I can remember, in the past, a dreary dullness and sort of low achievement that there was there, awful boredom that must have done an awful lot of harm. But, well, when I visited a school where this (freer kind of teaching) was happening, I had a feeling, this is really children being educated, growing, and all the things that they write, the things that they make all seem to be clear evidence that this is real education. . . . I still think that the essential virtues need not be aban-

doned. They are sometimes abandoned. I have seen enough schools run on these lines where they are not abandoned to know this is so. (2)

So also with the teacher whose children studied their country setting and worked for scientific accuracy in all that they did. So also with teachers who worried about progressive schools where there was too little content, just lots of activity. There has to be something to extend the child's interests, to encourage his involvement and the pursuit of his own questions. "I wanted them to get some feeling of the control of language, . . . I would not have anything that was just careless and slapdash" (38). So also with the teacher whose students took more top places in the 11+ exam than their allotted number. And as one teacher put it, parents and voters have a right to expect results from schools, and the most convincing argument for activity methods was that they produced results.

Many people with whom I talked made this point that good results convinced opposition. It worked in two ways. First, parents were often invited into the school and went away pleased to see their children obviously happy and absorbed. Second, there were measurable results like the 11+ exam, or, better, standards of reading, writing, and mathematics which children could achieve in the service of their own investigations. In one otherwise traditional school, one teacher built on the children's interests and the headmistress regularly marked one-fourth of all the children's written papers; she was amazed by the quality of this teacher's children's writing and gave far more top marks than in any other class (38).

But there was opposition, and there is still. Much of it comes from ignorance or misunderstanding of what these schools are about. Some opponents felt that all children do is play, quite confusing the common idea about play with the much more sophisticated, psychological interpretation of its great value to children and the possibilities which it contains for real education. One such person was taken to see a good film about a school, and he saw children making a study of their village, looking quite carefully at the houses, discovering how they were made, dressing up in costumes of the period, and doing all the map-making and measuring and writing that went along with this:

> He said, "Oh, well, I agree to that, there is nothing wrong in that." I said, "Well, this is what we are saying." Then, you see, he said, "Oh, all you people think of is the children with sand and clay and throwing it all over the place, and having a lovely time." I said, "You simply

34 / ACTIVITY AND EXPERIENCE

> haven't been into a school if that's what you think. You see, when we both look at something like that, we both agree that is worthwhile." Well, he can see the children doing something worthwhile in anybody's language. (5)

Unfortunately, it is easy to be trivial in this kind of work, as the teacher mentioned who discussed people simply shoving in all kinds of material and worrying if anyone were idle. It matters less what the material is than how the children use it and how they are helped to learn from it.

On the subject of standards, another teacher has this to say:

> If anyone asked me now to talk to teachers, I would take the subject of standards. I don't think that our standards are high enough. I don't think they are minding enough in this freer work about what genuine scholarship comes out of it, what genuine habits of hard work and care and thought are put into it. It is much harder. It is much easier if all the questions are identical, then the answers are either right or wrong. That is easy. . . . Most teachers are conscientious, and they were afraid of moving because they knew they could get standards in their own way, standards that they could test and could get across to the parents. You could only win them over when you proved that this freer work got higher standards. If it is done properly, there is no doubt that it does. But what worries me now is that most of the teachers did not begin in the days when you had to get things as reasonably correct as you could, and write with as much care as you could. As long as everybody is busy and happy and all moving about and doesn't make too much noise, they are supposed to be up to date and the rest of it. They have not got those standards, and they do not realize how much more careful the children can be, how much harder they could work, and would like to. I think there is a very great danger now that we have gone too far. (38)

The problem with competition for standards is that it teaches something other than what the school is aiming for. It forces a child to do work which may or may not be right for him, and it places an extrinsic reward ahead of the intrinsic satisfaction of a worthwhile piece of work well done:

> "A shilling a week extra if you get all your sums right," I do often hear parents say. "Unless there is competition or unless I do give him some money, he won't do it. I have to motivate him by those means." But this is a competitive society, and it is hard to persuade people. It is often, in parents who I know have in fact been extremely

good in competition, and they can't understand maybe competition is a pernicious thing and teaches some rather bad things. Parents are so wrapped up in, particularly, having the child at least keep up to the same level that they were earlier, or the child has got to turn out better than ever they were. But the parents' point of view has nothing to do with the child. (26) (36)

Without such competition and the "rather bad things" it teaches, a child can feel satisfaction in his own work in one area of his choice, and that confidence will help him in all other kinds of work. This refers, of course, to a child's need to develop self-confidence, a secure sense of his own powers that comes from competence.

Another way of convincing opposition had to do with the general attitude of the community towards teachers and toward the head in particular.[14] In bringing about change to a freer way of working with children, one famous head was able to rely on the great respect which everyone had for her. Her long-time associate writes:

> About your query about whether we had to face opposition or antagonism in the early days, Miss Simpson said, "We didn't really, did we, Dorothy?" The real reason lay in Miss Simpson herself. Her philosophy of life, and every aspect of her as a person contributed to her considerable capacity for establishing good human relations with children, parents, teachers, other heads, janitors, administrators. And it was this which created a climate of good feeling in the first place. We *did* have some anxious parents and critical head teachers who were to receive our children as "juniors" following their infant school life. We did have a janitor who complained about the "mess," but Miss Simpson's capacity for establishing good relations, and her obvious concern for the children, and for the anxieties of the above-mentioned people, quickly resolved problems which may have developed. . . . people respected Miss Simpson and her ideals, and it was this factor which operated to a large extent before our methods per se could be evaluated in terms of long-term results. I well remember that one cause for concern was that we did not *push* reading too soon. We didn't just wait and do nothing; but we did not push the mechanics. Some parents (and this is true today) who couldn't see overt progress, in terms they understood, became anxious and harried *us,* as well as their children, but eventually they saw that the children did read, and so when we had younger brothers and sisters, they did not worry about them. Perhaps the most worrying feature — and this is true of any approach, but it is used most frequently in criticism related to child-centered

education — is when you have weak teachers or ones who don't care and who misinterpret the whole idea of what you are trying to do. Then, *their* misinterpretations *rightly* attract criticism, but this should not be a criticism of the method, but rather of the weakness of individuals. (12)

Such concern for children's sound growth and such ability to achieve high standards and convince all opposition can create a school in which excellence is truly possible, in one area or another, for all children. And note that there is no competition in the traditional sense in this kind of school, and there is no reason for it, since each one is working, alone or in a small group, on questions he cares to answer. There is no setting of one child's accomplishment against another's and judging which is better or worse. Rather, each child is helped to compete only with his own past level of achievement, in the knowledge that increasing maturity brings with it increasing powers. This noncompetitive atmosphere includes acceptance of the work of others. If one's own work is interesting and fully appreciated by a sympathetic teacher, there is no need to denigrate that of another, or to imitate it, but only to compare with interest:

> ... it was all right because there was no temptation to imitate. There was just pleasure in watching somebody else going at the thing you were trying to do yourself. ... I think it is an acceptance through all the things they do, whether it is writing or painting or what have you. It is a pleasure when somebody else does something that is interesting. They have great compassion if they know a child is weak and that child pulls off something for the first time. I think it stems very much from the whole attitude of the teacher, and the quality of the work they do. (11)

> When once you get a standard in one thing, you see, it pulls up the standard in a lot of the other work. Because they all begin to know what excellence is. You know when you are doing your best. You know what it is to work hard at a thing, and achieve something. It is really satisfying. Once you have that experience, it is likely to spread. You know what it is to go all out and do the very best you can do. (20)

The positive effect of excellence on the work of a single child is also observable in a whole school. For many HMI's the best way to help a school improve its work was "to find something that a school really can do well, and get it to do that as well as it can" (20). The music in one school was the focus of much work at a very high standard: "success in this would spill over into their success in other fields" (28). "A school moves ahead very quickly indeed if you have got a good standard in anything, be it dancing, or art work, or whatever" (24).

Seeing the value of maintaining high standards makes one more aware that a teacher must have a sure grasp of what she is working towards:

> The ideas are not difficult to come by. They are everywhere around. To understand them and to manage them and to know how to get the results that you want from them, that is another matter. The hardest thing, I think, for the teachers to develop is a sense of standard, knowing what children can do and what you can expect from them. That is the most difficult thing. (20)

The teacher must have a kind of inner sense of the standards which are relevant to a particular child or group of children, a sense which is born of experience with children and close study of them over long periods of time as they grow:

> Then there is the question of standards. There are teachers everywhere who in this situation will accept things from children that they would never dream of accepting if it were a regular class. They think they don't understand what good standards are because they no longer have the competition element. A teacher has to learn to rely on her own standards ... that is the quality of being a teacher. (18)

The Life of the School

What were the schools like? As the development of such ideas moved along, every aspect of the school was made use of for teaching. No detail was ignored or left to chance; everything about, around, and in a school was considered for its educational possibilities.

Teachers were quite clear about what was *not* a good school, since most of them had been to what they later knew was a bad one. Few had been to a school based on the interests of children, but, rather, they were all too familiar with the kind of school that "keeps children under" (18), the school filled with boredom and lacking joy or spontaneity, classes in which "reading round the room" was common, with set questions to be answered, teachers who were formal and remote from their children — in general, schools in which authority and conformity ruled. For many such teachers, it was with excitement and joy that they heard about or observed child-centered methods at work or felt their own powers happily absorbed in doing work of remarkably high quality. For them, the hallmarks of a good school became more and more clear. One HMI, already quoted, put it thus: "The whole atmosphere of the school was one in which you felt that this was a place where human beings could grow " (2). Another teacher described a now-famous school which she saw in the 1930's:

> All the children were extraordinarily good. Nobody was keeping them in order. All the children were beavering away at everything that was going on, absolutely absorbed. And I never saw one child misbehave or be crossly spoken to during the day or two that I was there. It was such a very personal school, and every child was important. There was no question about these are the bright ones and these are the dull ones. (5)

An administrator, visiting schools, saw some things he had never seen before, and his idea of a good school gained new definition:

> I know my definition. A school where the children could be left to get on. This is what impressed me enormously when I first went into a school and there was no teacher in the classroom, and the children were painting with powder paint and water, and it was dangerous, lethal stuff in a crowded classroom, and I had never in my experience seen this before. I didn't understand what the children were doing, but it was obvious that they were completely absorbed in it. (7)

Another HMI described a good school more fully:

> I like to hear a gentle kind of noise. I don't want to hear silence unless there is something happening that there should be silence for. I like to be met by friendly children who are willing to look after a stranger if necessary, who treat you civilly as they would in their own home. I like to see them busy about something. I've got to find what they are being busy about. It might be worthwhile, but I like to see that they are engaged in something that is of some sort of vital interest to them if possible, and I certainly like to hear some sounds. I like to see the teacher going among them as a friend. (17)

Similarly:

> I should be very surprised if I went into a primary school and the children were not friendly and open and understanding and responsive and helpful and self-disciplined. It varies very much, but that would be the expectation. (20)

The idea that children in a good school can be left to "get on with it" reappeared often. Two teachers said, "They were completely helped by this method in teaching to get on with things. And the business of being able to take something and get on with it is very important in life" (26) (36). The process of learning, then, was just as important as the product, as teachers watched for "the absorption when the work was just right for the children" (9). One remembers, also, the school where the children could not get at their work fast enough and were reluctant to go out to play or to go home at the end of the day, so busy were they, so absorbed in "beavering away" at their own personal investigations. "You'll find the children are extraordinarily law-abiding and the schools are almost silent. They work like mad, but they are free to come and go and move and take. Time is not the thing that rules you at all" (34).

In general, the consensus seems to be that the result of sound methods which are based on thorough knowledge of children and a willingness to let their interests govern the curriculum is schools where children are busy and self-contained, absorbed and achieving at a high standard.

What have been the means toward this end? Again, the curriculum of the school is based on the "activity and experience" of children, not on information to be memorized or skills to be practiced apart from their use in real life. All the teachers with whom I talked felt keenly about that statement; many quoted it to me verbatim, as a key statement which got to the root of everything they had done in their schools. But none would have said that activity for its own sake was enough. "Anything like this craze for do as you like all day long I would not stand for" (3). "You must give them something in their lessons that their minds can work on. There must be meat in your lessons, yes, meat that they are ready for and reaching to swallow" (26) (36). The curriculum begins with activity, but it does not end there. The difficult task was to extend interests beyond the children's first, active expression into their more abstract or conceptual representation. The work of the school was to encourage concrete, personal expression of interests and then to be a "bridge between the concrete and the abstract" (12). There are many aspects to this process: children getting involved in an activity which they enjoy and then being helped onward into a deeper understanding of its significance by means of discussion, writing, reading, "maths," or some artistic, creative representation of the experience. Here, indeed, would be the source of a definition of "worthwhile interest" — namely, an interest that can be thus deepened, built upon, and developed into knowledge.

This is the way in which what is called "subject matter" or "content" originated after all; material that is put into textbooks is really no more than various experiences with the world, organized and codified after the fact. Children in good schools can begin with their own experiences and be helped to organize and express them in a way that is meaningful to them. Or, as one teacher put it more simply: "We don't begin with sums. You begin with sums, and we end with them" (8). Children can achieve a body of knowledge which is for each separate child what the great areas of human knowledge are for humanity at large — ways of understanding and controlling human experience:

> We did a class project on Harrod's store. We were very close, we were situated in the back streets behind Harrod's, and we had been doing shops and towns and things like that. A lot of the parents worked there. I remember one boy's father ran the butchery. Because they were so interested in shops, I wrote to the manager and explained things, and wanted to bring this whole gang of over 50 children to have a look around. He wasn't very enthusiastic, but we did and were such a success we kept going. Well, we built up Harrod's stores in our school, with groups taking the different departments and finding out things from their fathers, and it was real for those children. I kept their notes and everything, and it went on to other things, but that is how it got started. I can't tell you all the interesting results. Their English was so extraordinary, the fluency and the accounts of everything written and spoken. (3)

It is clear from this and other accounts that the three R's were seen as indispensable aids along the way, and the standards to which these essential skills were developed were often very high indeed. But they were never made ends in themselves, only necessary means:

I don't see for the life of me how children can appreciate size, dimension, number, proportion, anything, except through their own experience. If you offer children lots of opportunities for counting and understanding, presently, of course, they will want to write it down. It is amazing the zest and interest with which they take to it, provided you let them have plenty of material to build it on. (11).

Work of this kind blurs subject-matter lines, of course, but their boundary lines have always been considered artificial by these teachers in any case. When was the careful drawing of a leaf nature study and when was it art? When were the descriptive records of a growing guinea pig simply careful observations and when were they English? Work based on active, personal experiences and growing from them cannot be divided in traditional ways. Still, subject matter is thoroughly learned when it is connected with experiences which matter to the learner:

> One child made a shop, and made all these models. A lovely, big shop with an orange box. And he made the dolls. And then we discussed ages and prices. You see — is it art? is it writing? is it clothes for the wedding? We did a lot of baking, and then decided to have a party for the mothers. This meant we had to multiply the recipe four times. Well, they had all this multiplication to do, to make new recipes, and then the time to bake was for so long, so there was also a time element in it. (12)

When these children set the tables for the party they had to count out four cups and four plates, and they were "getting a much clearer concept of the fourness of four." In the same way, one teacher said:

> We explored our school environment to the full. We used the school canteen as one study, for example, and the children explored the sources and manufacture of the cutlery they used and the plates stimulated uses and experiments with local clay, which led on to a study of the potteries, supported by film. Similar studies were stimulated in fruits, vegetables, and meat. The children had looseleaf files and made really quite good records of the school canteen, which included geography, science, mathematics, and history and which were very well illustrated. (24)

One slightly unorthodox way of teaching French was observed by an

42 / ACTIVITY AND EXPERIENCE

HMI in a secondary school. It was rare then to see a secondary teacher willing to try an unusual method:

> Just after the war, I went into a secondary school in Manchester and walked into a classroom where the children were supposed to be learning French. There was a young woman on a bicycle riding around the room, and the children were all shouting directions to her in French. I came in, and she went rather pink and got off rather hastily, and said, "I hope this is all right." I said, "I should think that it is very well all right. Tell me about it" (2).

Aside from making use of the environment of the school or the immediate surroundings, teachers in these schools took the children on expeditions. Sometimes they went into fields or nearby woods to bring back leaves, insects, flowers, and so on. In the city, journeys were undertaken to spots of local historical interest and to extend the horizons of children who seldom went far from home. Often I heard the statement that such trips need very careful preparation. Not only did teachers feel that children needed to have a good idea of what they were looking for and specific questions they wanted to have answered, but also they worked on acceptable social behavior while in the public eye and safety rules to make sure their trip would be without hazard. Although such trips thus meant a great deal of extra work for the teachers, the results were satisfactory for the children's experience, since trips always stimulated new questions and investigations:

> I remember going with some children on the underground, and soon they said to me, "This is the furthest I have been into London before." That was a thing that shook me. To me London meant Westminster, and so on. You see, they had never been. They just lived in the slums of London, but they had never been anywhere else. Somebody had to stand at the bottom of the escalator to put them on, and somebody to take them off at the top in case they got worried about it. We took them to the British Museum . . . and we did just the two rooms of everyday life in Greece and Rome. It was so exciting being with these eight-year-olds. They had their little notebooks and their pencils, and they had been handling for several months the catalogues of that room, with tiny little pictures and the descriptions. We never went further afield than the part that they knew. . . . You see, we worked up to it for a term. They knew just what they were going to see and knew just what they wanted to find out. This was in the thirties. (38)

Later, this teacher told me that other teachers tried similar city trips, but had "devastating experiences because they had not planned in sufficient detail."

One teacher in a poor section in the north "always took the 6's and 7's on a railway journey, and that inspired them" (35). The people at the district office were concerned about safety, of course, because that was the time when motor cars were just coming in:

> I explained very carefully that I thought that this was the best means of safety training. I gave the children the safety training before they went, and it was a practical example. Entering trams, what to do, and the care you had to take, and when you crossed roads, what you had to do. It was the best training. These people, I don't think it is stubbornness or stupidity. They just haven't the experience of children. They don't know their needs. (35)

As another example of work in a country setting, here is the same teacher who took her children out into the field and later the stream:

> We kept chickens and rabbits and we had two goats. This gave rise to many aspects of education — the making of homes for them, the feeding of them, and the keeping of records. The senior boys took the rabbits to market for we were very short of meat then. . . . Some of the children learned how to milk the goats and we kept in close contact with the farmers; and the bigger boys used to do quite a lot of work (particularly in mathematics) on the fields. One could just trust the children to go out into the fields alone, and a visitor might well have found a group in the fields and another in the lanes. We grew crops such as thousand-headed kale for the goats. We had to learn an awful lot about food, what constituted a good diet, how much we could grow and how much we had to buy. And we had to make money on this project, at least enough to cover expenses. It was part of their training to be businesslike about it. We tried to make it all as scientific as possible. They used also to keep a personal diary of one living thing and one field throughout the year, and often before school officially opened each morning they wrote down their observations. I took into school magazines, my own books of identification, and brought as many books on trees and flowers, in fact as many books connected with their interests as possible, but choice in the early forties was extremely limited and money had to be raised to buy them. These were always displayed on a long desk and could be readily referred to. (24)

Even teachers in the city could make use of a nearby park for observing nature, and often they found surprising things. One enterprising teacher worked from an interest centering on houses:

> Houses in history. They made the models, and they would go out and visit the houses in the district, and so on. I mean, you start off with a thing like, "Go and look at your own house. Go and do a drawing of your house, your room, and tell us about it. Measure it, and find out where the water comes in, find out where the gas comes in, find out where the electricity comes in, find out where the sewage goes out." Complete with drawings and so on, from there. I can remember one or two little boys would come. They were so excited because this sort of thing spilled over outside the school, and this is really what you aimed for, that the school should come into the home, learning should come into the home. You see, it always sort of ties up. One little boy did a marvelous drawing of the way the sewerage system worked in his house. He put in some wonderful descriptive phrases how some of the sewers got bigger and bigger until you could drive a bus through the middle of some of them. (39)

From an interest in houses, these children wrote letters to the various officials who dealt with matters about housing, heard some of them speak, visited nearby houses of special interest, and saw deeds and mortgage papers; all this resulted in a great deal of very careful work based on close observation and record keeping. The teacher meanwhile "has got to have a very clear idea of what you are doing, and how you are doing it, and how the development is coming on" (39). Otherwise, such activities and experiences would be haphazard, not promoting children's learning.

Discussion was a technique used by many teachers I met. Discussions were used to lead children from their immediate experience into a more conceptual grasp of its meaning or to move from it into related lines of inquiry. The teacher and the other children would come together and look at something one child had made or brought to school and wanted to share. The teacher encouraged him to speak about it and asked questions or made suggestions that would "get a development in their thinking" (12). Often this meeting came just after a morning spent in creative play, during which the children had been busy making things:

> One development out of this creative play, one step forward, was when we had a discussion period. As you often see in school now, they all

gather 'round you; they brought along the things they'd been making or doing. The general idea was that if they've got something in their hands that they'd actually made themselves, then this gave them confidence to speak fluently about what they'd been doing. It certainly was a great advance on the old language lessons! It was all at a practical level, you see. If a child had made a lorry or a bus, I would butt in and say, "Well, how did you make those wheels so that they would go around?" Or, if they had stuck the wheels on instead of making them go around, I would say, "Well, I wonder how he could make these wheels go around." I would try to get a development in their thinking, about dealing with a practical problem. . . . Again, interesting things happened. We got these wonderful sidetrackings of a child who'd painted a picture of the Tower of London, because he'd been to London, you see. "I've been to London," said one, "and I went on the underground." And then we'd get a discussion about underground tunnels, and what other kind of tunnels were there, why did we have an underground tunnel in London. So you get the basis of this kind of subject emerging, subjects they're going to pursue all through their lives, coming from these discussions which may just have started with Peter's picture about the Tower of London. (12).

Again, it would be hard to specify what subject matter was being learned here, but, as another teacher put it, "after all, knowledge is indivisible; it is really just a set of hooks" (18). In the following example, however, it is more clear that mathematical judgment and reasoning are being quite deliberately developed by the teacher:

I will give you one example. It was to do with the roofing of the gang hut. We had to buy our materials. They wanted so much a square foot. The children said, "What's a square foot?" I said, "Well, we could make a square foot, and we could make another square foot and another square foot, and we have got to put nine squares together out on the playground on the ground." Well, we did this out of doors. I said, "Well, that's one square yard." Then they went on building 2 square yards, 3 square yards, 4 square yards. They did the whole thing, with their 9, 18, 27, 36, 45. When we came inside, I said, "Now, you call the next one out for me. Eighteen, 27, 36, 45, . . . all the way down to the end." "Now," I said, "do you see any magics?" Immediately they could see that all the digits made nine. I said there were others, and we could go on like this to the end of the world. I said, "Nobody knows the end of it, this rhythm." One child said, "Only God." (8)

Although the children learned some formal arithmetic by these means, "it was always in connection with something" (8). This same teacher was surprised when she heard a child singing the multiplication table as she skipped down a corridor as a pleasant way to keep the rhythm. Although many teachers spoke to me about ways to develop mathematical reasoning in children out of their experiences, many more talked about growth in language work — reading, writing, listening, speaking — as well as an appreciation of the literary heritage of their country. Of particular interest to me were several accounts of the importance of helping the children to speak fluently before they could learn to read:

> [I wanted to] teach children to read in a natural way, and long ago in the very early days [1920's], I thought it was no good attempting to teach reading until the children spoke in a natural way. I felt so strongly that it was stupid to learn to read until you could speak properly, until you could converse. (6)

Again, at the nursery level:

> My point is that if a child can talk easily and freely, a child like that will find very little difficulty at the next stage, to read. Reading comes very easily if they have been encouraged to express themselves freely. (13)

Certainly, that was one aim of the teacher who used discussions and "sidetrackings" with her children. With something in his hands which he has made, even a shy child will loosen up and speak easily, given time and encouragement:

> I pointed out we couldn't start the teaching [of reading] until they could speak. You know some of them couldn't speak. You know there are children in homes that aren't spoken to, or are in a terrible way. They could swear all right, but you've got to get them really talking. (3)

Attempts of a great variety were made to make the classroom a rich verbal environment where reading would be needed to undertake projects that the children wanted to do. Here and there about the room, signs would be put up which gave instructions or made suggestions about the use of materials. Name tags and labels of every kind helped. Real children's books were brought in, shared, discussed, and enjoyed by all. Under a child's paintings, words were written which he asked for or dictated about the work he had just done. One teacher (39) encouraged his children to keep personal diaries with their own words and drawings of the work they were doing or whatever was going on. Such frequent and personal writing, he felt, helped their fluency very much. In all cases, children were encouraged to keep a record, whether it was a description of a blossom coming out or an account of a trip just taken. Discussion and conversation continuously flowed through the work, with the teacher always trying to sense "the teaching moment" to intervene and "get a development in the children's thinking."

Another frequently used way in which teachers enriched the verbal background of their children was telling a story. I heard repeatedly about the story as a center of interest, a stimulus to the imagination and curiosity of children. I also heard how vital it was to choose the story with the greatest care, to plan it just a little above the level of the children's current vocabulary, and to plan exactly how the story would be dealt with — what phrases would be repeated, what words relished, when a question would be asked, what comments (if any) would be made. Teachers who made such use of a story were working within a long tradition in schools that a story was read to the children as recreation on Friday afternoons after the real work of the class was done. But these teachers saw more possibilities in the use of a story than just a pleasant pastime. Like everything else in the school, it was used as an opportunity for teaching. It was a starting point for dramatic work, for painting or writing, for the growth of vocabulary, for an appreciation of different uses of words in different settings, for literary enrichment, and so on. This was a far cry from the rather casual reading of a story after the "real work" was done. But such stories, again, had to be "very carefully chosen and very carefully prepared, with the children brought in and really got to discussing things. Otherwise, it would just be recreation and wouldn't be worth doing" (38):

> *Treasure Island* is such a wonderful example. You can sense in the first few sentences that there is going to be adventure here, there is going to be a mystery. Now, why should a man be going to the cliffs night after night and looking through a spy glass and seeing nothing? There were clue after clue. I worked them all out once. All of them would just adore seeing how a story is built up and leads to a climax. You see, if you don't do that kind of thing, all they will tell you when they have read *Treasure Island* is about Jim and the apple barrel. That is the thing they will remember, but the skill of the opening is just so

that children can follow clues of that kind. You are finding out and sharing together a delight in what they can understand at their stage. We all see more in a picture or in a piece of music if we are just given an idea what to look for. Oh, dear, to make teachers see that the sharing of literature and seeking what was behind it could be so exciting! (38)

This same teacher, eager to interest children in really good literature, brought in her own childhood books, bought a few really handsome books, and ransacked nearby secondhand shops for books, to build small libraries in every classroom. Another teacher says:

> I took in all the books that I was brought up on myself, and I put them all into a cupboard. Books that were far too old for them, but I let the children just go and help themselves. Well, the inspector appeared to inspect me and my students. She said, "These students read extremely well." They did. They could all read. They wanted to. She said, "What system are you using?" I said, "Well, I'm not, really." They didn't learn to read from the readers. I used to read to them, and I told them endless stories — I could make up stories, and they liked that. I used to say to them, "Now, what do you want in the story? Who do you want in the story?" I had to make a story up to cover all the different people they would mention. They would all wait for their person to come into the story. I think story telling is one of the most thrilling ways to really teach. I think they ought to have a great many books, and I think they ought to have books that sound far beyond them. (17)

Another device to improve the children's use of language was the post office. In one "big, tough school," a young woman teacher achieved a remarkable development in the boys' work simply by seeing and using an opportunity that was spontaneously offered to her by one of them. Her HMI reported:

> Apparently what happened was that, after she had been with them a few days, they obviously responded to her. First, a piece of paper appeared on her desk. "Dear Miss Taylor, Thank you for lorning me the sounds. Billy." She knew what to do with it. She wrote an answer and put it on his desk. Eventually all of them were writing letters to her so that she would answer them. The next development was that after all of them had written letters to each other, they made a letter box. They finished up by writing a play, and the play was called "The

Sword and the Anvil." It was a legend, and they wrote it as a group. Line by line. They suggested lines as to what was going to happen next, and this was printed on the board. The first scene was set at Uther Pendragon's castle, and Merlin was to appear, carrying the baby. He was to knock at the door and a knight was to come to the door. There was a long pause, and one boy said, "Well, you better say, 'What's to do?,' Miss." Again, she didn't say anything, and presently another boy said, "Miss, that's the way *we* talk. He couldn't say, 'What's to do,' could he, Miss?" So they began to realize that there were good ways of saying things and bad ways. They produced this play, and they dressed and made armor for it with the help of parents, and they finally performed it in front of a large audience of parents and brothers and sisters and the headmaster. It was a wonderful thing of transforming this class. Incidentally, the boys' attendance at juvenile court dropped wonderfully. After our discussion, she showed me an account she had written of her work, which was later published. (Taylor's *Experiments with a Backward Class*). (2).

Here is another classroom post office, a particularly busy place around Christmas time:

Children from all over the school put their letters into this post office, and then for the last half hour on each afternoon they would put on a postman's hat and go and deliver these letters. Well, we did make quite a scene about ones which were badly addressed and the names all misspelled, because we were really trying to run a post office, and letters wouldn't get delivered if they weren't properly done. Of course, it was pathetic for some of the ones from very poor homes who had never received anything, the excitement to think that some friend from another class was just wishing them a nice holiday or whatever, to receive just that little bit of paper that was folded up with their name on it. (38)

Again, standards of accuracy were kept, but always in connection with a written communication that someone really wanted to send to someone else.

Writing for important purposes worked well with other teachers, too. One had a great many projects going on constantly, which meant that materials were needed and had to be sent for:

We did a lot of writing to businesses to get materials for our projects, so that they wrote letters and they received letters. Then we put them up on the wall and talked about what kind of sense that letter made, and what it meant to you to receive it, which kind you liked best. Of course, if we went to anything, we wrote letters of thanks. We wrote for open days, children wrote to their parents. They didn't copy out a letter that I had made up, but we did agree together and put up on the board that you must put in the day, and the time, and the place, and so on. Then they wrote it as an organized letter. We generally agreed that if it was going to somebody of the general public that we got it right. It was the way they wanted to express it, but we saw that it was correctly spelled and correctly set out, and so on. (38)

Thus in a variety of ways, teachers tried to provide an invigorating verbal climate for the children, using many means to surround them with words having real connection with experiences they could understand and enjoy.

Materials and equipment were similarly considered with care. In the early days of child-centered education, there was very little available to buy that was suitable for use by children. Teachers had to use their imaginations, and children and parents brought materials of all kinds from home. One teacher had her retired father nearby, and he made all kinds of things for the school (18). Children themselves made things they wanted, using creatively all kinds of junk material from every conceivable source. Especially during the war, when materials of every kind were scarce, scrounging was an accepted and valued talent. Some teachers felt that having the children involved in making or finding their own equipment was a positive benefit for them, since they were actively engaged in furthering their own interests. The boys who made the "gang huts" in the school field learned a good deal about math, but they began by wanting to build their own small shelters. From this wish grew much work that was energetic and thoroughly worthwhile in many senses:

In those days when I taught those children, anything for them I had to make. You couldn't go to educational stores and buy anything of any interest. There were no good toys for children, no blocks, absolutely nothing. (14)

The arithmetic apparatus I made myself in my spare time and lunch time. A lot of the equipment was made by the parents. But you see the staff and I would stay in the evenings and provide the tools, and the LCC (London County Council) would provide the timber, and they made the big toys. We had blocks and bricks and this sort of thing for the little ones. Sand and clay and then the table games, and anything so that they could do things with their hands and not be talked at all the time. (3)

Gardens were dug and pets were kept and observed. Jigsaw puzzles and other games were used. There was much material in the classroom to be counted, sorted, weighed, and compared. One teacher working many years ago sent me a description of the materials she collected and how she used them in her infant school:

> I was always searching for means to provide my children with the opportunity to create, in their play and throughout the day, to provide every type of material. Waste material (cartons, boxes, cotton reels, etc.), natural material (sand, water, clay, wood, paper, etc.), good safe tools (saws, hammers, scissors, etc.), materials to create in art (paints, easels), musical instruments (pipes, percussion), for drama (dressing up material, space and opportunity for puppet theatres, material for puppets). To provide the knowledge and stimulate interest — picture books, festivals (May Day, Thanksgiving, Christmas with its Nativity play), and for the 6+ and 7+ year olds, a park, anywhere suitable and available. Discussion periods — to look at anything interesting or which a child wanted to show. Teacher to provide more material or discuss ideas. (35)

Teachers like this one were emphatic that manipulation preceded and is necessary for the development of concepts and must therefore be freely allowed for. That idea is now a widely held Piagetian notion, but in the 1920's and 1930's it was based on the intuitive grasp of observant teachers. Further, it points to their conviction that materials alone cannot teach. The teacher must see that, in her choice of materials and in her work with the children, learning does in fact take place:

> There is much more a feeling of growth and involvement, rather than just setting the stage and putting out the clay and the waste material and all that, and waiting for it to happen. I think this is where some teachers go wrong, because they provide so much material that they spend all their time mopping up and not really observing children. It is only when they observe that they have got any idea of what kind of preparation they are subsequently going to need. (22)

Not all the work of these schools was aimed directly at cognitive growth. Much attention was paid to the development of the artistic, imaginative

52 / ACTIVITY AND EXPERIENCE

side of children. These two aspects of a school's work were not in isolation, however, but very much went hand in hand, and it was the settled conviction of many teachers that successful work in creative areas did positively affect the more academic work, if only because it built a child's sense of confidence in his own powers:

> Immediately, a house was formed by a folding screen and a single piece for a roof. Another child brings her homemade ladder up to the house, saying, "I'm the painter. I paint the house." This gives the hint for the next day's work. Incidentally this dramatic work, being the painter — if I am the painter, I work like this — is the kind of reasoning that will be needed in mathematics, reasoning and experimenting carried out in the imagination. Sometimes I wonder if there is any connection between the wholehearted construction of imagined situations and mathematical ability. It has been a distinguishing feature of all children I have known with this ability. (8)

This emphasis on the importance of developing the imaginative potential in children was also a break from tradition:

> Normally, in those days [the 1920's and 1930's], you never saw any painting as you see it now. Once a week, at the most, children had a little bit of paper and they painted at their desks. I remember vividly the first time in my life when I saw a group of six-year-olds on the floor with newspapers, jam pots, and paint, all painting. At once I saw how different it was. It had a quality. . . . They were painting on newspaper because there wasn't any other paper to paint on. (29)

Here is a now-famous HMI and artist describing his work in 1929 in a very bad section of London, where the children had only a penny to buy a doughnut and some pickles for lunch:

> Now this was only 1929. You see, in 1929, notions like education through art — good Lord, children's art wasn't heard of. But this [headmaster] liked me, and he let me do what I wanted. You see the only thing then you did with your hands other than some pitiful drawings was horrid cardboard modeling, they called it, and cutting out little bits of paper. So, he said, "What do you want to do?" I said, "Let's make books." So we ordered no more books. We made our books. We lettered, we wrote, we made patterns, we printed patterns, we painted pictures. I thought these children were born

artists. Well, this was quite a new notion. Then there was an idea abroad that, yes, young children were imaginative but that dies in them at the age of puberty. Well, I proved it was a lot of nonsense. If they handled the materials that were right for that age, oh, their imagination went right on. The 14-year-old did work that just astounded me. It was remarkable. (34)

The next selection shows the excitement that teachers felt when they released the children to use a variety of materials for their own purposes:

> I think that the understanding of child art and the introduction of it into state schools was one of the biggest factors in freeing teachers in their ideas. Because when they found that children given paper and paints and brushes could make pictures without being told exactly how to do it and shown how to do it, it really opened up a whole new world of understanding. It takes a long time for people to grasp that. (26) (36)

Again and again, I heard how teachers were surprised at what extraordinary results children could achieve, given freedom and encouragement to invent:

> I think the teachers got excited by the aesthetic things — they were certainly pleased with what the children were able to do. It isn't only the aesthetic thing, when I think of a child making a study of a plant. It's very beautiful, and one says, goodness, how on earth did the child do that at that age; but it is something to do with the way in which the child is seeing in his own way this plant or whatever, and then finding the right tool for what that child wants to say. This in itself is an important thing. There is a great deal of oldfashioned craftsmanship coming into this, too. (7)

It was the high standards that children could achieve that overcame any opposition to such artistic work. But the process was equally important, for these teachers believed that the way in which this extraordinary work was produced helped a child's growth in imagination. In many ways, they tried to get "this imaginative development, the encouragement and the exercise of the imagination" (33). Artistic work was one way; climbing equipment, movement, drama and pantomine were others. Here is an example of building a dance right into the activity of the day:

> One day we decided to make an omelet. We didn't decide, but a child

54 / ACTIVITY AND EXPERIENCE

> knew about it, and had one at home, so we provided the egg. The frying pan went on the heater and the butter swizzed around, and she said, "Do it this way," and took the pan and swizzed it around. She said, "I could make a dance out of that, you know," so she called it the fat dance. We went in, and later that was one of the contributions for assembly, the fat dance. I played a sort of skinny piece of music of some sort, and it described her spinning around and then the fall flat — her fat dance. We had music grow out of experiences like that. (8)

Another teacher carefully planned the room arrangement so that:

> If we were reading Alice in Wonderland, let's say, and you came to one of the poems, they could just slip out into the space and create a little dance or dramatise a scene. If we were doing PE [physical education] the children knew exactly where every desk went, and they pushed them around very quickly and so created a bigger space. We had our quiet reading area, our writing area, this space for activity, and then at the end of the room a craft area, and this was over 30 years ago. (24)

The children were being given an opportunity to recreate in imaginative representation their inner world of fantasy and feeling. The importance of this opportunity was underscored again and again by the teachers I spoke with. A vital part of children's growth is their exploration into and gradual control of fantasy in play of every kind, but especially in dramatic representation. In this way, they bring forward their feelings in safe, acceptable ways, they are praised and encouraged in this, and they try on new roles or new points of view in imaginative exploration.[15]

Teachers' reports varied as to the particular kind of artistic expression which they used; obviously it depended on their own gifts and training. But many used dramatic play in their rooms as a standard activity, and much good work grew from it. And all used clay, sand, paint, water, and often junk material for creative work as well.

One particular development, especially in the West Riding of Yorkshire, was the work in movement (derived from the work of Rudolph Laban). Some teachers were able to get that absorption I heard about so often that comes when what a child is doing is exactly right for him at that point. In movement, one teacher told me she felt that:

> The person is so deeply involved. The person is the instrument and the medium. He is the painter, he is the picture. I think we can show

that success in any field is a vitalizing thing. I can, therefore I am. And I think, because the person is the instrument, realization in movement is such a realization for the person that it probably does carry over more into other things than other media. But one can't possibly tell. (11)

Sometimes children absorbed in movement, especially in working out a story in their own way, can express feelings one would not have thought they had yet experienced:

> Well, I will give you two instances. They were doing a version of the Pied Piper, and a group of boys were the corporation. They had been sitting in a little ring of chairs, while the populace waited outside. And they decided they couldn't employ the Pied Piper. They came out of the council chamber and walked the length of the hall, surrounded by the populace (it was the street, you see). One little boy stayed behind to straighten the chairs, put the place in order. When he came out to walk between the people, there was a big gap between him and the rest of the corporation. The kids who were the parents had simply watched the corporation go past. But when there was one solitary one, they were able to make a gesture to him. But he couldn't look them in the face. Now, how do children know that? There was another instance, in the Pied Piper, where the lame boy came back from the cave without the other children. One little girl, clearly in her own house, suddenly drew the curtains in front of her face and couldn't look. How did she know? (11)

Even without a story to work out, movement can be used to help children get absorbed and concentrate:

> If you have a class that is chattering, instead of saying, "stop chattering," you might turn them onto slow movement, and it would very probably disappear absolutely because they become absorbed in the quality of what they are doing. Then you can bring them into a quick movement, which they will not be able to do. Or if you get them to step slowly, they can't do it. They get absolutely absorbed, and the moment they are absorbed. . . . One chooses the quality of movement, but it would very much depend on the class. If a class came into a space with me, and they were very bubbly, I would probably give them something that was exuberant, and when they got pink and panting, they settled down. If they were like that . . . if not, I would much more likely talk quietly to them. If they were standing, I might say, "How slowly can you get right down on the ground." (11)

In some few areas of the country, movement of this kind, wholly without reference to a story line, developed in schools where teachers were taught it or experimented with it. In these schools children learned to concentrate on movement itself, on space, time, energy, and flow, and on how they could express their own personalities within that framework. The teacher might give the first impetus for ideas to come, and then "moving gives rise to the idea, and the movement plays back into the idea" (11).

Many ways of helping children develop creatively, then, were employed by these early teachers. Each used the materials in the school, her own imagination, and the inventiveness of children to bring out the imaginative side of a child's personality. And such work was considered centrally important, not peripheral or merely recreational.

Other aspects of the school were also considered carefully for their contributions to the all-around growth of children. The whole question of the plan for the day, the schedule, received very close attention, and many teachers told me about how, as they experimented and felt their way in this work, they simply had to "break bounds of the day" (12). It seemed unnatural to break off what the children were absorbed in doing, just to adhere to a preplanned timetable:

> One example was with a group of children who had decided to make a town in the playground, and they were using the bricks and the planks of wood, and they were making things with boxes, and it was a large-scale town. It was in summer. Each day, of course, it got more complicated. Each day more children were involved, and each day before they could start, they had to set everything out. Well, each day, of course, this took longer, so that they'd get to the same point each day, and there'd be ten minutes or so to get along with the next idea before it was time to pack up. I was always coming to apologize, "Well, I'm sorry, you see, but it's time to pack up, now." So this is how I put it to the children. I had them all together, and I said, "Well, you know, we're going to have a rearrangement," and I quoted what had been happening. "You know, when Janet was making so and so, and she wanted to go on with it, and she was so disappointed because I wouldn't let her. And someone else was in the middle of his story, and so on." And I said, "Well, I've decided that I'm not going to do that any longer, but you'll have to help. I think it'll be a bit difficult — it'll take a lot of organization." (12)

So they replanned and reorganized their room and rearranged the day, all together. The results were enjoyed by everyone, especially one little girl: "One little girl brought me her lunch, she was so pleased. 'I'm going to give you a present,' she said" (12). Examples of such rethinking about schedules abound in the material I gathered from teachers who wanted children to extend and develop their interests through activity and experience. The artificial time restrictions of the conventional timetable were hindrances, and, with due consideration, they were readjusted. I recall the teacher whose boys got to work on Elizabethan England and had to spread out over two periods and finally most of the morning. She puts the matter thus:

> Most of modern, progressive education in England began in the late 1920's and early 1930's, with the idea to develop a child's potential and to encourage him to think for himself. Education had said this, but the schools didn't provide for this at all. Instruction was given in various subjects orally by the teacher or by means of textbooks. So a child of junior school age was supposed to be able to concentrate for about half an hour. So the school day was divided into half-hour periods. It didn't seem to occur to anyone that some children might get so interested in what they were doing that they resented being forced to change arbitrarily at the end of half an hour and go on to something else. This to my mind only created a lack of concentration and a lack of the things we were trying to help children towards. The emphasis was on repetition and the main motive was competition. (37)

For a teacher who had a large class with a great span of ages among the children, there seemed no other way to work:

> If you have a class of children from 7 to 14, what do you do with them? You can't teach them as a class. It was necessary for some children to be getting on with some activity, maybe some practical work, whilst I was concentrating on the teaching of some skill to another group, and then they would do some follow-on work whilst I concentrated on others who were needing my help. What we now call an integrated day was the only possible way of coping with children of such different abilities and different ages, but it was just common sense and didn't need a label. (24)

Such teachers had to work out ways to use the time they had with the children they had to the best advantage, and also "they didn't see why any children should stop doing what they were really interested in" (26) (36). Another reason, teachers felt, for allowing children to continue the work they were absorbed in was that by watching the children they could pick up clues for further work.

58 / ACTIVITY AND EXPERIENCE

Several schools planned the day to have a certain definite rhythm, placing creative and active play first, then a quiet time for discussion, then a chance to work on the skills needed to continue the activities to a higher level next day. Some felt that a definite rhythm for the day was wise, allowing for activity and repose in turn, with due allowance for individual differences. But "there was always a screened corner where an individual child can leave the group, perhaps for just a few minutes" (13). The main idea was to provide big blocks of time for children's activities — for group discussions, quiet reading, or skills practice — all based on the teacher's observation of the children at work and their apparent needs.

Record keeping, too, was an important matter for teachers in helping children to grow:

> It is very important what you record in your mind. Obviously you must have records, but you can go wild on records and spend so much time writing up your records that you don't really remember what has happened with the children. Each child will have his own folder to keep his own papers in, and a teacher has those periodically, and looks through the work that he has done and sees what his sums were, and drawing, and of course, it is so much more interesting when children are doing different things. (26) (36)

Grades or marks were gradually eliminated where possible, and so was the competition that they engender. Rather, children were helped to evaluate their own work by discussion with the teacher and to set their own standards of individual achievement. Some teachers kept a checklist of points to observe every day, and these were particularly useful for new teachers coming into the school. Others wrote notes after the day was over about the work that children had done and the way tomorrow's room might be set up or experiences provided to further the interests expressed. Some teachers felt that record keeping could be so excessive and so time-consuming that there would be no time to be with the children. Consequently, they developed their own "shorthand" methods of noting progress in reading, math, writing, and so on. No teachers filled out standard forms; rather they worked out their own most congenial ways of keeping track. The purpose of doing so was always to help the teacher think about the child and his progress over the school year and to consider how best to work with him as he went along. Records, then, were yet another device used to promote children's all-around growth.

The same may be said for what one teacher calls "social training." The noon meal, when introduced during the war, was often a social meal, with the teacher sitting at the table and conversation going on:

> They paid great attention to the social quality of the meal that they served them during the day. They served it themselves. It certainly was a very conversational affair. We had eight at a table, and they talked very, very well. (26) (36)

Another teacher, this time in a slum school, said, "I think I put what I mainly called social training as high as anything else that anybody learned at all." Her children were taught, on expeditions, "how you behaved to other people, and how you give up your seat on a bus, and how you don't crowd into the underground — all this kind of thing" (38). Her feeling was that children should be given the social training they need to feel at ease anywhere.

In at least one school, great care was taken about school messages, that they be courteous and clear. Several teachers told me about experiences like this one of an HMI visiting a school in a bad district:

> You saw children you had never seen before. Very poor children. Wonderful work with great confidence, and dirty little things they were. And yet they treated you so marvellously. (11)

As already quoted, visitors in such schools were met "by children who are willing to look after a stranger, who treat you civilly" (17). Children were also expected to be "friendly and open and understanding and responsive and helpful and self-disciplined" (20). The point was not simply to impose good manners upon the children but rather to help them develop the respect for one another on which true good manners are based. Another purpose was, as one teacher (38) put it to me with great emphasis, to provide children with civil manners and speech so that nothing would stand in their way socially as they grew older. Children were invariably treated with courtesy and were expected to treat one another in the same way. Care was taken for everyone's rights as well as duties. In this way, the example set by the teachers helped the children learn social habits which would stand them in good stead always.

Chapter 3
THE TEACHERS AND THEIR WORK

> The only uniformity of practice that the Board of Education desire to see in the teaching of Public Elementary Schools is that each teacher shall think for himself, and work out for himself such methods of teaching as may use his powers to the best advantage and be best suited to the particular needs and conditions of the school. Uniformity in details of practice (except in the mere routine of school management) is not desirable even if it were attainable. But freedom implies a corresponding responsibility in its use.

It is certainly true that, for the teachers whom I met, "at the heart of the educational process lies the child." But there is another sense in which the work of the teacher is also at the heart of it all, because she[16] makes it happen. It is her responsibility, and she has the freedom, to ensure that sound growth does in fact come about for the children in her charge. And in this connection it must be remembered that head teachers are teachers, too. Their leadership and their demonstration of sound methods are crucial to the schools they head.

In the preceding chapter, much has already been said about the responsibility of the teacher. At the risk of some repetition, I now focus more specifically on the work of the teacher and the head teacher; I then turn to the various arrangements which have been worked out to prepare teachers and to help them forward as they experiment and grow into their own special ways of working with children.

The keynote is, of course, sounded by the quotation from the 1918 teachers' *Handbook* that opens this book and is repeated above. Teachers and heads are remarkably free in England. They have long been considered professionals who knew their job and were expected to get on with it. But as the quotation wisely points out at the end, with such freedom comes the responsibility that the work be well done. Still, an American visitor cannot help being startled at the freedom which British teachers have, particularly the heads, who are truly captains of their ships.

The Good Teacher

What makes a good teacher? One answer lies in the descriptions of good schools quoted earlier, since schools are the best evidence of the teachers' work. But the people with whom I talked also had other ways of expressing their ideas about good teachers. Here is an HMI:

> The conclusion I came to after all the years that I was working was that if you could find a common factor, it was that the children really had to know that you liked them. They had to know that you thought they were interesting and wanted to teach them. Your feelings went out to them. This isn't a sentimental thing. The children responded to someone who really liked them, who really cared about them and thought that they were important. (2)

The importance of this fundamental attribute was attested to by many of the people I interviewed; no one can teach children well who dislikes them. One talked about the need for "affection for the children" (39); another about "the power of love" and emphasized "enjoyment of children and the desire to live with them" (34); another stressed the importance of "being in touch with children" (17). The book *Primary Education*[17] puts it well:

> The teacher's power to influence the children depends on the regard they have for him. At best, this regard has in it something of affection and something of respect, and especially of trust. A child wants to be sure that his teacher likes him and understands his difficulties. Children expect that their teacher will "look after" his class. Where there is a warm relationship between him and them, they do what he asks of them because it is he who asks it. They obey because they trust his authority and respect his judgment.

When a child is secure in the knowledge that his teacher likes him and finds him interesting, then an atmosphere of trust and acceptance is established within which he feels safe, and can try out his emerging powers. And children know instinctively how a teacher feels:

> I think that this reinforcement comes enormously from the quality of

voice and gesture. The kids know. I think with teachers, the way they stand, the way they move, what kind of gestures they use, the sound that comes into their voice . . . I think that makes more difference than we know. (11)

One HMI always looked first of all for this sort of thing:

> I think what I looked for at first was a relationship between children and teacher. It was always the most important thing, and I didn't much care if the methods seemed oldfashioned and stuffy, if I thought there was a good personal relationship. (15)

Another similarly focused on the "attitude of the teachers to the children, and then the attitude of the children to what they were doing" (28).

"Minding about children," as one HMI (17) put it, comes first. But this is not a sentimental, casual, or weak-minded attitude. Although some people did talk about children in a somewhat romantic way, none would have left it at that. The attitude of the teacher toward her children is clearly and inescapably linked to the attitude of the children toward their work and toward one another. Learning is changing, and changing means taking risks, trying things out that may fail, figuring out how to solve a problem, and being willing to let go old patterns of thought and action when new and better ones are found. All that can only happen in a safe environment, where a child knows he is valued for what he is, not for what he does at any particular moment. And for the teachers I met, such an atmosphere is essential for the learning that they were dedicated to assist:

> I had a very, very good member of staff for those seven-year-old children. The atmosphere she created was so free and so peaceful that the children could really express themselves very freely and very honestly, and the results of their creative writing were so interesting. (37)

There was an expectation that growth would take place, and the teacher provided the supportive warmth that permitted it to happen.

Children come to value people who value them, and to want to learn what they have to teach. Thus, not only must a teacher sincerely love children and create an atmosphere that bespeaks her feelings, but she must also have something of value to teach them. "I think one comes to this, because I think the children value what the teacher values, when they value the teacher" (29). If the teacher has confidence in the children's powers, so can they. Her work, then, is to challenge the best that is in them and to develop it with them, to the highest standard they can achieve at their stage. When there is a good relationship between child and teacher, the teacher's adult mind is open to the child's, and there can be a genuine "companionship in thinking" (8) from which a child learns much. Another teacher says, "I myself learned much more from contact with other minds than any other way. . . . I believe so much in mind touching mind" (15).

In this connection, it interested me that several administrators told me they preferred to hire people as teachers who were alive, vital, civilized people who clearly cared about children. These qualities came before paper qualifications, in their minds. Others noted that a teacher must be, primarily, a mature and stable person for informal classroom teaching. It is very demanding and one's powers are constantly "at full stretch," so one needs to be soundly put together. "A teacher in this kind of a situation needs to be aware of herself, her own feelings, her own likes and dislikes of children, and so on . . . of her own personality" (12). Some head teachers and HMI's were particularly sensitive to this dimension, and gave much understanding help to teachers who were unsure because of inexperience, upset by an absent husband during the war, or disturbed in other ways. They knew the impact a teacher's feeling can have on the children and were therefore just as concerned about the well-being of their teachers as about that of the children, knowing that an unhappy, angry, frightened teacher makes the learning atmosphere tense and anxious.

A teacher, then, must care about children, must have something to teach them, and must provide a mature outlook. She must also be willing to study children, to know them, and be constantly learning from them. This essential ability to observe children and respond to their needs in ways that challenge them to do their best work has already been discussed, but bears repeating here. Knowledge of children and a clear notion of the quality of work one can expect go hand in hand. This is true both of the overall work of the school and of separate activities like "maths," art, movement, or the story. It depends on "the material being there that produces the question" (9), which is what Dewey meant by his famous phrase "psychologizing the curriculum." The job of the teacher in each situation as it arises is "to take them that step further . . . to get a development in their thinking" (12):

64 / ACTIVITY AND EXPERIENCE

> I suppose the whole point is that teaching is such a complex and highly developed skill that it can only be achieved after years of practice and experience. . . . You have got to know what is in the book yourself, and what is in the child, and combine the two. (26) (36)

One HMI describes the complexities and difficulties of teaching in the informal classroom:

> A teacher has to learn not to attempt more than she can take. I think some of them try to do too much and some of them don't know why they have got so many activities going on. That is the weakness, but they have got to see learning comes out of it. I don't think that in the last resort you can absolutely describe what it is that makes a good teacher. I think it is a very unique, creative act. You have got these children in these circumstances in this classroom, and you have got your ideas about what might come out of this. And whether it does or not depends on the relationship you have created with the children, on the sense of standards you have got into them — whether or not they are really doing their best. It depends on timing and knowing when to interfere and when not to interfere. It depends on your expectations from the children and their expectations from you. It depends on a great number of very sensitive, intuitive actions, knowing just how to instill into the children the spirit of going all out to do their best, the ability to get concentration from the children that enables them to achieve and know what achievement means, instead of just playing about on the level all the time. It is infinitely complicated. Some people have it naturally, I think, but some people get it with experience. When I see it, I take off my hat and sit humbly and try to learn. (20)

It is clearly not easy and requires quite special personal qualities. An important essay in this regard is Nathan Isaacs' "What Is Required of the Nursery-Infant Teacher in This Country Today?"[18] He goes into the whole subject in great detail and makes clear how demanding and sensitive this kind of teaching is. One HMI in talking about this topic said:

> I think one of the things that has rather horrified me in the last ten years is the calm way which anybody thinks they can go and be a teacher. We used to have some standard. Now, the most astonishing people say, "I want to be a teacher." In order to teach you have to have a real conviction, and an obvious love for children. (17)

Again, one has to remind onself that not *all* teachers met these high standards; nor do they now, anywhere. The freedom British teachers have to shape their own work means that they can do very bad work as well as very good work. But the attributes discussed here have been consistently held as ideals, especially among teachers whose work is based on the children's activity and experience.

In general, the teachers whom I met came from cultivated backgrounds, both socially and educationally. Therefore, they had much to give the children whom they taught, not as "Lady Bountiful" but out of genuine concern that children of rather narrower circumstances should enjoy the broader resources of the culture. Some of these intrepid women had been to university, some were themselves poets and writers, some had highly artistic or intellectual parents, some had traveled widely. But some, indeed, had come from poor homes, like one teacher who knew just how slum children felt because she too had run about the streets barefoot as a child. Yet these teachers too made excellent use of the resources offered them for personal cultivation and enrichment, and they lost no opportunity to further their own education. Then all that the teacher had ever learned or done became resources for her teaching:

> Teaching is an art as well as a science. No matter what you are going to do, in this particular situation it can't be done by a computer. It is that creative element in a human being which uses its resources and then creates a situation. (29)

Another attribute of the teachers whom I met, although they did not discuss it directly, was the willingness to work very hard. Evenings were spent writing records, making equipment for the children, planning how to encourage an interest or talent, or devising ways to move beyond the classroom into the whole environment of the school. Evenings were also spent talking with parents, or giving parties for them with guest lecturers and plenty of socializing, or providing tools and encouragement for parents who were helping make things for the school. Holidays might mean camping trips with the children. Evacuation, of course, meant 24-hour supervision in strange surroundings and all the work of organizing the children in their new homes and making sure that school continued. Scrounging for materials, haunting secondhand bookstores, and making anthologies for children's use were all part of the job. Teachers went to courses of lectures for weekends or longer to enrich their own backgrounds and to give them ideas about good ways to work with children. If children were to go on a trip, the teacher went over the route first and checked every detail of planning. Some teachers in country settings lived in the schoolhouse and were very much leaders in the local village doings. Some had to do battle with recalcitrant authorities who did not approve of their freer methods, or who were slow to provide the needed material. Head teachers often took a class, while the regular teacher could visit another school. All these demands, and many more, meant that a teacher who opted for this kind of teaching was undertaking an immense task.

The Teaching Moment

What does such a teacher do? How does she know "the teaching moment," the critical moment when her intervention will bring a "development in their thinking" — or when she should step back and let matters take their course? No teacher answered in the same way as any other, but they all aimed in a similar direction. One has to rely on intuition, but one must cultivate it as wisely as possible. One has to develop one's own resources, to study children carefully, to "keep in front of them" (18), as one teacher put it, when she was talking about a teacher's constant effort to understand what children are saying as they handle material:

> Your contribution is to take them that step further, whether it's some material, whether it's a question, whether it's a challenge of any kind. You are evaluating as you go along, and your curriculum making and curriculum planning are related to your own evaluation of what's happening. You see, if you know your children well — and this kind of work means that you do — and you've got the examples of their work and you know just what stage they're at and what you're going to bring in the next day — all this supplements your observations. You don't see everything, you miss a lot. But then I would ask the children to recall the stages they had gone through, so that I could see what's happened that I haven't seen, and that's very impressive. (12)

Sometimes, however, children need to be left alone to do or to think what they need to. So the question is "skilled intervention and skilled nonintervention" (13). Particularly when the teacher sees a child fully concentrated, she should leave him to explore that experience which is so obviously absorbing all his attention and energies, "the absorption when the work was just right" (9):

> Pioneering teachers were constantly thinking about children and developing their work, and trying things out to see what gave the children most in terms of imagination and learning of skills. (9)

This tentative or experimental attitude seemed basic to any discussion of just when to intervene and when not to. It meant, of course, that one could never be sold on one method as a sure-fire way to teach all children:

> One must listen for the child's questions and then make the adjustment in the situation if necessary, and leave the child to his own solution. This listening technique is so important. (4)

Another teacher put it in terms of hearing the child's question: one should hear the question and put it back to the child in a different way, and then provide the means whereby he can find his own answers (7). Another teacher was constantly asking herself, "What do I do now with them? What next? What do I put into the environment?" (24). Anything to provide "the right challenge at the right moment" (18):

> I think it is up to the teacher to see what a child is doing and lead him on, by producing the books or whatever — something to stimulate him a bit. Or, one might say, "I really think that you have done that long enough, and what next?" I didn't like leaving the children just to do what they want ... All the time he must be given something to lead him on, to the next stage and the next stage. (26) (36)

One teacher used discussions, with all the wonderful "sidetrackings" that might happen, following the children's thinking and contributing the adult point of view along the way (12). None of these teachers could possibly give an exact formula for what to do in each situation, nor, given the nature of their work, would they want to. One must simply, in the nautical sense, be always "standing by."

Freedom and Discipline

The teacher, then, is quite free to work things out in her own way, and

68 / ACTIVITY AND EXPERIENCE

the children are free to express themselves in a wide variety of ways. But what kind of freedom is this? The teachers whom I met were quite clear that freedom does not mean license. It does not mean a child can do just as he likes all day long, and it does not mean that a teacher is free to abdicate her responsibility to help the children learn. Freedom goes hand in hand with responsibility, as the quotation from the 1918 *Handbook* says. There are sane limits within which sound growth can occur; freedom which is license can lead only to chaos and a weedy kind of growth. It is really a question of giving a framework within which the children feel safe and can go about the business of learning. The materials provide one kind of structure; the teacher plans them and uses them with the children, and this interaction provides another kind of structure. The children are not simply provided with a great array of materials and left to make of them what they wish, for that is giving children more freedom than they can use fruitfully. "In a good school, the children are given as much autonomy as they can take, but not more than they can take" (20). The teacher must know what the children need and provide suitable materials. She must also provide the climate, the setting within which children can use and learn from the environment she has arranged. There is a kind of "invisible armature" (18) underlying the informal classroom. "You know that the children are not conscious of it, and yet their freedom comes from the fact that the teacher holds the reins" (18). Thus, adult choices and decisions enter in, subtly and crucially. The teacher must "make it possible for children to learn" (11).

In my discussions with teachers about their attitudes toward children and toward standards of work, it was clear, first, that the children must be free to make real choices and follow them through, and second, that the teacher must make sure that sound work is the result. In a noisy or chaotic room, those things are unlikely to occur. There must be structure — structure born of the planned environment and which results from joint agreements between adults and children about ways in which the materials and space will be used by the people who are there. Simple rules of courtesy are important, especially if the children see that, by being considerate of one another, they themselves can get on with their investigations without fear of disruption:

> We would find very small classrooms, perhaps only 350 square feet, and about 40 or more children, and these heavy desks, and the

teacher had to squeeze between. The children adapted to it, and every little bit of corner and every little bit of space outside the children would fit into, and respect each other's work and climb over it, because they were enjoying life absolutely to the fullest, and it all meant so much to them. They took great care. (9)

In planning for freedom and its wise limits, a teacher has to be very practical. She must think ahead of time about actual possibilities. "You don't discuss freedom, you discuss whether a boy or girl should be free to go and get a book if he wants. If not, why not, and if so, why so?" (29). Like every other aspect of a child's life in school, freedom must be thoroughly understood and wisely planned for.

Another of the teacher's concerns is the child who finds it hard to settle down to anything and disrupts others. Many teachers I talked with felt that such children often came from disorganized homes or some sort of unsettled experiences. Given some freedom to express their needs, but within clear limits, such children usually respond in time:

> Although everyone hadn't to come in at the same time, I said, "Well, if you are not coming, you sit down there and be quiet." Although in the classroom I would have a quiet voice, I've always been firm, and I think that's what makes the happiness, the mixture. (3)

Another teacher put it thus: "I had a great feeling that some children who are disorganized in their lives often want to be quiet and to order things happily" (24). Still another felt that doing work at school in an orderly fashion should appear to the children as "the natural way to behave because this is what you went to school for" (28). She goes on to say, "I've always felt that it was important for the children to be able to control themselves and manage themselves." These teachers, then, set definite expectations of behavior and quietly but firmly insisted upon them. From this kind of attitude, they felt, the discipline which makes freedom possible can come. Besides, "if you have a school run like ours, you see the problems more than you would in any other type" (4). When the problems are visible, they can be dealt with. Although there are no magic recipes for a peaceful classroom, these teachers' experience taught them that when a child feels himself in safe hands, in a schoolroom where a teacher is kindly but securely in charge and where there are rules which are reasonable for everyone, he has a good chance of getting involved in some activity that interests him. To establish and maintain that kind of atmosphere is the teacher's responsibility. "Children have got to know that the teacher is steering the ship" (34).

Headship

Within each classroom, the teacher steers the ship. But the whole school is steered by the head teacher, and her function has been of the greatest importance in the development of informal schools, for "the staff take color from the head" (17). Continuing the nautical metaphor, "you must always have a captain, and in a school it is the head" (29). All the teachers with whom I talked emphasized the crucial role of the head. "The head of a school is in command" (19). Such absolute control means that a head is free to experiment and move her school forward, but it also means, as everyone pointed out to me, that she can run a very bad school indeed. That is the price paid for such freedom.

The best heads, of course, did nothing of the kind. They exerted their leadership in ways that enhanced the growth of their entire staff and of the children in their care. Their experience and leadership could make a great difference to the whole school:

> You must have an element of inspiration and outstanding ability present there. I always said that a really good head can make an ordinary staff look jolly good, whereas a very good staff is powerless if they have got a poor head. (2)

Like the work of the teacher, that of the head must be intuitive and creative. It is not limited to settling budgets, ordering supplies, answering letters, or the like. There were heads I heard about who did only that sort of thing and were never with the children, and they were severely criticized. The place of the head is with the teachers and the children – guiding, leading, helping all along the way. She needs to sense what kind of help is appropriate for whom:

> I think it is possible for a teacher, I suppose, to do things on her own. But it's much better if you've got a leader who is guiding you. There's an art of headship, really, because there were several of us on the staff at that time (1930's) and subsequently, and we were all very different and we all needed different kinds of help. I have seen heads help quite

ordinary people, ordinary teachers, to develop their own personality and to understand their own psychology — you know, the psychology of themselves, not necessarily the psychology of the teacher. (12)

A head has to work with each teacher in a way that brings out the best in her, another teacher told me (35), so that the teacher is using her talents well and feels the head is supporting her in her work. One head went about it with great care:

> We had an afternoon a week for clubs, and the idea was, not from the word go, I waited until I got used to the children and the teachers got used to doing things a bit out of the ordinary until I found their gifts. Then I would say to somebody, "Would you like some extra time for music," or "Would you like some extra time to get out of doors," if that was their particular gift. We decided that the children should choose, of course, but I have always believed that what you do in school is for worthwhile education; therefore, the staff set the framework and the children chose within a given framework. We decided with all our various interests and gifts what we could best contribute. (38)

In order to give a teacher extra time to work on her particular interest, this head teacher made a practice of "coming in on it," that is, doing some teaching herself to free the others and to make their groups smaller, too. Instead of about 50 or 55, then, each might only have 40 children to deal with.

Heads I talked with also took over classes occasionally, either to free the teachers to visit other schools to widen their own experience or to give the teachers some relief. Sometimes they took special groups for a particular project of one kind or another. One might take all the children who were having difficulty with reading, for instance, or another might come in whenever poetry was the focus of interest. One head gave her staff free time to make careful records of the children and also to have a rest period:

> We kept a weekly record under headings of each child, and materials used alone and with the group. I could easily manage the children, so they had time off to do it, when I taught the story to the whole lot and they told me stories. All my staff had a period of the day, which was most unusual in schools. But you see, it is a strain, this sort of work. (3)

72 / ACTIVITY AND EXPERIENCE

In order to fit in like this, a head teacher had to be thoroughly experienced and resourceful:

> In my experience, most of the best head teachers are teachers who were once heads of small schools, because you have to cope with every situation. You have got to cope with every aspect of education. Having done this yourself, I think you are so much more able to help other people. (24)

The wise head teacher, then, stood by to use her own experience as needed. She did not dictate, but rather encouraged and supported the good work of her staff by whatever means she could. Thus her own very considerable authority was delegated to the teacher, to the extent possible:

> The head, you see, if he is wise, passes on as much autonomy as he can to the teachers. He tries to make the best of his teachers and give them their head to work the best out that they can, and get staff meetings to work together. It will be a poor head that dominates a school. He will inspire it, if you like, but not dominate it. (20)

Community Relations

If she is wise, a teacher spends part of her time in building good relations with the community around the school. And the head, even more so, must be available to the parents of the children she is responsible for. However, such relations are very different from those in the United States. "Your parents expect to control the schools, but ours don't" (29). This is the key difference in attitude between the school systems of the two countries. In England, as I have noted earlier, head teachers and class teachers are considered professionals, and they are expected to do their job as such. "The freedom of the teacher has never been challenged" (34). Teachers and heads are free in the way described by this chapter's leading quotation: free, but responsible for the work they do.

Many heads made substantial efforts to bring parents into the schools, especially if they were trying to bring about some changes in their methods:

> There were always mothers in their children's schools. They come, and of course they see and experience the relationship. They see the children happy, they see them learn, they see them paint, these things

which they think are quite wonderful. They see them reading books, they see them sitting down quietly. Two mothers will see all this, and of course they go home, and there is a turnover of mothers in the classroom. They will stop and chat, and really feel at home. So that it will be continually home to school and back again. (29)

All the teachers I spoke with felt that this kind of pleasant experience for mothers can only help the children. There would be no great break between home and school in such schools, unlike more formal ones which might retain the old sign outside: "Parents not permitted beyond this point." There was a genuine attempt made by teachers and heads to know something of the family from which the children came, a further insight which could be useful:

> [This headmistress] was really wonderful. She gave up all her time in going into rooms and sitting with children. It was her leadership that made the school. She knew all the families, and all the families came to collect the children. (9)

Sometimes a head could serve a very useful function, especially in a poor neighborhood, as friend and counselor. "If somebody was drunk and wanted to row with me I'd just say, 'Sit down, Mr. So-and-so, and tell me about it' " (3). Another head in a very bad slum area managed to make contact with parents who had long been alienated from the school:

> The thing that I found most appalling was the attitude of the children to the school. They hated school and they regarded the teachers as enemies, and so did their parents. I think the best compliment that I had paid to me was two mothers talking underneath the window. I heard one say, "Oh, well, you go and see the governess, you can talk to her," and they hadn't been able to talk to me before. I think this was a way into understanding children, when the parents did come and talk to me. (28)

One result of such good relations with mothers for that particular head was that when her HMI came once, he thought she was having an open day, because there were so many mothers in the school.

Another teacher in a mixed area often made opportunities for mothers to come to the school; she also made sure they were welcome and helped with whatever problem they might bring to her. Some of those mothers came in and talked with children and enjoyed themselves in a school for the first time:

> Some of my children did come from poor backgrounds, living in poor tenements, in large, old, shabby, converted houses, but most came from good artisan homes. The value of our Parents' Guild was that mothers came from both types of homes, those with low paid incomes welcomed and able to come (no cost involved). I provided tea, milk, sugar for the welcome cup of tea, two, three, four, or even five mothers in turn voluntarily promising and providing their inexpensive home-baked biscuits or buns. Often recipes were exchanged.
>
> One mother was distressed because she said that the information about the birth of a baby given to the senior girls by a trained visiting nurse on "mothercraft" was too detailed for schoolgirls, so I persuaded the Mothercraft teacher to come and talk to my mothers about her aims and contents of her talks, allowing time for questions and discussions after the talk. This and talks on problems raised by members were welcomed, proving informative and helpful. (35)

Still another teacher was asked to open a nursery class in connection with her infant school. She had very little money for equipment, but she called in the parents:

> I talked to them informally and said, "We shall want somebody to sew, and we shall want someone to wash these things [smocks] every week. We all sat around and went into one of the classrooms in the evening, and two or three of them brought sewing machines. Then a mother who could do smocking very beautifully showed us how to smock, and we all sat around smocking, and that was the beginning. Then we decided that we would begin in a formal way. So we had a formal meeting, and we had the room packed. We used to turn people away. And we were great on socials. Whenever someone came to give a talk, then we would push the tables back and have a social. (8)

Mothers were thus made to feel really useful in the work of this school, just as in another school parents built much of the equipment for the children, with the staff providing tools and materials (3). And the school became a pleasant meeting place, with time for a chat and a cup of tea.

This role that a school could play was important in a country village, too, where the teacher was very likely the best-educated person living there:

One was always in touch with the parents. The children took home a lot of work that they had been doing and parents began to be interested. They participated in our Fair Days, by organising Teas, and Rabbit and Poultry shows. I lent them books. I did form a parents' association and had people come and speak so as to widen their horizons, but I think parents felt to be very much part of school and I hadn't any trouble with them, ever. I started a young farmers club too, which brought in farmers and the older generation. (24)

During the war, particularly, when no one went away for holidays, this teacher was a leader in developing community projects and entertainments. She reintroduced the old country dancing which she had known but which had never been kept up in that village. So, over the many years she was there she served the whole community. Her school was a familiar place to everyone, and she was trusted to do all kinds of free experiments, because everyone knew her and she knew everyone. Nor is her story an isolated example; I heard similar accounts from a number of other people who had taught or knew teachers in rural areas.

Clearly, such friendly relationships between home and school ultimately worked to benefit the child. Teachers made themselves available to the community and came to know the members of it. The parents entered the school and often worked with it, but they did not expect to control it; instead, they trusted and respected the teachers and especially the heads as trained professionals. Thus, all the adults in a child's life were communicating with one another in a helpful way.

Pre-service Teacher Training

One topic discussed frequently among the people whom I met was teacher training. Many had retired from years of active teaching and had gone into training colleges, so they had one particular point of view on the subject. Others saw the process from outside, as administrators or local county advisors. Opinions differed considerably. Some felt that, by their very nature, training institutions are out of touch with schools and therefore remote from realistic contact with children. Such institutions, these people felt, emphasized theoretical subjects — philosophy, sociology, and psychology — at the expense of the more practical ones having to do with children and their growth and development, so that the first real training which a probationer (first-year teacher) would receive would be in the school itself. Other people, on the contrary, felt that pre-service training could be useful; they spoke particularly of the long-established Froebelian three-year training colleges, with their focus on children and their natural ways of growing.

Two main points were emphasized to me by those who were involved in pre-service training: first, the need for ample opportunity to work with children in a variety of settings while gaining necessary theoretical preparation, and second, the use of the same activity-centered methods which teachers would later use with children. The first of these points I have already touched upon in Chapter 2, in discussing the necessity for observing and studying children. Practice in doing so could be obtained in the training college, especially if it was Froebelian:

> Yes, I think they do a lot of observation of children, but I think, more important, they do it at the right time. You can't observe unless you know what you are to see. I think they need to get into a classroom fairly early on, and then I think they need to discuss a lot of what they have seen. Then they go back into the classroom. They have lots of time to observe. (7)

One person involved in training infant-school teachers planned her work thus:

> I don't think you can get very far unless you train people to observe. I think the foundations of growth in teaching are because you are able to see the children and see what happens. Sometimes I have tried it with groups going to see a group of infants, and then a group of top infants, two contrasting ages. I give them questions, quite simple questions, simple counting and seeing what ways the children move about the playground and the classroom. And they come out with the fact that the little children hop, skip, and jump much more, and the other ones move more rhythmically. So you get this idea of control, and they see it happening. They ask about certain features of the playground and the furniture — which is suitable and which is not. Then you take another question: What does a child seek a teacher for? They write down, in a half hour, two of them side by side, every time a child goes up to a teacher, what it's for. Of course sometimes they see, as they are following the child and he is going up to the teacher, that what he wants isn't what the teacher thinks he wants. Of course, when I have a group of twenty all out in different classes, you can

summarize and you get some very interesting graphs out of this. And they enjoy this, they enjoy the contact with children and seeing all this. (21)

All this had to be very carefully done, by someone who knew exactly how to move from theory to practice and back again, or else the work would become haphazard and somewhat trivial. This particular teacher had been an early student of Susan Isaacs' and had a similarly thorough grasp of child development.

In order to keep in touch with reality, many teacher-training colleges had demonstration schools attached. There the students could work with the children, and the staff could demonstrate the methods they were talking about in lectures. One instructor said, "I never let a year of those students go through without a systematic observation in a school with me teaching" (4), and she encouraged other members of staff to work in the same way, both in college lecture halls and in school classrooms:

> This tie-up between a school and a college, I think, was one of Froebel's insights, because it meant, you see, that no college lecturer in education was able to stay far away from children and had to use students' observation as a basis for theoretical content. This, I think, made the theory meaningful, relevant, and therefore likely to be fruitful. (4)

The second point emphasized was the need to develop an acquaintance with activity methods — at first hand:

> You see, unless they do this, they don't realize the importance of putting certain problems in front of children in order to develop them. They themselves don't know the materials sufficiently well to understand what the child is saying. (33)

It was particularly interesting to me to hear, from people whose own training had been very different, about the desirability of helping training-college students to learn from their own activities and experiences. For example, one HMI I spoke with had been to Cambridge, where the approach to learning is certainly traditional. When he went into training-college work, however, he saw the importance of providing experience for students in exactly the kind of exploratory work that they would later want in their classrooms. In doing environmental studies, he found, "They needed a bit of instruction, because it is easy enough to say you must get outside, but in sheer practicality they need some practice" (2). On one occasion, he took them to the railway station and had them ask questions and look about them. "Then the next time we met in college, we said, 'What shall we do? Is there something here we can do with children? How shall we do it?' " Later, he did a more extensive piece of work in his own village, carefully warning a few neighbors ahead of time. His students explored many aspects of the village and then came back for a discussion. A final piece of writing was required: "I told them all this has got to amount to something. You must try to get a finished article at the end." Altogether, "this gave them some idea that this can be done, and that you could organize it." Thus, they began to see how one could go out into the environment, explore it, and come back with interesting topics and questions for further work, just as they would be working with children later on. Another teacher agreed: "You have to *do* an environmental field study before you know what it is all about" (20).

Two others, in a Froebel college, said:

They didn't decide what age they were going to teach until the end of the first year. They gathered as wide experience as possible, in different schools, and subjects, and methods. They spent a whole term on an active approach. I think we called it exploratory sessions. And at the same time they were having related child psychology. Then, when they came on to the more formal studies they had a basis to build on. (26, 36)

Thus, among people involved in training students to teach, there did seem to be agreement that, just as in schools, the child was at the center. The training included a careful combination of theory and practice in the area of child development and active involvement of students in various kinds of work that they would be doing later with children.

Not all training colleges were doing this kind of work, nor are they all now. In general, it was chiefly the Froebel colleges that were child-centered until, by the end of World War II, Froebel-trained teachers headed the infant departments of nearly every training college.

Further, the importance of the two aspects of teacher-training work which have been described is not that they were or were not prevalent among training colleges but that they were considered essential by the kinds of teachers I talked with. There was, therefore, a congruence in their views of how children should be taught and how teachers should be taught, just as there was a congruence in the way they felt a head should treat her staff and the way a teacher should treat her children. All these views were based on the same general attitude toward working with people at whatever stage or in whatever setting one found them.

After World War II there was a great need for more teachers in England's schools, and special arrangements were made to train people quickly. These were the Emergency Training Colleges (ETC's), and to them came mature, highly motivated people coming out of the armed forces, wanting something more relevant and more personally involving than the schools they remembered. One HMI found that these students were very different from the usual ones:

> Oh, yes, when they had come back from the war, indeed they were men and women who had been in the forces, and so they were older and more experienced. It was very intensive training and on the whole a very successful one. (20)

Staff for the ETC's was often recruited from among those who had been actively teaching rather than from among academicians, and that had two beneficial effects. First, it gave these practicing teachers an opportunity to articulate and pass along the ideas they had been experimenting with. "This was very good for me," said one, "because it meant that I had to do an awful lot of reading and had to consider why I had been doing all these things" (24). Second, it meant that the ETC students were talking to people who were in close touch with schools and children and had worked effectively with them:

> I think there were some marvelous selections of devoted and well-informed teachers for that scheme. I can think of one who had been headmistress of a primary school near here and had been recommended for emergency training staff. She was absolutely first class. (4)

Although some ETC's did not last very long, they could be very exciting places.

> The students were very mature, they had confidence, and they were desperately anxious to get to work. The enthusiasm was simply terrific. The college I knew was actually fizzing with enthusiasm. They were

80 / ACTIVITY AND EXPERIENCE

absolutely terrific. They got a very good start there. When this lot got into the schools, of course, they galvanized them. They weren't at all anxious to do just what they'd done in school, but rather the opposite. I think that all this was very important. (2)

One administrator testifies to the effectiveness of the ETC-trained teachers when they got into schools:

They were more mature, of course. I remember looking some years ago at the people from these colleges, and many of them had senior posts. They went right ahead. (7)

The ETC's, for the short period of time they existed, met a pressing need. They seem to have been realistic about the students they enrolled; they seem to have given their students the experiences they wanted to set them going in the right way. This is a general impression I received from the people I talked with; no doubt not all Emergency Training Colleges did as well, but I did hear considerable testimony to their effectiveness at a critical time.

In-Service Training

Whatever the pre-service training, no one assumed that a teacher was fully trained when she completed her formal qualifications. It was expected that teachers would go on learning and improving throughout their careers. Expert teaching is a highly developed skill acquired over years and demanding all the resources one can muster, especially with informal, activity-centered methods. Without a set syllabus or prepackaged curriculum, but with high expectations for children's learning, a teacher needed all the help, support, and counsel she could get:

This is my point. Nobody suggests that a young teacher of twenty-one is adequate to all these things that are coming in. But at least she ought to know where to find out. (5)

Further, she needed to recharge her own batteries as a person just as much as she needed specific answers to her problems in a classroom.

Possibly the earliest in-service training opportunity came in the 1920s:

The first in-service training, as far as I know, was in the 20's, when the master of one of the colleges at Oxford suggested to the minister of education, "Wouldn't it be a good thing to get teachers to come to Oxford in the vacation? They could live the life of the university for a fortnight, and they could have courses." I believe this was the first example of it. (2)

Courses in the early days were run by the National Union of Teachers, mostly consisting of lectures given to large audiences. There were also Saturday mornings at the Froebel Foundation:

> I went to the Froebel Foundation in London in Manchester Square, and we used to go up every Saturday for lectures and discussions, and we discussed Susan Isaacs and Nancy Catty, and all these people, and we visited schools where this work was going on. (5)

Training colleges had lecture series from time to time, and people like Susan Isaacs gave widely influential lectures for many years to experienced teachers on a wide range of topics, but often on child development specifically:

> From the time I came out of college [a Froebel one] they had the monthly lecture, and they also had a bookcase in which they had progressive books. By the way, I used to go to the library and spend one night at least every month after tea, reading primary plans and primary educators' papers and American papers. Yes, I got a lot of incentive from there. (35)

In some places teachers got together themselves, to share experiences and discuss ideas:

> It was the teachers' initiative that got things going. It used to meet every month. Now there is so much more. It went on for 60 years, I think. (35)

The New Education Fellowship also ran courses and held lectures for anyone interested in experimental ways of educating children and leading figures such as Maria Montessori came to speak. The Froebel Foundation had an annual conference and held summer schools for years. Libraries and courses were established for teachers:

The London Council had the most wonderful teachers' library. You could not only choose your books, you could ask for them and they were delivered to the school every month, and then we had the most interesting winter lectures too. You could go and take a course on speech training, for instance, or music or art, and you met a teacher or head teacher who had made a special study of this for her school. (3)

Thus, in-service training in England goes back a good number of years. There were always opportunities for the enterprising teacher to build up her own background and hear new ideas, but since World War II they have increased substantially. Now there is an extensive network of teacher centers for conferences; there are local advisers who travel to many schools; there are courses of a great variety, materials centers for teachers to use, and so on.

One of the first efforts after the war was to increase greatly the series of national courses for teachers which had been run by the Ministry of Education since the 1920's. Their purpose was, in effect, to revive practicing teachers, who were weary with the war years of just being sure the children were cared for and who were now ready for some "recharging":

> There was the need to revive, because during the war education had resolved into: who pays for this boy's boots or haircut, or how do we get this child away from the foster parent who isn't looking after him? Education was down the gutter, so after the war we had to do something to revive it. (17)

Top people in many subject areas were recruited, and carefully selected teachers were taken through two weeks of inspiring talks and discussions. The aim was not only to get them thinking about education again but also to get them to reawaken themselves as people of culture:

> Not only did you need to learn more about children's needs, but you had to fill your own wells in order to do this. And each of these courses laid aside a certain amount of time for the development of each one that was there. Staff and students together came away from the course with the feeling of movement. (17)

As one teacher put it:

> You know how you suddenly feel that you've given everything out

of you. What I felt was that they had out of me all that I'd got to give them, and I had to have something poured into me. And it brushed my thinking power up again. (18)

Then, when it was all over, the focus returned to the child. Groups came together to discuss, "Now, what are we prepared to give to children out of that? What can we give the children?" (17). Discussion groups formed in local areas among teachers who had been to the national course, and some of them still meet to discuss ideas, share experiences, and hear talks about new ideas. By now, local authorities have started their own courses for teachers, for heads, for custodians, for anyone concerned with schools, often at residential centers where, informally and freely, colleagues can meet and talk.

Another well-known course that was run after the war was a one-year course at the Institute of Education at the University of London. It was a one-man operation, with one very experienced HMI (29) working with a group of twelve students. He chose only experienced teachers with a positive attitude toward children and a record of imaginative work with them. Each day of the week they met with him, visited schools, had discussions afterward, observed again, and so on. There were no examinations; none were needed because the director knew each person's work so well. For some of the people whom I met, this course was "the supreme educational experience" of their lives. It was at an adult level, the work was challenging and very relevant to their professional concerns, it opened new doors into new ways of thinking, and, perhaps most importantly, it formed among the members of the group a strong bond that still persists.

The course that Susan Isaacs ran, carried on by Dorothy Gardner later, was also widely influential in helping teachers develop their thinking and their work with children.

These are some of the ways in which, for many years, teachers in England have been provided with opportunities to learn and grow long after their preservice training or probationary year. The assumption is that teachers go on learning, and great care is taken to make it possible for them to do so, both for personal enrichment and for professional brushing-up.

HMI's

One supportive service for teachers and schools merits separate discus-

84 / ACTIVITY AND EXPERIENCE

sion: Her Majesty's Inspectorate.[19] It has no counterpart in the United States; it enjoys a very large measure of professional independence and its reports cannot be influenced by party politics or by ministers or anyone else (2). The HMI was founded in 1839, when government money was going into schools for the first time. The plan was "to have an educated, civilized man going to schools to meet teachers who weren't very educated themselves. This started things in the right direction" (2). Some of the early inspectors had no experience with young children at all, but some did a remarkable job, with sympathy and understanding. They had then, and still have, a sort of "roving commission" to look at the schools in their districts, and they are very little bound by regulations from London. Originally conceived of as a purely advisory body, the Inspectorate was nevertheless very much feared for many years because of the policy that the HMI came to the school and examined the children's skills, and the teacher's salary depended on the report he wrote. This "payment by results" system "did enormous harm to the relationship between inspectors and teachers and to the whole conception of primary education, which tended to narrow itself down to the things which could be tested" (2). It lasted from 1863 to 1898, and after the turn of the century the official position changed, and teachers were urged to use their own initiative, as the lead quotation to this chapter points out. Yet even in the 1930's, "there were plenty of people who were still really afraid of the inspector, as a person who might do them down" (2).

In the early years, also, HMI's were selected from among "educated men," so that few were either women or teachers. But gradually, inspectors of both sorts began to be appointed, with women usually filling posts at the infant-school level, and men higher up. I met many HMI's, and their way of describing their work, especially as it became more advisory and less inspectorial, was of particular interest to me. Often they had been teachers and heads themselves, so they had particularly realistic notions of what schools could do, as well as a sympathy for children and a humane outlook on life. The HMI's whom I met had been responsible for spreading freer methods of teaching in their designated areas. They were "bees carrying around ideas" (19), involved in what some even called "pastoral" work: counseling, supporting, advising, but no longer the stern inspecting of earlier days. And for some, the years just after World War II, when the educational ideas of previous decades had begun to take hold widely, was an exciting time indeed, "real missionary work" (38).

One HMI, who had entered the Inspectorate in 1924, described his work with teachers thus:

> All I tried to do was to put them in touch with each other, encourage them, praise them, and sometimes suggest various other ideas or tell them what somebody else is doing. Once people begin to work in this way, I think, what they do need is encouragement. I used to feel in those days, and I still do, that my job was to provide help, opportunities, and resources and stimulus, and so on. (29)

Another describes his work in somewhat similar terms:

> I've got one law to myself that has, I think, helped me tremendously, and that is going into a classroom and not saying anything unless it's something which can grow. For me this has worked considerably, but it takes time. I say, too, that any fool can go into a classroom and criticize. One's professionalism comes out in looking at what is there and blowing the flame. The more one does that, the bigger flame you can grow. It sort of eases out the other. What it also does, it brings about a relationship which allows you to say things which are taken into account rather than dismissed. (33)

Another, quoted earlier, tried to find out what a school could do well and encouraged that ability, since he felt that excellence in one area spreads into others. This idea of focusing on a "growing point" (9) reappeared often during my interviews. It is similar in effect to the method of teaching that the informal classroom requires: help the person, child or adult, to achieve for himself the best that he can, and many-sided growth will come about; a positive relationship will be built; and ideas can be exchanged or introduced without fear of criticism or hostility.

Chapter 4
THREE INFLUENTIAL BOOKS

Over the years, the gifted and enterprising pioneers in England worked out their ideas in scattered classrooms with what seemed like "precious little theory" (29). Nonetheless, there was also a steady growth of published work describing, analyzing, and supporting them. Today there are many books about informal schools, each explaining them and the principles that underlie them from a different point of view. Earlier, however, such books were rarer, and much less widely read. It is difficult to assess the degree to which any one book or group of books did in fact influence teachers, aside from hearing their own testimony, yet such books did exist and were used by at least some people in the educational world.

The ideas and practices that these publications present strike one as remarkably contemporary, yet the original expressions of them are all but unknown in the United States. In general, although these works differ from one another in style or content, essentially they deal with similar themes: all are concerned that education build a better society and that careful study of children's natural ways of growing and developing should be the basis of school reforms. There is little detailed concern with administrative or curricular arrangements as such: the focus is and remains on enhancing the child's activity and experience in the microcosm of society that is the school.

Many well-known books are discussed at the beginning of the bibliography (page 203); here I deal at length with only three. They were chosen because they were often referred to by people whom I met, because they were clearly influential at the time of the publication but unknown in this country, and because they represent three quite different kinds of books from three different periods, yet they are in fundamental agreement.

Sir Percy Nunn's *Education: Its Data and First Principles*

Probably the most influential book of educational theory in its day was

Sir Percy Nunn's *Education: Its Data and First Principles.* Published in 1920, it went through 14 printings before 1930; there was a second edition in 1930, which was reprinted 8 times, and a third, revised, edition came out in 1945. R. J. W. Selleck has this to say about it:

> F. A. Cavenagh, writing in 1936 and surveying English education since 1920, remarked that it was undoubtedly "the outstanding book of the period." "The studies of a generation of teachers in training have been based on it," he claimed, "and it has profoundly affected their outlook and subsequent practice." Almost all his contemporaries agree with this estimate, even those who do not agree with the arguments advanced in the book. It gave the progressives a textbook.[20]

Nunn's book is sensible, moderate, and intellectually thorough. It lays out a full theory of human development and demonstrates what he means by "education according to nature." He asserts "the development of individuality" as "the supreme educational end," and goes on to place that aim in a theoretical framework, explained and clarified with sound English common sense.

Briefly, his argument runs as follows. The aim of education is the fullest possible development of the unique individuality of each person. The individual finds his fulfillment in self-expression within the social framework into which he is born. Indeed, society itself, especially a democracy, serves precisely to enhance the individual lives of its citizens. Here, he argued, "the good of all is the good of each," for "individuality develops only in a social atmosphere where it can feed on common interests and common activities. . . . individuality is by no means the same thing as eccentricity" (p. 16). Then, his progressive zeal burst into full flower:

> . . . that freedom for each to conduct life's adventure in his own way and to make the best he can of it is the one universal ideal sanctioned by nature and approved by reason; and that the beckoning gleams of other ideals are but broken lights from this . . . that freedom is, in truth, the condition, if not the source, of all higher goods. Apart from it duty has no meaning, self-sacrifice no value, authority no sanction. It offers the one sure foundation for a brotherhood of nations, the only basis upon which men can join together to build the city of God. Dare we, then, take a lower, and can we find a higher, ideal to be our inspiration and guide in education? (p. 17)

For Nunn, life itself should be seen as a work of art at its best. A work of art has a controlling unity in its diversity, imposing upon its materials a deliberate and purposeful pattern, using the materials but transcending them. It is also autonomous, in that it comes from the mind of the creator alone, not from any external law which governs its form or expression; however influenced in various ways that mind may be, yet the work of art is a unique and free creation of it, in the sense that a sonata cannot be written until it is in fact written. So with the individual life of each person: "To speak of individuality as the ideal of life implies, then, that life as a whole is autonomous and that it constantly strives after unity." (p. 21)

Although man has clear links with the whole animate world, the difference between the amoeba and humanity lies in the degree of complexity and subtlety of responses to the environment. The operations of consciousness, the sole possession of man, are the highest form of such responses. All life is a "striving toward the individuality which is expressed most clearly and richly in man's conscious nature" (p. 25). And an education that aims at fostering this conscious individuality is the only "education according to nature." In this view, the work of the educator is to study the unique, creative responses to the environment which each child makes, and to adjust the school situation so that this individual consciousness can be most complexly and richly expressed.

As each human being develops, he or she demonstrates a powerful force that Nunn calls the "will to live" or "self-assertion." It is an urge to be, to protect the self and at the same time to expand and express it; thus it has a conservative strength and a creative one. Conserving the self means actions that are self-preserving and stabilizing, and in a school they may well take the form of routine and ritual; creative activity, in contrast, comes out in growing, developing, exploring, and in many ways increasing the complexity of the person's self-expression:

> [A] school fails in its purpose unless it gives its pupils some understanding and appreciation of the conservative basis of their nation's life and of civilization as a whole, and fits them to play, efficiently, intelligently, and dutifully, some part in its maintenance. It must, accordingly, be on its guard against the tendency of every type of education to stiffen into a closed and static system and be too little responsive to the changing needs of the social situation.
>
> [A] school fails unless the spirit that pervades it gives its pupils a zest for at least some modest form of adventure in life and some confi-

dence in their power to carry it through. Here the standing danger is that didactic and dogmatic methods of instruction should receive too large a place, too little room being left for freer methods of learning based upon a belief in the average pupil's gift of spontaneity and a due sense of the importance of developing it. (p. 36)

Thus, tradition has its place in school, in practices that do not stifle but express the natural conservative force in each person. Provision should be made for them, and they can be counted on as the "flywheel" whose momentum can be constructively harnessed from time to time, to get through the duller aspects of schoolwork and its routines. Some effective rituals, too, provide a sense of identification with the past and with the present school as a community and are naturally attractive to children as they develop a group spirit.

Play, the expression of the natural creative impulse, is of particular importance:

> The spirit of play is an intangible and elusive sprite, whose influence is to be found in corners of life where it might be least expected. Everyone agrees, however, that childhood is her peculiar sphere, and that she manifests her presence there in activities whose special mark is their spontaneity—that is, their relative independence of external needs and stimuli. . . . In play, . . . the child gradually enters into possession of his own body, and raises his command over it to the highest possible power. . . . he finds and exercises in play his intellectual gifts and powers, and often discovers interests that are to fill the central place in his adult life. . . . he finds and establishes his moral and social self largely in corporate games. (p. 79)

In the development of an individual life as a work of art, play is essential. Though its "peculiar sphere" is indeed childhood, yet the ability to play well as a child prefigures the ability to work well as an adult, and the line between the two grows blurred. "Nature invented play . . . as a device for using that energy to prepare him for the serious business of life" (p. 80). Play among children must, then, be fostered by the school for many reasons: play can be a "cathartic," an opportunity to express safely "the ancient tendencies to cruelty and vice," and a means by which they are transformed (one assumes by sublimation) into actions of "ethical value." Play can also be therapeutic: "A child's self-chosen activities have a virtue that helps to straighten out the crookednesses and entanglements that distort some children's minds and behaviour" (pp. 85-86). And for the wise teacher, carefully observing play is the finest possible way to learn about a child's abilities and interests. Play is no trivial waste of time but rather is "full of high seriousness" and should be freely allowed:

> It is hardly extravagant to say that in the understanding of play lies the key to most of the practical problems of education; for play . . . shows the creative impulses in their clearest, most vigorous and most typical form. [These impulses] are, in fact, continuous in the development of individuality. . . . All truly effective reform, both in education and society, is motived [sic] by the desire to enlarge as much as possible the field in which that central function of life may find worthy and satisfying exercise. (p. 99)

The freedom Nunn refers to is not the kind of freedom whose "ugly synonym is license," but rather "the higher values of freedom emerge only when it chooses worthy ends and in pursuing them submits itself to the control of well-inspired forms or methods" (p. 100). This concept of responsible freedom, or freedom with inner discipline, is characteristic of the progressive movement in education as Nunn saw it:

> Expressed in broad terms, the principles of the movement are that the old authoritarian attitude of parents and teachers should be modified, that more responsibility for their conduct and progress in school studies should be entrusted to the children themselves, that methods of instruction should be made more flexible so as to meet better the widely differing needs of individuals, and that more account should be taken of varying tastes and abilities. In a word, it is a movement to exploit more fully than heretofore that spontaneity of the individual which we have described as the essence of play. (p. 105)

Lest the reader believe that this kind of schooling is mere dreaming, however, he says that "there is already good evidence that such a system is not only practicable, but is capable of yielding fruits better than those of the older system, even when measured by the older standards" (p. 107).

Under such a system the role of the teacher and the whole organization of the school must change. The teacher, instead of giving one lesson to the whole class, must be an acute observer of each child, "standing by" in the nautical sense, always at the ready but refraining from fussing or interfering. He must keep minute records of progress; he must be steeped in the best that culture has to offer; he must know how by inspiration, suggestion, or demonstration new ideas can be offered to the child for his use; he must be an "idea carrier" for children, a liaison between the "great world and the school microcosm, infecting his pupils imperceptibly with germs that may fructify into ideals of sound workmanship and devoted labour." His role is complex, concerned with intellectual development and its expansion, with personal and emotional expressiveness, and the free growth of a sound morality in this small society. Always his work is in the service of greater and more complex self-assertion for each child's unique life force.

> Reviewing the whole discussion, we may say that self-assertion, as far as it is expressed in cognitive activity, has always the same immediate aim—an aim that may be described as the intellectual control of the world in face of which the individual maintains his creative independence. (p. 237)

Just as the teacher's task becomes more responsible and complex, so the school's environment must allow child and teacher to work well together. The social world of the school ideally provides the correct forum for the individual's growth into creativity and service. It is a special society, however, in some ways and not merely a replica of the larger one:

> [It is a] natural society, in the sense that there should be no violent break between the conditions of life within and without it. . . . There should be no cramping or stifling of the citizens' energies, but room for all, whether teachers or taught, to live wholly and vigorously; no conventional standards of conduct, but only the universal canons and ideals; no academic separation from the interests of the great world, but at least an intellectual participation in them. . . . a school must be an artificial society in the sense that while it should reflect the outer world truly, it should reflect only what is best and most vital there. (p. 253)

Thus, large-scale social reform can be brought about only, as John Dewey said also, by reforming the small societies which are a nation's schools, by developing within them the kind of citizens toward which a democracy aims. And to this end "education according to nature," as Nunn has defined it, is the only way to produce a truly humane society:

> [T]hough our children cannot build a fairer world on any other foun-

dation than our own, yet they are not bound, unless in our folly we will have it so, to repeat for ever our failures; . . . they have in them a creative power which, if wisely encouraged and tolerantly guided, may so remould our best that, as the dark shadows pass, 'the life of the world may move forward into broad, sunny uplands' and become worthier than any we have yet seen. (p. 276)

A. L. Stone's *Story of a School*

Story of a School, written by A. L. Stone,[21] was published in 1949 by the Department of Education and Science (formerly the Ministry of Education). A small pamphlet of only 36 pages, it was subtitled "A Headmaster's Experiences with Children Aged Seven to Eleven." It concerns Mr. Stone's work with the children of the Steward Street Junior School in the older part of Birmingham, to which he went as head in 1940. The air raids had already begun by then; many houses were without glass, and people spent many hours in shelters. The crucial point that Stone makes is this: children, even though they live amid "stark ugliness," "when they were allowed to express themselves freely, . . . they created something which was beautiful" (p. 7). This story of the work in Birmingham was very widely read when it came out. By 1970 it was in its seventh printing, and it is still on sale at Her Majesty's Stationery Office.

The booklet has a number of other important aspects. First, Stone had done a good deal of sound teaching before he was appointed to this school. He was familiar with child-centered methods and theories and was able to apply them from the start of his tenure. To be sure, he learned from the children as he went along, but before he came there he had already developed the kind of attitude that would allow such learning to take place. Second, this school was not the stereotypical village infant school with its devoted headmistress, but quite the opposite. And it demonstrates that good work can go on under very bad slum and wartime conditions, not simply in the isolation and beauty of the countryside.

Stone's book begins at once by describing the milieu of the inner city:

Of the 240 [children] who attended, the majority lived in back-to back houses, very few of which had bathrooms. . . . Most of the houses in some way or other were suffering from the effects of raids. . . . Many of the school's hours were spent in the air raid shelters. The school itself was bounded by factories on three sides. The playground

Story of a School / 93

was entirely overlooked by factory windows and nowhere was there the possibility of encouraging a blade of grass to grow. The nearest park was half a mile away, and there were no open spaces in the near vicinity where children could play in safety. The majority of them played in the back streets, or crept into forbidden premises of neighbouring timber and builders' yards which afforded excellent opportunities for all kinds of imaginative play, but from which, all too soon and all too painfully, they were, without fail, ejected. . . . It is important that you realise how little beauty surrounded them. . . . The obvious fact was that the children in this school, with but little conscious awareness of what was beautiful, had within them, as their birthright, an ability to create true beauty within all the media of the arts. (pp. 7-8)

He also takes care to point out another important matter: he and his teachers were not specially gifted or trained, but "just an ordinary inartistic lot of people." Yet they wished to give the children the freedom to go ahead and do those things which would enhance their development, and that was their chief aim. The beauty of the children's work surprised and humbled them, one feels, and they clearly learned as much from the children as the children did from them.

Further, they knew that these children had developed some antisocial attitudes that could not be expressed in the school setting, or fights and disruptions would ensue. How, then, could the children be encouraged to express their feelings and find themselves in a more acceptable way? The answer was through the media of the arts:

> I knew we must be very careful that the very young child is doing what he wants to do and is not over-directed by another person. On the other hand, if we allowed the child to do exactly what he wanted to do we were giving him a licence, the results of which I was not prepared to face. The child has to live in a social world as a social unit. The laws of the herd must be well and truly known and kept if he is to become a contented member of that herd. But the child must be free to develop, and it is in the creation of beauty that the true development of the individual emerges. So I turned to the arts as the basis of the education which should pervade this school. (p.9)

What Stone was aiming for was "that confidence, that interest, that concentration" from each child which comes from total absorption in a task which he finds meaningful. He did not make use of crafts, with all the technical skills that would be needed, but rather such media as clay, paint, movement, and drama, in which a child could find open opportunities for expression, free of the need for specifically learned techniques. One must ask, what of the 3 R's? Did the school teach nothing by way of the skills of literacy and numeracy? It did, but first came the development of students' attitudes toward their work which prepared the ground:

> The three Rs, I decided, should become a secondary consideration, . . . It must not be thought that I undervalue in any way the importance of the three Rs. I believe, however, that there are things of much greater importance; the development of the personality of a child, his growth as a whole, demand greater attention than the three Rs. (p. 9)

And this development, so critical to all progressive educators, took place best, Stone felt, through work in the arts. As he introduced his students to one medium after another, he was careful to watch not for the quality of the work but for "interest, concentration, and imagination."
When these were evident, he was sure that the work was exactly at the growth point for a child, that it spoke to or answered a need in the child at that moment of his development. Then would come a saturation point, and the child's concentration would flag. For one child it might come early in painting, for another in clay. It became evident that children who went about their work in an orderly, self-disciplined way reached the saturation point more slowly than others who jumped from one thing to another. "The result was that we could be fairly assured that if we kept the child's interest, concentration and imagination at work, there would develop this self-discipline which would carry him through a greater period of time before he reached saturation point" (p. 10). Through the arts, then, Stone saw growing some "essential educational qualities." As interest and imagination were engaged, as the concentration grew, "this discipline was being developed." It was an inner discipline that was crucial for any further kind of schoolwork.

Interestingly, the teachers developed a special technique for working with difficult boys. Some boys, although they had the ability to show interest, imagination, and concentration, could not be trusted to work alone for long periods of time, for they quickly reached this saturation point and then began some mischief with other children who were still working. However, if these boys were near some adult while working, they kept at it a longer time and with more absorption than before. Stone lays this to a fear of freedom: give such boys freedom, and, because they have been badly treated outside school, they are fearful and do not know what to with the freedom. For outside, whenever they have expressed themselves, they have been punished for unacceptable behavior. Thus, they are afraid of what they might do given freedom, their repertoire of acceptable behavior is still small, and they are not able to discipline themselves as yet. But put them next to an encouraging and supportive adult, and that responsibility is not theirs; they can absorb themselves in creative work and develop self-discipline by its means:

> [M]y feeling is that, with the freedom that creative activities demand, the child does begin to assume, and to want, in spite of his earlier training, the freedom that is so essential for his development. I see these qualities of interest, imagination, concentration, self-discipline, freedom from fear, as enlivening the contact between the self and the world. (p. 11)

Particularly for slum children, that contact, that interest in reaching out into the world, is critical for their development.

Story of a School continues, after the introduction to the method and its purposes, with discussions of each medium in turn. The author is frank about failures as well as successes and at every turn points out how he and his teachers learned much from the children's responses to whatever they presented. In each case, they worked for "that complete absorption in the medium which I felt was important if it was to be used for a pure educational development." Thus, choral speaking was dropped, because it did not deeply attract the children's interest, and so also was puppetry. But movement, more and more free of imposed techniques, became the most important medium in the school and seemed to underlie the creative urge itself:

> That common beginning (of the arts) is movement—movement, something primitive and fundamental, so it seems to me: not movement for expressing emotion or ideas, which becomes Dance; not movement which makes us feel we want to say something, which is Drama; not movement for developing bodily strength or skills, which is Physical Training; but movement for movement's sake, the starting point of all the arts. (p. 12)

Building on the work in movement, and always watching for the child's absorption in the medium, the teachers tried many ways to develop the self-discipline and freedom which they felt were basic to education. With drama, for instance, a definite development took place. First, plays were introduced, with already written scripts. Although the plots were interesting, the children did not get fully involved in the plays. So they were encouraged to mime the story, to move and act it out silently. Then, spontaneously, the children's own words began to come, making the story come alive in their own way, especially the moments of crisis. First there were short monologues, then brief conversations. Stone encouraged them to write down what they had said, and a new play was born of the children's own spontaneous speech. Groups of children would rehearse in their homes, books of stories were pored over, especially the Bible, for vivid scenes, and the development from movement into drama, based on children's expressions, was complete:

> I would go so far as to say that, unless a child will take and use for his own development those activities which he experiences at school, we have not approached the activity in the right way. The approach to all subjects must be such that the child of his own volition will use that medium of expression in his leisure hours. (p. 19)

Here is the link between school and home, between school and society. School for these children was not isolated from home, different and hostile to it, but a lively, enriching place whose influence spread out into their total lives.

Stone is also very clear that cognitive reasoning, and the expression of it in numbers or in writing, comes after real, absorbing, creative experiences. "I believe that writing down thoughts in words too often stops the flow of imagination. . . . I am sure we expect the child to express himself in the written word at much too early an age" (p. 28). Possibly this is the reason that, in the spontaneous dramatic work, younger children were unable to write down their speeches, and they changed them from one rehearsal to another, whereas older ones could develop a real script and keep to it. And as to the teaching of arithmetic, "I feel that what we now call arithmetic is a reasoning process, and the child is expected to show results before reasoning can be based upon real experience" (p. 28). Certainly Jean Piaget's studies of the development of reasoning in the child similarly demonstrate that extensive manipulative experience is basic to the child's growth in logic and that unless such experience is provided, the child expresses his understanding at a verbal level only.

In observing a child's development in working with artistic media, Stone sees definite stages at which one aspect or another of the arts becomes particularly important. For instance, there is the early "repetitive" stage. Here the child uses the medium he has chosen in a rhythmical way, not in a representative way. Next comes the "expressive" stage, when a child represents the world, but only as his inner eye sees it, not as it might be in a photograph. Thus we get strangely shaped faces or trees, each expressing how the child sees the objects around him. Third, one sees the "communicative" stage, when the child is more aware of the world around him and more interested in having his artistic endeavors understood. In this stage he asks for help, and he can be taught techniques to increase his skill; in the first two stages, such helpful techniques are useless. "I feel that the young child should, in the early stages, as far as possible create" (p. 32). "Of one thing we were assured, that a child must be absorbed in his work before we could help him to widen or develop his experience" (p. 25). Moving through these stages took some children longer than others, and it was important for the teachers to observe carefully so that they could provide the opportune stimulation and guidance for each child. As they watched, and as the child became absorbed in the work, they knew he was engaged in an activity that was educational to him at that stage of his development.

Teaching like this has little to do with the teaching of facts:

> It was when we began to realise that what we were trying to achieve was the child's absorption in his work, and not the results, that we began to develop an attitude towards teaching which demanded more power and ability than did the teaching of factual knowledge. We were constantly searching for those things in which the child could become absorbed, and we were looking for the individual interests of the child. We realised that discipline was the outcome of the child's absorption in his experience and not a thing imposed by the teacher. (pp. 35-36)

Putting the child's expressive nature at the heart of the school was not new, as Stone well knew; it was his clear and appealing explanation of the ways he and his staff devised to put that idea into effect which gained this brief booklet a wide audience. The teachers at the Steward Street School

98 / ACTIVITY AND EXPERIENCE

were trying to give a child a chance to move and to express himself in many ways. They believed that the personal qualities developed in this way gave the soundest approach to academic subjects and a confident basis for social relationships as well. It seemed to them clearly wrong to teach the child to do academic, verbal tasks before he had had a thorough grounding in free, expressive activities along the lines of his own unique nature.

Primary Education

Primary Education[22] is the third publication of particular interest to this study. Published in 1959, it prefigures the Plowden Report in many ways; it had its fourth impression in 1968 and is still available at Her Majesty's Stationery Office. The book summarizes and analyzes the work of successful schools and includes all the important educational developments in the field of primary education — the various Acts, the Handbooks, and the Hadow Reports — which had laid the groundwork for current successful practices in schools. It then discusses up-to-date thinking about child development during school years and goes into every aspect of the work of the school from this developmental point of view. The book closes with a special section on education in Wales. It is not called a handbook, although it stands in a long line of the famous Handbooks that began in 1905. Its scope is broader than theirs, in that the authors clearly mean to give relevant background as well as current advice, although the book focuses only on primary education. More than a handbook, then, it is a compendium of past thinking, current work in the field of child study, and a description of good practices as the authors (all HMI's) had witnessed them in schools around the country.

The point is strongly made by *Primary Education* that successful schools of today were not invented after World War II, or during it, but had been growing slowly and carefully out of the experience of thoughtful teachers, chiefly in infant schools. England has had its tradition of separate infant schools, usually for children from ages five to seven, but sometimes including the "under fives" of nursery school age. These infant schools, dating back at least as far as Robert Owen's efforts at New Lanark in 1816, have seen over a hundred years of "steady growth and progressive practice inspired by generations of devoted teachers and informed by research in the educational, psychological, medical and social fields both in this and in other countries" (p. 5). The book continues:

It is fortunate that when primary education was at last established as a separate phase in its own right, it had this cherished tradition of infant education to draw on; for here the nature and needs of the children had become central to thinking and were accepted as the basis of educational practice. (p. 5)

Thus, the work in the infant school is considered the chief source of the child-centered attitudes and practices that have so influenced the development of English education. This "cherished tradition" was described as early as the Hadow Committee's *Report on Infant and Nursery Schools* of 1933. It is also true that progressive thinking and practice at the nursery level had an important effect on infant schools, particularly after the work of Rachel and Margaret McMillan in the early years of the century.

Not until 1944 was "primary" education officially so called and discussed as an entity, yet it was in 1931 that the Hadow Committee's *Report on the Primary School* came out. In *Primary Education* there is a long discussion of this earlier document, with its concern for the smooth and continuous development of the abilities of children, without a sharp break at any particular age, and without the sense that the lower age levels are chiefly preparation for the more difficult work at the upper level. On the contrary, as pointed out in the Hadow Report of 1931:

> The primary school should afford time and scope for general development in preparation for the more varied forms of teaching that will be adapted to the special abilities and aptitudes of the pupils at a later age. It should arouse in the pupil a keen interest in the things of the mind and in general culture, fix certain habits, and develop a reasonable degree of self confidence, together with a social or team-spirit.[23]

To be sure, the primary school is seen here as preparation for more specialized work later, but the preparation is not described in terms of skills mastered or information taken in; rather, the aim is to inculcate certain habits of mind and of conduct. Putting the point even more clearly, the Report goes on to say that there are certainly places in the educational system "where the curriculum is distorted and the teaching warped from its proper character by the supposed need of meeting the requirements of a later educational stage."[24] In opposition to this attitude, the Report emphasizes again:

100 / ACTIVITY AND EXPERIENCE

> [N]o good can come from teaching children things that have no immediate value for them, however highly their potential or prospective value may be estimated. . . . we must recognise the uselessness and the danger of seeking to inculcate what Professor A. N. Whitehead calls inert ideas — that is, ideas which at the time when they are imparted have no bearing upon a child's natural activities or body or mind and do nothing to illuminate or guide his experience.[25]

The Report then summarizes the whole purpose of the school in words which are often quoted in English educational circles, and which open this book, beginning:

> The curriculum is to be thought of in terms of activity and experience rather than of knowledge to be acquired and facts to be stored.[26]

The progressive nature of these comments is especially remarkable because the Report dealt chiefly with the upper primary, or junior-school, age (7-11) level. One might expect such sentiments about the infant schools;[27] the Report was far in advance of its time by including junior schools. Furthermore it should be remembered that although the schools which were famous in the twenties and the thirties were independent schools — like A. S. Neill's Summerhill, the school founded by Bertrand and Dora Russell, St. Christopher's at Letchworth, and others — the work which the Hadow Reports described was chiefly observed in state-supported schools. The writings of the progressives had some effect, as did their schools, but the state schools also were moving ahead in progressive ways, if without as much fanfare.

The historical part of *Primary Education* goes on to deal specifically with the "Handbooks of Suggestions for the Consideration of Teachers." Each Handbook reflects, to some extent, changes in emphasis or in expression, but there is remarkable continuity in the basic position toward education and toward children and their teachers which each one takes. The quotation above from the Hadow Report of 1931 is expressive of the point of view which also informs the Handbooks as to the most fundamental aims of primary education. The following paragraph is equally famous; it was written in the Handbook for 1918 and reprinted verbatim in the 1937 version, in 1944, and again in the 1959 book (part of this paragraph appears at the beginning of this book):

Neither the present volume nor any developments or amendments of it are designed to impose any regulations supplementary to those contained in the Code. The only uniformity of practice that the Board of Education desire to see in the teaching in Public Elementary Schools is that each teacher shall think for himself, and work out for himself such methods of teaching as may use his powers to the best advantage and be best suited to the particular needs and conditions of the school. Uniformity in details of practice (except in the mere routine of school management) is not desirable even if it were attainable. But freedom implies a corresponding responsibility in its use. . . . the teacher need not let the sense of his responsibility depress him or make him afraid to be his natural self in school. Children are instinctively attracted by sincerity and cheerfulness; and the greatest teachers have been thoroughly human in their weaknesses as well as in their strength.[28]

It is in this spirit that these Handbooks are called simply "suggestions for the consideration" of teachers and others; they do not dictate practice or urge uniformity in any way. Yet they do clearly represent the point of view, held in all the official publications, that "at the heart of the educational process lies the child."

The historical background thus completed, *Primary Education* proceeds to describe "the arrangements and practices which are to be found in the more successful schools, and to discuss these in the light of current knowledge and experience of children's capacities and reactions" (p. 10). That these arrangements and practices have deep roots is important:

> What is now to be found in the schools has gradually evolved out of the free working and independent initiative of teachers who have refused to discard the solid, proved and unassailable part of tradition in favour of what is apparently easy, bright and new, and have preferred to base their practices on the foundation of experience patiently accumulated. (p. 10)

Although HMI's see many schools, and although even today informal work characterizes only about a third of English primary classrooms, it is important that this book, following the tradition of its predecessors, describes those classrooms and no others. There are no descriptions of "successful schools" in which there is much class teaching, a fixed curriculum or timetable, rows of desks and chairs, and all the familiar features of the traditional classroom:

One salient feature of primary education today is the ever deepening concern with children as children, which has gradually spread from the nursery and infant schools to the junior schools. This concern shows itself especially in the awareness of the child as a whole with inter-dependent spiritual, emotional, intellectual and physical needs, and in the appreciation of the wide range of aptitudes, abilities and temperaments which any class of children presents. Another feature, of no less significance, is the increasing attention given by teachers to the worth of what is taught and to the quality of the children's learning. Equally important is the growing realisation that the capacities of all children, dull and bright alike, must be exercised to the full, and that to achieve this end the work must be made interesting and a sense of standard must pervade it all. (p. 11)

At one point, in discussing infant schools, a small section appears called " 'activity' and methodical teaching" (pp. 52-54), which well describes the essential differences between the two styles of teaching. It again makes use of earlier statements, this time from the Handbook of 1937. Good teachers, it is stated, have always know that a child learns best when his interest and activity are intimately involved in what is going on. The problem for the teacher is to "stimulate in the children the effort which makes learning successful and to use it fruitfully when it is aroused" (p. 52). When a child's natural curiosity or his expressive wish to make something or do something is effectively at work, then learning is allied with the natural developmental forces. "The best of what have been called 'activity methods' are the attempts to use natural ways of learning so that the children give their full attention to what they are doing and use all their desire to explore and find out, putting out their maximum effort" (p. 53). A teacher may not fully foresee what will engage the children's attention, but she can and should provide opportunities for work with materials and ideas which are appropriate for the children's general stage of development:

> The teacher's responsibility for what is offered to the children, for the ways in which they use opportunities and the attitudes of minds which lead them to make the most of them, and for the maintenance of good standards of performance in relation to the children's capacity, is in no way diminished, but rather increased. She is, in no uncertain sense, "in charge," and her powers of organisation are at full stretch. (p. 53)

However, focusing on activity does not negate the worth of methodical

Primary Education / 103

teaching. Every child needs it at one time or another. Such help is given when a child learns to dress himself, to tie his shoes, to handle fork and spoon, and so on. So also in school, as children learn to read and write, to take care of pets in the room, and to use numbers with skill and ease:

> But methodical teaching is effective to the extent that the children see it aiding their own efforts, and if it holds their attention and helps them to achieve something they want to achieve or have a use for or a pride in doing. In short, it is effective if it is given at the moment and in the amount the child's own activity of mind demands, and if it does not smother his ardour. (pp. 53-54)

The issue, then, is not activity methods *or* methodical teaching, but rather the judicious use of each, on the part of a teacher who thoroughly understands.

A final paragraph in this section follows up this discussion of activity and methodical teaching. It warns that the teacher must always remain in the world of practical, day-to-day classroom experience with children, not the world of theory about children:

> The ways of teachers differ; but should they attempt to elevate particular methods or procedures to the levels of fundamental principles, and cease to be critically aware of what they are doing and of the value of what the children are learning, unfortunate results are likely to follow. (p. 54)

Not that fundamental principles are useless or unsound, but they must always and continually be rethought and recreated in light of current experience. This is the only way in which sound change can come about, while the teaching goes on:

> [Each new idea or experiment must be] fashioned into new forms which reflect new circumstances and stand the test of new practices in the contemporary scene. The pioneers take such ideas and refashion and temper them in their daily work in school. Patiently, day after day, week after week and year after year, they make the pathway from the past through the present towards the future. (29)

A long chapter of *Primary Education* deals with "the working of the school," and the longest section within it is on "discipline." This topic of great interest and concern to all educators is dealt with in detail, beginning with the task of education in general. It is, the authors tell us, twofold: it must enable children to grow up as good members of the society of which they are a part, with a sufficient degree of compliance or conformity to the mores and standards of that society. It must also, and at the same time, develop a "proper sense of independence in thought and action which implies a power to choose and to make judgments on their own account." Those two aims, the social and the individual, are not in conflict but complementary, since the development of an individual occurs in large part by means of his "playing his proper part in society," and a good society can only be such if it is made up of men and women "fully grown as individuals, working together unselfishly, and appreciative of purposes common to all" (p. 78). These twin aims of education and their implementation lie at the heart of all the problems that are associated with the term "discipline."

The next question is, to what extent can an individual be free to develop his own personality, and what extent must that freedom be curbed? The basic idea of freedom is "that the children can make a choice." But these choices are made within comparatively narrow limits, limits set by the teacher, by the materials and resources of the schoolroom, and by the social arrangement of many children working together. A child may not disrupt the work of someone else. This rule is basic to the harmonious work of the school. Within it, and within the carefully planned opportunities offered by the teacher and her room, the individual child can choose work that will enhance his progress toward maturity:

> Between discipline in the liberal sense of the term — learning a good way of living as an individual in a society — and the kind of freedom the children enjoy in most primary schools today, there is no antithesis at all. True discipline includes the exercise of responsible choice as an important part of learning. (p. 79)

Discipline is to be understood, then, not in terms of restrictions and sanctions but in terms of "the fundamental importance of the quality of the human relationships and of the standards accepted and admired within the school, as within the home" (p. 82). The teacher is central and her work is clearly moral, in this view, reaching far beyond curricular concerns into the very fabric of the human relationships that grow under her care. Common problems and common purposes within the school are made known to the children and common solutions sought. What few rules are needed are understood and freely agreed to:

> In short, where the children are aware of, and sympathetic to, the general intentions, where their teachers are agreed about what they expect of them and the children know where they stand, where what must be done for mutual comfort is understood by all and there is consistency of standard throughout, then, even in a very large school housed in a bad building, a good life is made possible. ... The more that can be left to the children's general good sense, so that they feel personal responsibility for their own behaviour, the better. The teacher's respect for them, which such freedom implies, appeals to their self-respect and contributes to their growth as self-controlled and reliable people. Further, since personal responsiblity allows everyone to adapt his conduct quickly to particular circumstances, it makes for increased efficiency all round. (pp. 83-84)

Described in this way, it seems all pleasant and smooth, but any teacher who has had to deal with the complexity of school life, with many tasks and large groups of children to manage, knows that it is not so simple. It is a most exacting task to organize the work of the school to help the children grow as individuals, to become self-controlled and responsible in their relationships toward others and always ready to learn or try new things. It is, then, the teacher whose wisdom and tact are so essential to the harmonious progress of the school. Most of all, "his own example is the most powerful of all the influences he can bring to bear" (p. 89).

In this connection, the leadership role played by the head teacher is discussed. The English head is, again, first of all a teacher: she teaches the children, and she works with her staff, including teachers, custodians, and cooks, until all come to understand the purposes of the school so that all can contribute to them. "It is the Head's personality that in the vast majority of schools creates the climate of feeling — whether of service and cooperation or of tension and uncertainty — and that establishes standards of work and conduct" (p. 92). The ultimate responsibilty for planning and organizing, supervising, and encouraging the work of the school rests with the head. In an increasing number of schools, the authors note, some clerical help is available to make administrative details less time-consuming for the head, for the head has no business staying at her desk longer than absolutely necessary. Her place is with the people, large and small, who are the school. To a large extent, in England the heads are given a

106 / ACTIVITY AND EXPERIENCE

great deal of freedom, but it is also understood that that freedom brings with it a heavy responsibility. The rest of *Primary Education* is a detailed examination of the separate subjects of the curriculum, among which religion, physical education, art and craft and needlework, handwriting, and music are given considerable space as well as the more traditional subjects. And the theme is reiterated: the work of the school begins with the needs and interests of the children, and it is meant to help them grow into maturity. Two further paragraphs are worth quoting:

> Children bring their keenest attention to what satisfies their immediate interest, sometimes heeding nothing else; and what interests them may well be something which, from the teacher's point of view, is quite irrelevant or unimportant. It is only through discussion with his pupils and by giving them opportunity to record their impressions in various ways that he is able to discover what significance they give to what they see and hear. Through this exchange of ideas, questions, answers, and of critical comment and enquiry rather than through docile acceptance, children are helped to relate their experiences to others, to clarify them and to make them articulate. (p. 105)

> [M]ost children will enter with zest into certain experiences to satisfy their curiosity, their sense of wonder and beauty and their growing need to know the reason why. The course in the primary school can be said to be successful if the children have come to regard ignorance as a challenge to enquiry in which their own observations play a major part and if they have learnt to support and amplify these observations by referring to books and other sources of information. Their observations should have become increasingly careful and accurate and their recording of what they have discovered should have been honest. But even in normal children enthusiasm has often to be skilfully and patiently aroused and still more skilfully sustained; and it has to be aroused in a group of individuals where each reacts differently from his neighbour. If he is to succeed the teacher must himself be sensitive to wonder and beauty and must retain a fresh and curious mind, because the spirit of enquiry is fostered by infection rather than advice. (p. 313)

Chapter 5
THE JOURNEY HOME

Returning to my own country, I thought back over my eventful three months in England. I realized how much I had learned and how generous people had been with their time and ideas. I began to sift through the myriad impressions that will always stay with me, and in this chapter I want to discuss those aspects of the English scene which seem to me useful for American educators.

For one cannot simply transplant the successful English practices, the products of years of careful experiment and slow growth in a country quite unlike our own in many ways. Yet, I believe that there are some parts of the English experience which Americans would do well to ponder. We must be eclectic, just as the English are: we can consider what others say and do, and then take what we can use in our own work.

Basic Attitudes

To me, an extremely important point about British informal schools is that they have developed not simply a new approach to the same old task but a wholly different way of working with people in schools, children and adults alike. This approach essentially reverses the more formal, authoritarian methods, for the center of attention now becomes the learner, not the teacher or the book. To be sure, not all the teachers whom I met had done their work in the same way, and there were certainly differences of opinion among them as to particular points of emphasis. But there was fundamental agreement, first, that "the initiative for learning comes from the learner" (5) and, second, that schools should promote a child's "all-around growth" (9). Once these attitudes are adopted, formal methods which demand docility and compliance can no longer be used, but, rather, one must begin with the present activity and experience of the children. In this way, one arrives at the mastery of subject matter by starting with the child's natural interest in the world. For instance, one can help the children develop historical insight by beginning with their immediate environment — perhaps a nearby Norman church, an ancient stone wall, the family tree, an old story — and moving with them toward more and more organized and explicit representation of that experience. But one cannot start with the history textbook, which is the result of someone else's experience and investigation. The learner must be the active agent of his or her own learning.

If one begins with the twin propositions that schools are to promote all-around growth and that the initiative for learning comes from the learner, it follows that the process is as important as the product. The approach to an investigation is as important as the final map or display or report. The product that is finally achieved and shared with others means as much to the learner as to his audience, since the process by which it was made was his own and not in compliance with someone else's ideas of what should be done.

Another corollary is that the school is adjusted to the nature of the children within it, not the other way around. Here, understanding the developmental needs of children is of the greatest importance: English teachers spend far more time on such study than their American counterparts. Teachers who are concerned about children's growth believe that curriculum is less important than the basic attitudes toward children which prevail in the school. This is not to say that development of curriculum and materials is useless, but, again, every teacher must be eclectic. What other people develop, she must consider for her own particular set of children. And since children differ very much, no single method or curricular device will suit each one. The judgment must be the teacher's, based on her intimate knowledge of her children.

Not only in the area of curriculum, but in every other aspect of the school, life within it can be planned to enhance children's experience and growth. The school can represent a sane, understandable institution to children, with ways of working that clearly suit their needs and with adults who are concerned about them. Perhaps this is one of the greatest contributions a school can make to growing children, as they try to understand and grow into the world around them.

Further, all the people in a school can be treated with respect and trust and encouraged to show their natural talents and to develop them. I constantly noticed that the ways in which adults dealt with children were similar to the ways in which they dealt with each other. There was the emphasis on helping a person's sense of self-confidence by developing a supportive relationship and by giving positive encouragement for work that showed possibilities for growth. In this way, each person's special contribution to the school could be made, to everyone's benefit. All the people I met felt that such an atmosphere produced far better work from everyone than did one of formality and distance.

Finally, this whole set of attitudes is not a catechism or list of propositions, laid down years ago for all time, but still living and growing. As the understanding of child development has grown, so have ideas about sound ways to teach children. This is being progressive in the radical sense: teachers hope that they will progress, that each day they will do things for children better than the day before. "We saw education as a march forward," said one (15). The term "progressive" has become a pejorative one for some, but, rightly understood, it need not be. Building on basic notions about children and the springs of their learning, one can constantly improve ways of helping them grow:

> We are not on the shifting sands of fashion. What you're providing for children changes according to the changing needs of society and the changing environment of children. But if the way in which you're teaching is based on sound principles, then the needs – the psychological needs – of children remain similar.(12)[29]

All of the other aspects of the scene I was studying are derived from this basic point of view. For instance, the teaching of the 3 R's, "the basics," was done in connection with work that was meaningful to children. Formal teaching of reading starts with the symbols of language; informal work begins with their meaning in experience, and arrives at the symbols after meaning is thoroughly explored. Thus, children are urged first to talk fluently, to express their inner worlds in language, to discuss the work of others, to plan next stages – all to develop their confident use and control of language. Then, when reading and writing come to be necessary tools for the work they want to pursue, the symbols can be mastered in the process. And because children do value what adults value, when the relationship is sound, children come to care about books and writing when they see that their teachers care about these things and make use of them. This may seem like an unsophisticated and simplistic point of view when one considers the great mass of work done on methods of teaching reading and the large numbers of remedial teachers being trained and hired. But in fact it accords with children's development; it takes into account the whole child and the way he or she naturally makes sense of the world; it does not stop with the ability to decode.

The same can be said about the development of mathematical concepts and arithmetical skills. In the context of the whole child's growth, he begins with manipulation of concrete things which he is interested in, with comparing, measuring, weighing, pouring, lifting things in the real world of his experience. Then, later, his observations can be symbolized as the need for recording experiences arises. Again, this corresponds with the way children develop concepts. Learning that does not connect with the child's experience but remains at a verbal level only cannot be used later in new combinations or to solve new problems. One recalls Whitehead's famous warning about "inert ideas."

Play

Connected with this approach to developing the basic skills through real experience is the belief in the value of play. Play can be used in a number of different ways to enhance children's growth, since it is the natural expression of their wishes and abilities. "Play is the child's work," Froebel put it. Dramatic play allows for imaginative representation of the child's inner world, as he works out a particular story that moves him or experiments with different roles he sees adults play around him. Physical play of all kinds can help a child assess his own agility and powers of balance and competence. "I can, therefore I am" (11). Play can also help him express his feelings outwardly and acceptably, so that they are not locked up within him or disruptively loosed on others. Creative play, using all sorts of materials to make things, can tax a child's ingenuity and help him develop ways of solving problems, which will stay with him always. Also, play in all its varieties serves the teacher as a vital diagnostic tool, for in it she can see the child as his natural self and can plan how best to promote his growth. Thus, play, while it may seem like wasting time, is in fact a way of gaining time for the child to grow.

The importance of play has long been understood in England, especially since the advent of Froebelian ideas in the mid-nineteenth century. Because these ideas had taken root, the impact of Maria Montessori's methods was less than it might have been. She came to England in the early years of this century and several times thereafter to lecture and to lead workshops. As her ideas and techniques were studied, it became clear to many progressive English educators that only part of her doctrine was useful to them — a good example of the eclecticism so often evident in English education. It was soon seen that she had two great contributions to make: first, she released the child from class teaching and class responding, to work individually and at his own pace with materials in an environment specially designed for his learning. Second, she presented a theory of child development, derived from her medical and educational experience, which described a child's normal progress through the growing years, a theory on which the planning of the "prepared environment" was based. However, English critics were not able to agree with her relative unconcern about the child's imaginative life, as expressed most naturally in play, and they were equally unable to agree with the authoritarian way in which she and her disciples insisted that there be no deviation from her ideas or her didactic materials. The English felt that she was ignoring a very important aspect of children's growth, imagination, which they had long understood and encouraged, and that no one set of ideas or materials was the final word for all children. They therefore took from her work what was of value to them and discarded what was not. The basic commitment to children's all-around development was the guiding principle.

The School Schedule

If one puts the child's natural activities at the center of the educational process, the formal schedule must change. Movement toward what is now called a "free day" or an "integrated day" happened quite naturally, as a response to children's needs. It was not a new idea that someone thought up and that teachers might try now and then. Formal schedules had previously been planned on the basis of what was assumed to be a child's concentration span. But this span was what a child could manage while being instructed; it had nothing to do with the amount of time a child would happily spend when absorbed in a task of his own choosing, a task which exactly met his developmental needs. The progressive point of view is that the best preparation for the future is a full and satisfying life in the present; formal instruction usually focuses on work that will be done later or on drill that helps a child get ready for the next stage. By contrast, child-centered practices focus on getting a child fully absorbed in work that is currently meaningful to him. Uprooting a child from his self-chosen task in order to adhere to the schedule would reduce, not improve, the quality of his concentration and therefore of his learning. This way of using time appropriately for children's growth was very striking to me.

Not only were the bounds of the school day broken through, but the school year was viewed in a leisurely way as well. Not every skill had to be practiced every day at great length. Especially in schools where the child is in the same classroom for more than one year, the teacher and the child have plenty of time. Again, this point of view responds to the real developmental needs of the child, since no stage of maturity can be hurried.

Individualization

"Individualization" is a strategy much praised in some quarters, but progressive teachers think of it differently from the way it is often meant. In a more formal situation, material is individualized: that is, schemes of work are devised for the child, who is by this means kept busy. In many cases he is also isolated both from other children and from the teacher, since the individualized program material is deliberately planned to do the teaching.

In informal classrooms the child plans and develops his own curriculum, often in discussion with others. He works out his investigations in ways that are his own, tailored to suit his own needs and guided by the teacher, who understands them. The difference is the involvement of the child in the work he undertakes. The focus can be on the process of planning and organizing work that he wants to do, rather than on passively going from one workbook or reader to the next. The emphasis is on worthwhile activity, rather than on the development of skills separately from the arena in which they might fruitfully be used. And there is less importance placed on the number of workbooks completed than on "getting a development in his thinking" (12). Although progressive teachers do use workbooks, they are selective in their use, since the practice afforded by them may or may not be relevant to the work the child is involved in or to his particular style of learning. This individualization of children's learning is by no means the same thing as individualization of material.

Art and Movement

Still another striking aspect of the work of the best English schools and their teachers is the attention paid to art. Early interest in developing children's authentic art has been described, as over the years children were gradually allowed to create their own artistic statements instead of simply imitating adult work. *Story of a School* placed art at the very center of the school. By now, art work is an integral part of every good informal school; it is a natural way for children to represent the world outside them, and their inner world as well.

One art form in particular has no counterpart in the United States at all — namely, movement.[30] Taught by competent teachers, it is not athletics or drama or modern dance, though it contains elements of each. It is movement for its own sake: exploring a person's space around him and his own ability to move expressively within it, in response to inner ideas and feelings. I saw a videotape of a superb movement lesson, and the children in it showed a lack of self-consciousness and an absorption that I found very impressive. The teacher set the tone of the lesson, so that the children had confidence in her seriousness of purpose and her respect for what they were doing. She also provided enough guidance to get them started, made suggestions for development of movement, or helped them combine with others in a variety of ways.

In the United States, physical education is chiefly confined to games and gymnastics. Both are competitive, in that some children are clearly very much better at them than others, and some must win and some must lose in contests. It is certainly important to develop physical agility and control, and also to learn how to play games within the rules, how to lose a game without feeling it is a total disaster, and how to win without becoming overbearing. But the movement lessons I witnessed and others I heard about provide an additional opportunity for children. They help children express themselves in ways not governed by rules or by comparison with the performance of others, but only by the idea within and the space without. Physical actions and emotions are closely linked, and to help a child use his body expressively is surely to help his all-around growth in a very significant way. My observations were that such work produced relaxed, serene children.

How the Schools Evolved

To return to the historical growth of English informal schools: I often asked people how they felt that changes had taken place, both in their own individual work and across the country at large. The process seemed to be similar — ideas spread after seeing them work out in practice and reach a high standard. There is no polarity between the traditional and the progressive points of view, as long as a teacher cares about children. A teacher can move along the continuum which stretches between them at her own pace, as through experimentation she sees the children happier and working better. Meetings with other teachers helped very much, providing opportunities to share problems and hear colleagues' ideas. People of like minds often knew one another and exchanged views in that rather small country. And a whole range of advisory and supportive services have grown up to extend and support the work, as well. Successful teachers and heads were asked to go into teacher training, and there they were able to pass along their ideas: examples are Nancy Catty and Lillian de Lissa. Lectures, courses, and conferences with speakers from various frontiers of educational research, like Susan Isaacs, D. E. M. Gardner, Molly Brearley, and others, also helped provide support for teachers who were trying freer ways of working with children. One effect was to draw teachers' attention over and over again to the nature of children. In general, change was brought about, slowly and spasmodically, by the impact of one person on another. There was the freedom of the teacher to develop in her work, and there was also the expectation that she would continue to learn and progress. It is not possible to point to one person or to one institution and say that that was the source of change. Rather, the picture is of like-minded people coming to know each other in a great variety of settings, to share ideas, and to work together. Conviction about the value of the new methods came when the standard of the children's work rose beyond expectation and when teachers saw the children absorbed and happy.

In certain counties, like Oxfordshire and the West Riding of Yorkshire, teams of people found themselves working very harmoniously together, and the schools moved ahead rapidly. Thus, for example, the combination of Robin Tanner as HMI and Edith Moorhouse as local advisor in Oxfordshire worked particularly well, as did the team brought together by Sir Alec Clegg in the West Riding. It was people working with other people and spreading the fruits of their own successful experience that brought about change; it was never by fiat from above or by a single extraordinary and charismatic figure, although there were certainly some of those. The development was varied, as ideas were continually tried out in real situations and perhaps reworked or altered to suit the needs of the children.

Junior Schools

One minor point about the history of these methods and schools might be made here. It has been said that the chief growth of English informal classrooms has been among the infant schools. To a certain extent this is true, for they have a long tradition — since Robert Owen's early infant school — of being separate and of being less formal than schools at a higher level. "Infant methods," too, was a term used to connote informal, activity-based ways of promoting children's growth. But I was struck, when searching for some of the origins of less formal ideas and practices years ago, that they appeared among teachers of junior schools as well, despite the long-standing effects of the competitive examinations for entry to grammar schools, especially after these no longer charged tuition and high test scores were the only criteria. One of the most influential books written and widely used by teachers and students of teaching was Nancy Catty's *Learning and Teaching in the Junior School* (1954). Edith Warr did her investigations into the interests of children, later published and widely known, at the junior school level. Several of the pioneer teachers with whom I talked, among them E. R. Boyce, Monica Withers, and A. L. Stone, had done their teaching in junior schools. Others, like Edith Moorhouse and Sybil Marshall, had worked in small schools with children of a wide age range. What seemed to me more important than the age level of the children with whom any one person worked were the fundamental attitudes their work exemplified. The pioneers clearly believed that their way of teaching worked with and not against children's natural development, at whatever age. So it seems that, although infant schools have indeed been historically separated and allowed to develop more freely than older ones, teaching based on children's activity and experience was characteristic of at least some important work done at the junior level as well.

Teachers' Freedom

In considering the work of the English teachers, at whatever level, there is another phenomenon which is striking to an American. It is the freedom of the teachers. Over the years, teachers and head teachers in England have been genuinely free to work out their own ways of dealing with children. Again, this can mean a very bad school or a very good one, for such is the price of delegating responsibility.

By contrast, teachers in the United States tend to be caught in a position which leaves them frustrated in their work. Their principals are often removed from the classroom and therefore out of touch with the work which is going on; they can too easily judge a teacher by criteria which are not the relevant ones having to do with the observed growth of children, and the teacher's job and salary depend on that judgment. Nor do American principals continue to teach, typically, and so teachers are without leaders who can demonstrate and encourage sound techniques and who thoroughly understand the work on a first-hand basis. Third, American parents expect to control their schools, and English parents do not. This is particularly true in the well-educated suburbs, although there are other places where parents are either indifferent or hostile to schools. But efforts to bring such parents into the school generally aim at increasing their control over it, as much as anything else. The American teacher is continually forced to answer to parents for what she does, and the tendency is to try to produce measurable results in order to prove her competence. Political pressures by parents on the local school committee, a far more powerful body than English LEA's, can be brought to bear to direct what and how the teachers shall teach. Reading programs or standardized testing plans can be imposed by outside people who know nothing about teaching or about child development. Further, there are few supportive or advisory services regularly and easily available to teachers who want to move in new directions, and there is little encouragement for them to experiment with new methods. Even entry to the profession is controlled by people outside it, namely, state legislatures which determine certification requirements. All this leaves the American teacher rather powerless, without leadership or support, and subject to considerable outside, nonprofessional pressure. By contrast, the trust and respect granted to teachers, the leadership of heads who are truly teachers-in-chief, and the many opportunities for in-service training are striking aspects of the English educational scene at its best.

Teaching Method

In either England or America, teachers working along informal lines tend to be much less intrusive than their formal counterparts. It is too easy for a teacher to intrude upon a child who is exploring and trying to make sense of his world. The temptation is great to move in with directions that will speed things up, with corrections or judgments about good or bad work, or with ideas which are not the child's own. The informal classrooms are planned specifically to minimize rewards and punishments handed out by teacher and to maximize opportunities for children to explore the natural world and succeed or fail without the intrusion of another person's subjective attitude. The natural world is nonjudgmental: if a child tries to create a tower out of old boxes and cans, it will fall or it will stand, according to the child's mastery of concepts about balance and weight. Human approval or disapproval are at best irrelevant, at worst intrusive. They seem to imply that a child cannot know he has done something well until someone in authority says so: he must surrender his own powers of judgment to someone else. But this means a loss of self-mastery which can damage a child's growing confidence and sense of himself, the very feelings which are so basic to his all-around growth.

The only way to help and not hinder the child, to encourage him or her to take the next step and the next, lies in moving with the child's mental current. Just as one would not enter a conversation between two people until one had listened enough to catch the drift of it, so a wise teacher does not intrude into the internal conversation of the child with the material he or she is handling until the teacher is sure she has something useful to offer. The adult point of view is by no means dismissed here, for an adult has much to offer a child in terms of greater experience and maturity. But the adult's contributions are useless to the child unless they are actively related to what the child is experiencing. Children's growth through the various stages of their development is marked by their attempts to make sense of the environment. It is done, finally, by their own efforts and no other's. Therefore, attempts to control, shape, or disrupt this process are harmful to the child's sound growth, and, in fact, they are unlikely to succeed. A school, to promote sound growth, must work with the child, not against the grain. Here lies the true meaning of "relevance," another term much misused. When a child is given an opportunity for activities which are right for his stage of development, and when he is helped along by someone who is attentive to his needs, then he knows that what he is doing is relevant to him. Such work strengthens and extends his grasp on his present experience, and in this it prepares him for future stages of development.

Teachers who practice such methods know that they are far more difficult to use than formal ones, for one must constantly work from the current situation, watching, estimating, questioning. There is no preset guide of work to be covered by all seven-year-olds, no lesson plan that proceeds from point to point according to the thinking of the teacher. And since this kind of teaching is more difficult, there is the danger of incompetence. Some people whom I met were all too well aware of teachers who used masses of materials in classrooms because they thought it was the thing to do, but who did not understand the principles that should govern their choice and use. There is no magic to materials: everything depends on how they are used. To pack a classroom full of a profusion of materials may confuse children by presenting them with too much choice; to pay too much attention to arranging and then clearing up materials may distract the teacher from observing the children's use of them; to set up a room according to a printed plan may look attractive but may not relate to the work the children want to do; and to get the children active for the sake of activity may not be attentive to their need for reflection or quiet from time to time. Mere "frivoling about" (15) is not good enough. A teacher must see that learning takes place. Some of the people I met felt that this kind of teaching, in fact, exposes incompetence more quickly than the more formal kind, because at least with the latter there is a lesson guide to lean on, and some standard of work can be achieved, whereas in a badly run, chaotic informal classroom very little worthwhile is accomplished.

Aiding or Stifling Development

The danger of misinterpretation or incompetence is particularly great when the children's all-around development is the aim of the school, for that includes their emotional and social development, as well as the intellectual. When school deals chiefly with cognitive skills, children's fantasies and feelings can be ignored or brought by one means or another into the semblance of conformity with expected norms. However, the child-centered classroom is deliberately planned to help the whole child to grow, and this is far more difficult.

Helping children develop suitable ways to express themselves and their feelings, directing their energies into worthwhile channels while accepting their natural emotional responses, can at times stir up in adults some of their own "unfinished business" from childhood. It is much easier to provide children with outlets for feelings which adults can tolerate, reinforce them, and keep the peace. Allowing children to express themselves freely and safely demands much forbearance, but it can enhance the child's self-image and help him develop along lines which are uniquely and personally his own. And sound relationships among all the people in the classroom can be fostered when the teacher's feelings and needs are not all-controlling.

To put it in other words, a child needs to express his emotions in ways that are both satisfying to him and at the same time acceptable to those around him. If he cannot, peers and adults will disapprove and turn away, and those feelings may be driven back inside him and eventually excluded from his conscious mind. However, when that happens, such feelings do not vanish but may be expressed differently, often in ways that are psychologically damaging to the child. For example, a child who is not helped to express his feelings and to assert his needs appropriately may become disruptive, overly docile, or withdrawn. The first process is sublimation, necessary for sound personal growth and an important goal for teachers. The second may be repression or some other unsatisfactory way of dealing with forbidden feelings. Again, accepting and dealing with children's natural feelings requires great maturity and wisdom.

Sir Percy Nunn's book, already discussed, contains an example of how best efforts can misfire for lack of insight into the true nature of children. In Chapter 13, "The Growth of the Self," some rather contradictory attitudes toward the emotional and social growth of young Jack emerge. Sir Percy is all for individual development, as he made clear in his earlier chapters. Here, he analyzes how it comes about with a particular boy, Jack, and he pays due attention to Freud (and Susan Isaacs' interpretation of his work) and to the work of Piaget. He speaks of Jack's appropriate ways of self-assertion; his curiosity, which leads him to investigate the world and, in fantasy play, to recreate it for himself; and of his expression of feelings in his increasingly successful interaction with the world. As the discussion moves along, Sir Percy is pleased to report that Jack enters school "an intelligent and docile child," that he wins a place at the county grammar school and so can go on to the university, and that as an adult he has subdued all inner conflicts and become an ideal Englishman:

> Thus Jack at the age of forty will not be merely an enterprising electrical engineer. He will be also, we may imagine, a devoted family man, keen upon backing his wife's social pretensions, and on securing his children's future; an esteemed churchwarden who stands well with

the vicar and is not indifferent to his reputation for serious views and good works; and, perhaps, a golfer sternly bent on reducing his handicap. (p. 202)

I read this account with a mounting sense of incongruity, especially recalling Sir Percy's earlier lofty paragraph about "the freedom for each to conduct life's adventure in his own way." Jack's whole childhood seems to be a tale of increasing repression of his natural feelings and reinforcement of his outwardly conforming "docile" behavior, with emphasis on the "control" developed over his less-than-acceptable behavior. With all his early liveliness and interest, Jack at forty is no more than the stereotype of the Englishman. One wonders why Sir Percy used his very lucid understanding of the "growth of the self" to reinforce a stereotype that may do much damage to teachers reading it who hope to help their children break away from mere stereotypes and live their own, more adventurous lives. Moreover, adopting Sir Percy's views allows one to put disturbing feelings away, because one can seem to give due credit to the child's early emotional development and then fail to follow through, assuming that when he is grown he will in fact conform to socially accepted patterns. This reflects a superficial understanding of children, because it means that adults can continue to hold the norms of behavior constant and by various means make sure that the children adapt to them. It also reflects adult anxiety about allowing children to grow up as their own people.

Susan Isaacs was similarly concerned; in her *Social Development in Young Children,* in the chapter entitled "Education and Psycho-Analysis," she speaks of the "enormous opposition" that met the first introduction of the ideas of Freud, the "shock and horror" which people felt. After the shock was over, however, some educators seized upon these ideas without fully understanding them, sometimes with unfortunate results:

> [In] most cases such reformers of education on supposed psycho-analytic lines have taken no account of the actual later course of psycho-analytic studies, and omit, for example, all reference to the guilt factors or the reality of those forces in the mind that lead to repression. (p. 404)

This does not mean that teaching and psychotherapy are the same thing; they move, in fact, in opposite directions. An important work in this regard is Richard M. Jones' *Fantasy and Feeling in Education.* In his chapter "Insight and Outsight," he deals quite specifically with that difference and explains how a teacher can make wise use of children's feelings in her teaching:

> In developing instructional methods of cultivating emotion and imagery, should we model our efforts after the more polished and practiced methods of psychotherapy? . . . Yes, provided we are very careful to reverse everything. A therapist's first concern is anxiety. A teacher's first concern is learning, i.e., *human* learning, i.e., creative thought. (p. 77)

He goes on to explain that anxiety is produced by the imagination working in a person who also feels alone and helpless. A therapist's work is to develop a relationship which will reduce those feelings and thus alleviate anxiety. A teacher, on the other hand, aiming to bring creative learning about, should cultivate the workings of the imagination or fantasy world, in a situation that provides the child with a sense of community and that permits him to develop a sense of his own mastery:

> Imagination plus helplessness produces anxiety, which may be relieved by psycho-therapy. And instruction may lead to imagination plus community plus mastery, which produces creative learning. (p. 77)

There follows a description of the two methods in some detail, and it is well worth consulting.

All this brings us back to the point raised earlier in connection with the danger of incompetent teaching in a child-centered classroom. Adults who teach in such settings must be mature enough so that they have no psychic need of their own to dismiss or suppress children's immature feelings; they must be secure enough to embody for the child an adult model of patience and tolerance, honesty, and a sense of proportion. I asked people if, given this level of demand, they felt that only gifted teachers could manage these methods. Everyone whom I asked said they thought not; they said that although child-centered methods are more difficult to learn and to use, that with understanding leadership from a competent head, even fairly ordinary teachers could go quite a distance. But they also stressed that what matters is the basic attitude toward children that a teacher brings to her work.

The Role of Women

Looking back over the long development of this kind of teaching, there is another striking feature which deserves far more attention and recognition than it has received: the extraordinary contribution of women. With but few exceptions, the influential teachers, heads, lecturers in training colleges, writers, and intellectuals were women. And they worked under great difficulties. After World War I (and to a lesser extent after World War II), for many there were no men to marry, and in any case marriage would have meant cutting off a career. So these women "married" their jobs, pouring into their schools all their creative energies. Many worked in isolated schools, wholly devoted to the village and its children but otherwise quite alone.

Further, teaching has commonly been considered a woman's profession. Froebel himself wrote that a woman is uniquely fitted to work with children, because women have a natural affinity for the maternal role. And if a woman wanted a career, at least teaching was considered respectable, and there were few other occupations that were. Also, places at university were few, for men or women, and many very intelligent women who wanted higher education chose teachers' colleges instead, which in England did not carry the same stigma they do in the United States. Thus, the relative absence of men and the opportunity to work in schools meant that some very able women did go into teaching. Eventually they held the majority of the responsible positions in the educational world.

There were, to be sure, some very able men involved along the way, and some of them pay sincere tribute to the "terrific women" (2) who were working in the field. "They are the people to whom we owe where we are," said one (29), and he went on to report that he deliberately chose women to work with him because of their "more imaginative, creative way of thinking." In the Inspectorate (and throughout the British civil service), however, men had always dominated, although women inspectors had been appointed for subjects other than housecraft as early as 1896. But even when a woman inspector had equal responsibilities, she was never paid as much as a man, she could not inspect in a boys' school, and she had to resign if she married. "They suffered hell for their convictions. These women were fighting for their lives in a man-oriented world" (34). Yet the promotion of liberal ideas about teaching by some of these women HMI's is among the most important that was done, particularly by those women who entered the Inspectorate from the ranks of teachers and heads.

The seminal books used during the early years, especially those dealing with practical problems facing the average teacher who wanted to move ahead, were written by women. These women had a gift for teaching, and also for making their experience available to other teachers.

Training colleges, especially the Froebelian colleges, were for the most part staffed by women, who, as tutors, demonstration teachers, lecturers on child development, and principals, exerted considerable influence on their students. Some of the women in the training colleges had been to university, so they were highly educated themselves and could pass on their sense of intellectual standard.

Women like Susan Isaacs were particularly influential. From her psychoanalytic point of view, she contributed immensely to teachers' understanding of children and their emotional and intellectual needs. Her experimental work at the Malting House School and the two books which stemmed from it (see Bibliography), her indefatigable lectures and talks with teachers all over the country, her own teaching at the Institute of Child Development of the University of London, her clear and concise written style, which helped make difficult psychoanalytic ideas understandable — all made a truly extraordinary contribution. Many people whom I met testified that her books and her support meant a tremendous amount to them, for they had been experimenting in an intuitive way, and she provided the necessary psychological basis for their work. "Then I knew where I was," said one (3). "She had a *mind!*" said another (8). Although she was a practicing psychoanalyst, she was "always thinking about children" (38), and that emphasis made her work relevant to the teachers who learned so much from her.

In another important area, women made their contributions: as members of the Froebel movement. The impact of the thought of Friedrich Froebel (1782-1852) was much greater in England than in the United States, owing to the fact that his followers fled from Germany in the mid-nineteenth century to England and established kindergartens there beginning in 1873. In 1875 the Froebel Society was founded, and then the National Froebel Foundation was set up as a national examining board for teachers; the board was a body of people who knew about children and could judge the effectiveness of a teacher's work from that point of view. The Froebelians also founded a large number of training colleges, with the result that Froebelian ideas influenced the whole teaching world as graduates went out to their work in schools. The National Froebel Society sponsored summer courses, lectures, and meetings, and it published what is now called *The Froebel Journal* (formerly *The Journal of the National Froebel Society*). Most of the writers in the pages of the journal were women, and the executive bodies of both the society and the foundation were chiefly made up of women. During World War II, a group of women formed a "members group" to propagandize Froebelian ideas, a group which included people like M. H. Bradley, Edith Warr, Molly Brearley, Barbara Priestman, Elsa Walters, and others — all women of great ability and influence.

It seems quite clear, then, that in the growth of humane, child-centered education in England, able women have played a major role. This is not to denigrate the men involved, but only to point to at least one important area in which, over a long period of time, a large number of women have operated creatively, and with very considerable success.

America

Turning, finally, to the American scene, is there anything we can learn from the development of nontraditional ways of working with children in the English school? Again, it is certainly unwise to think that such methods can simply be transplanted and made to grow here. Americans must sift through successful practices and ideas and make use of the ones which suit the American situation — they must be eclectic. The comparative viewpoint, however, is very helpful when it is time to look at one's own situation, and it bears reexamination. Over the years of educational history in the United States, schools have been assigned to perform two rather different tasks: one suits the needs of society, the other the needs of the child. On the one hand, schools have been expected to produce informed citizens, skilled workers, patriotic Americans, and "college material," and to promote general social equality. Schooling has been seen as an unqualified good, and the more a child has of it, the better his chances for high income and status. All this has nothing to do with the child but rather with what society assumes goes on in the schools and what it wants schools to produce.

On the other hand, from time to time there have indeed been American schools that have the child and his or her development at the center of their work, like their English counterparts.[32] These schools see their role quite differently: instead of the product, the process of growth and development in the child is stressed. Education, in fact, becomes an end in itself — an opportunity to learn and grow. These schools, however few, are just as much a part of the American tradition as the more numerous ones mentioned earlier. In fact, during the very time when English schools here and there were working out experimental ideas, there were American ones doing the same. And English thinkers and writers, too, can be matched by American ones of the same persuasion.

So, one thing we can learn from the English experience is that if we look at our own, we will find a similar past. Another is that we can and should follow their example in paying very close attention to the remarkable knowledge, stemming basically from the work of Freud and from Piaget, that now exists about child development. The English have done so to a far greater extent than we, and much needs to be done to make the average American teacher more aware of her children's natural needs and interests, and of how she can use them in promoting their growth. One possible side effect of taking such ideas seriously is that we may develop smaller schools, on the English model. If what matters is the relationship between people in a school, then large, impersonal schools hamper children's growth, however much they seem to increase efficiency. Similarly, we must think through all the consequences of putting the child first, and plan our expenditures and arrangements to suit that aim.

Careful study of what we know about children's development can teach us that the first demand made of schools — to serve society's ends — has not worked and cannot work. The strategies we have planned to produce the attitudes which we approve do not follow developmental lines. They are constructed by adults and implanted in children, with some hope of success. But unless the learner participates in the learning, unless he is the self-aware agent of his learning, such learning remains verbal only. Citizenship, for instance, cannot be directly taught, although a classroom which embodies democratic principles of personal and social behavior can do much to inculcate democratic attitudes. One cannot hope to produce future citizens by teaching them about governmental organization; rather, one must help them see what it means to be a citizen in the classroom that they inhabit every day.

There is one particular myth which Americans have long held about the effect of schooling and which is now being destroyed, namely, that equalizing educational opportunity for children will result in greater social mobility

126 / ACTIVITY AND EXPERIENCE

and higher income for them when they are adults. Again, the emphasis is on the hoped-for results of the school process, not on the process itself. Evidence is mounting that this myth is quite far from an accurate picture of what happens to children when they leave school.[33] On the contrary, the best predictor of a school's effect in later years, when measured in terms of status and income, is the background and status of the children who come there in the first place.

This is not to say that schools do not matter but only that they do not and cannot serve at least one function which has long been assigned to them. It is time to stop measuring the success of schools in terms of later results, especially material ones. It is time we began to consider the contribution schools can make to society because of the quality of the life within them. Judging schools, then, by measurable effects may be just the wrong way to think about them. As Jencks says, "The long-term effects of schooling seem much less significant to us than they did when we began our work, and the internal life of the schools seems correspondingly more important" (p. 13)

This iconoclastic view of what schools can do may shatter one myth, but we have the other strand in our educational history to turn to. Like England, we have had schools where the "internal life of the school" was the central concern. "What the best and wisest parent wants for his children, that must society want for all its children," said John Dewey. We can make schools suitable places for children to grow in. When schools and teachers refuse to be used as means for distant social goals but see education as an end in itself, then they can be free from distractions, impositions, and all the pressures that force them to do work they cannot do. Schools cannot eradicate poverty and inequality; but they can be sane, understandable places fundamentally concerned with the sound development of the children they serve. The best preparation for an uncertain and changing future, on this view, is a fully developed life in the present and at every stage.

NOTES TO PART ONE

1. See Bibliography, especially references to the *Handbooks for the Consideration of Teachers* of 1905 and subsequently and the *Reports of the Consultative Committee*, "The Hadow Reports," of 1926, 1931, and 1933.
2. *Children and Their Primary Schools,* "The Plowden Report," 1967. See Bibliography in Part Two (p. 203) for full bibliographical details for this and other works referred to.
3. *The New Republic* articles.
4. One of the best such references is Blackie's *Inside the Primary School.*
5. For a brief description of the English educational system, see pp. 7-9 of this chapter.
6. Except where the speaker has specifically edited his or her own words, I have added only punctuation and an occasional word or two, for the sake of clarity.
7. "A group of persons who are engaged in first-hand efforts for improving the education of children, and who have all shared in the general movement that has brought about a more scientific study of them." From the pamphlet of 1917, about the bureau's purposes. The major work of the bureau was expanded to become what is now the Bank Street College of Education. See Charlotte Winsor, ed., *Experimental Schools Revisited: Bulletins of the Bureau of Educational Experiments.*
8. Conducted for the Progressive Education Association by its Commission on the Relation of School and College. See Cremin, *The Transformation of the School: Progressivism in American Education, 1876-1957,* p. 251 ff.
9. See also Chapter 3, the sections "In-Service Training" and "HMI's."
10. Later published as part of an article in the *Froebel Journal* of October, 1969.
11. See W. van der Eyken, *Adventures in Education,* Chapter 3, "Art & Craft: Marion Richardson and Robin Tanner."
12. See Chapter 5, p. 107, for the differences between these two approaches.
13. See Chapter 3.
14. See Chapter 3, "Community Relations."
15. See also Susan Isaacs, *The Children We Teach,* for a full analysis of the benefits of dramatic play.
16. In this chapter, as elsewhere, I use the feminine pronoun for teachers and heads. This is not to say that there were no competent men in the field, for that is not true. But it is a fact that the vast majority of professionals in education in these early years, especially in the infant schools, were women. This issue is discussed in somewhat more detail in the final chapter.
17. P. 83. See the further discussion in Chapter 4.
18. *Froebel Journal.*
19. A thorough description of the Inspectorate is Blackie's *Inspecting and the Inspectorate.*
20. R. J. W. Selleck, *English Primary Education and the Progressives, 1914-1939,* p. 47.

128 / ACTIVITY AND EXPERIENCE

21. Stone is not identified as the author, since the custom of the government is not to do so with its publications. Extracts from this book and from *Primary Education* are used with the kind permission of the Controller of Her Majesty's Stationery Office.
22. The authors, although also not identified, are chiefly Mrs. Ellen Mee, Miss Stella Duncan, and Mr. Robin Tanner.
23. The Hadow Report of 1931, as quoted on page 7 of *Primary Education.*
24. *Ibid.,* p. 7.
25. *Ibid.*
26. *Ibid.*
27. As in the report of 1933.
28. From the Prefatory Note to the handbook of 1918, as quoted in *Primary Education,* p. 9.
29. Mrs. Glynn said that she was here paraphrasing the words of Miss Dorothy E. M. Gardner.
30. See *Moving and Growing* and also the paper by Ruth Foster reprinted in this book. (p. 189).
31. *Intellectual Growth in Young Children* and *Social Development in Young Children.*
32. See, for example, Gordon's *My Country School Diary,* or Roetzel's *The School at Rose Valley.*
33. See especially, in this connection, H. Perkinson, *The Imperfect Panacea;* M. Katz, *The Irony of Early School Reform,* and C. Jencks, *et al., Inequality: A Reassessment of the Effect of Family and Schooling in America.*

PART TWO

INTRODUCTION

Part Two consists of original source material by some of the pioneers in English education, chosen for their variety and intrinsic historical interest. Chapter 1 consists of seven documents and a number of pictures by Mrs. Dorothy (Alderson) Glynn, stemming from her work as a teacher in the Park School, Doncaster, Yorkshire. The head was Miss Dorothy Simpson, about whom there is an article in *The Froebel Journal* for October, 1969. At the age of 31, in 1924, she was appointed head of an old school in a poor area, and in 1935 she was transferred to a new one in a large park nearby. This was the Park School, historically a very important school in the development of child-centered education; it was there that Miss Simpson and Miss Alderson spent almost twenty years together, experimenting and developing their own successful practices. *Creative Play in the Infants School* (1950) comes from those years, as do the documents and pictures used here. Another reason for this school's importance is that Susan Isaacs, among many other important educators, visited the school over the years, seeing it as a fine embodiment of the theories about children and learning which she had been developing and spreading around the country. The third reason for its importance is that Miss Alderson and Miss Simpson, working as a remarkable team, kept careful records of their work with the children. Discussions in the classroom, observations of individual children's progress, check lists of pointers for observation, reflections on past weeks, experiments along various lines — all were put down on paper. So for this school, many more records are available than for others, and some key documents and pictures have been chosen for inclusion here. They give the flavor of on-going work with children aged 5-7 in a real school, dating from the 1930's and 1940's, as well as the careful thinking and planning that went into that work. Throughout this section, where appropriate, names of individuals have been changed to protect their privacy.

Chapter 1
ONE TEACHER REPORTS

EARLY INFLUENCES

I would like to reëmphasise the part played by the Head teacher of an Infant School — particularly in a teacher's initial post. If I had been appointed to a school other than the Park School, provided I had not been expected to be unkind to children, I feel pretty certain I would have absorbed the pattern of *that* school. (e.g. a school *I might* have been posted to was run on a strict interpretation of Montessori principles and great stress was laid on the apparatus — everything was "cut and dried" and one knew exactly what one was expected to do each week, etc. I don't think I would have had sufficient strength to have resisted this in my first post.)

Many teachers I have observed have been strongly influenced by the philosophy of the Head and the practical interpretation of this encountered in their first post. So that those of us who were fortunate enough to be placed with people like Miss Simpson* and Miss Vint* had a head start and were given confidence to experiment under expert guidance.

PERIOD ENDING NOVEMBER 20, 1941
OBSERVATIONS AT THE PARK SCHOOL

Two and a half weeks ago we began our new experimental day. We had decided previously that the 3 top classes should take part in this experiment and after several discussions (in which we all felt that although there were many difficulties, perhaps these were not insurmountable), we de-

---

*Respondents numbers 30 and 35. See the List of Respondents at the back of this book.

132 / ACTIVITY AND EXPERIENCE

cided that we would organize what space, equipment and extra help was available, to the best of our ability, and embark on the new experiment as quickly as possible.

First of all we organized our classroom libraries and in our bookcases we placed several books of many series and some suitable to the reading level of all those children in that particular class. The covers were clearly marked in a certain colour – each colour representing a certain stage and the children were made aware of this grading. We rearranged our rooms so that the tables at one side could be used for writing work, number work and quieter practical number activities and at this side of the room the cabinet with 'helping words' was placed. The other tables were arranged for box-modelling, painting, art paper work, clay-modelling and sewing and work with any waste materials. The woodwork was placed outside during the day time. We had hoped for a quantity of P.T. apparatus but all that was available for the time being was a tree trunk, a ladder and several planks.

Children working in reorganized classroom

One Teacher Reports / 133

Miss Alderson helping a small group

Simple playground equipment

134 / ACTIVITY AND EXPERIENCE

Simple playground equipment

We had a helper each for most of the day and there were certain periods a day when those children who wished to read as a group could go to the head mistress and read in her room.

On the day before we began to work in this way I explained to the children very simply how we were going to organize the day; that we should cut out the mid-morning break and also milk time, but there would be a milk table for four and they could go as they wished to eat their lunch and drink their milk during the morning. I told them that one side of the room would be an office and one side a factory and that they would wash in the appropriate place. I could easily explain the reasons for the change because frequently during the last few weeks I have found myself in the position of forcing somebody to stop his handwork when his interest was at its highest and similarly in the case of children who have been drawing or working. They were very quick to see the point and on the following morning when they arrived at school Christine Potter looked around the room and said in a surprised voice, "You've done what you said you were going to do and now I'm going to give you something for that." She produced half of her lunch as a token of her appreciation.

From the outset nobody missed the mid-morning break and the milk table service ran very smoothly. On the first day a child who was playing in the house brought the bell to the milk table and Richard who was doing woodwork was sitting there. They said it was a café and they had arranged to meet there for lunch.

My first impressions of the first few days were not at all clear cut and I haven't really quite sorted them out yet, but here they are briefly.
1. There was a much more peaceful atmosphere about the classroom.
2. Although I did not appear to have had many groups or individual children to read to me during the day, at the end of the day when I looked at my notebook I found that one group had been to Miss Simpson and that with the exception of the top eight (fluent readers), I had heard every child read.

I have found that the reading has presented very few problems. The children have made good use of the library and individual children have practised reading a book precisely similar to their own grey reader quite without direction.

Many individual children have asked me to hear them read and all the groups have been very keen to come at odd times and read as a group. They

Children absorbed in reading books

have also been quite pleased to follow up their reading by some writing and drawing to help them with the new words and phrases.

I have noticed a marked improvement in the more backward readers.

The written news has been disappointing; not many children have chosen to do news and those who did do so produced poor writing and drawings until today November 22nd (the third week) when the news table was occupied by five or six children all trying very hard with both their writing and their drawing. The written number, again, has not been chosen by many but I have noticed that those children who have chosen it have put far more effort into it than even they did previously, e.g., Graham Smith – Christopher Johnson.

I arranged a table for the Practical Number Activities of measuring water and weighing various materials such as sand, beans, peas, silver sand. The helper was in charge of this table and she kept a record of the children who use it and how they used it.

There were always children wanting to use it and many of them would

Miss Alderson gives ten minutes of help to a child

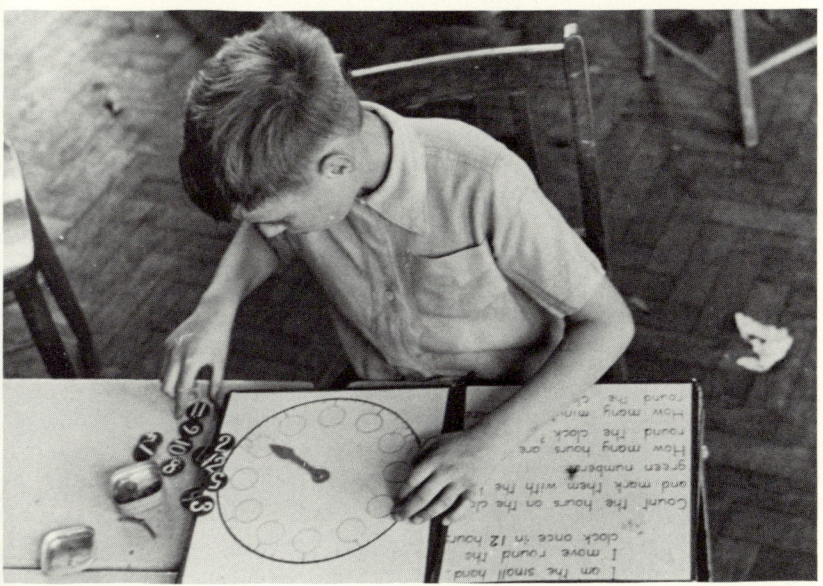
Ten minutes of tutoring — combining reading and number work

become absorbed for a considerable length of time. It was particularly noticeable in cases of children who found it difficult to settle to anything else, e.g., Garry Parker.

He worked for the best part of the morning finding out the answers to the various problems suggested by the cards.

The helper said that all the children approached the activity in a sensible way and found satisfaction in finding out for themselves.

I found that several children chose the work with money and bus tickets and shops, but there was not the competition for it that I should have expected.

At first the paintings, on the whole, were much more careful and detailed than hitherto. The box-modelling had a set back and many children did not continue at it for a little while, but interestingly enough, they all came back to it after several days. During the first few days it was inclined to be messy and had not a great deal of finish.

One group of children made a bird table with some old wood and it was full of really purposeful activity which involved reassuring and many discussions together. They painted it, varnished it, and set it up in the shrubbery. It was really an effortful activity.

Ann Hill and Wendy Jones finished their large house but Christine left hers and has not returned to it since. Bruce Jameson and Richard Holden returned to their ship after several days and worked with much more enterprise, finish and detail.

An interesting piece of work developed a few days after the experiment had begun. Tommy Bristol had made a rather cute stage for a Punch and Judy show a week or so before and this was put out for him to finish. He did not return to it but Richard Powell found a Quaker Oat Box and cut out the man's head from it, stuck it to a wood spill and said, "I have made a puppet." Nigel, Trevor, Harold and Jim Moore followed suit and soon they had all cut out the heads and mounted them on sticks. In the discussion they told what they had been doing and said they would like to use Tommy's puppet theatre for their play. I said that their idea was a good one but I asked them how they could make a play when all their puppets were exactly alike. They told me that they were going to dress them differently and they were going to make others with cardboard. Next they fastened cardboard arms with paper fasteners. They had some fun and enjoyment from making their puppets work and giving private demonstrations to each other. Then I noticed that they fastened long cottons to the heads.

One Teacher Reports / 139

These they threaded through holes which they had pierced in the ceiling of the theatre. So far they had no directions but I felt that this piece of group work had now reached a stage when a lot more could be gotten out of it if it were pulled together a little with the help of an adult. I felt certain that as it was they would abandon it soon having exhausted the apparent possibilities, so I suggested to my helper that she should discuss with the group further possibilities. They did this and decided on a play to be produced to the rest of the class. The next morning I suggested that they should go to a quiet corner in the hall with Sheila and rehearse. They did this and in the afternoon they said they were ready to perform. The puppet were very crude but the story (Cinderella) was quite well portrayed with the narrator (Richard Powell) keeping the sequence of events in good order. They all spoke up and everyone was quite sure of his part; even shy Jim Moore came in with his contribution at the right time. The other children were very appreciative and after the show we discussed its merits and its faults. The merits were those I have commented on. The criticisms (by the children) were that it was too small, that the puppets weren't easily identified because they were too much alike, that they were too crowded. The interest was so keen that I asked which children would like to learn how to make bigger puppets and to produce a play. Many of the children were very keen so we chose a group and gathered together the materials and they stayed with Sheila to discuss a story and choose characters.

They decided on "Little Red Riding Hood." I had a talk to them about puppets' heads and explained how the features were exaggerated because otherwise they did not show up at a distance. On the following morning they all arrived with a stick-bundle of material for dressing their puppets and one child with a book with pictures of the characters in the story. They set to work and modelled their heads from plasticine and then covered them with small pieces of tissue paper pasted on. When this was done they began to make the clothes. Margaret James (Red Riding Hood) had a very good idea of what she wanted and set to work on a kilt (a bit of Scotch plaid), a blouse and a cape and hood in a very business-like way. David Kent wanted a great deal of help but was keenly interested in talking about his puppet (the wood cutter) as though he were a live person all the time. Richard Powell dressed his wolf in a red coat and painted his head in a manner which indicated that he knew well what he was about.

Joyce Morris began to dress the grandmother who had been made by Alan. (Alan did not want to dress her.) At the end of the second day such concentrated effort had been put into this piece of work that the puppets were almost dressed, their heads painted and were, in fact, complete except for the "hair" which we have to find somewhere.

An interesting side issue of this activity is its effect on David Lewis — a boy with an extremely high I.Q., well grounded in reading and arithmetic at a private school. A child with obvious difficulties due in part to being pushed on the academic side, in part to having very old parents and in part to his mother being ill with asthma and bronchitis. The difficulties have shewn most obviously in the following ways:

1. twitching and nervous habits not unlike those associated with chorea.
2. an effortlessness in any creative activity — an inability to play without upsetting somebody's work.
3. an inability to choose an activity and a disinclination to do anything (even arithmetic), other than spasmodic reading.

He has shewn an interest in what other people have been doing and has brought various gadgets from home for other people's models. He has examined the contents of the waste material boxes from time to time but has not made anything, nor has he ever done anything except at my suggestion.

He was keenly interested in the puppets and after everybody had started he asked if he could make one. Unfortunately I had no plasticine left on that day so I told him I would get some but in the meantime he could paint some scenery for the show. He painted three or four pictures of trees — very crudely — but with real effort and satisfaction. This was the first really satisfying work with material I have seen him do. On the following day he again asked if he could make a puppet so I gave him the plasticine and a stick and shewed him how to make one. He decided on a witch. I kept my eye on him and from time to time I had a little conversation about his witch — what she would be like and what she would wear and what she would need. I found him a piece of black cloth for a cloak. He said, "I cannot sew." I told him I would show him how to sew and after I had shewn him a running stitch I noticed that he was sewing the cloak with great effort and concentration. There was a marked difference in his attitude to me and the other children that day. When I was shewing some of the mothers the puppets at home time he came up and in a really childlike way (again, something new) he said with real pride and a sense of achievement, "I have made one too, haven't I, Miss Alderson?"

On the next day he painted the witch's face and I noticed he had Harold Reed, another new boy, working with him. About one hour later he said, "Harold wants to make a puppet if you give him the plasticine." "I will show him how to make it." He did this and told Harold his puppet could be a wizard. Later still he told me that Trevor and Christopher both wanted to make puppets and he would show them..

In the discussion these items of interest were discussed and David said that in his group there was his witch, the wizard — the witch's cat and the wizard's dog and he said he would make a story for them to act.

There must be a feeling of satisfaction in what he is doing for him because he is putting so much more of himself into other things — into singing and offering to help me for example; before he was a typical example of a child unable to express himself. I feel that if we watch him carefully at this stage we may find that he is finding a creative release in this way.

Another interest which has developed during these last few weeks is that of doll making. Beverly Ash — a girl who is very scatter-brained and slipshod, one who has never settled to anything — wanted to make a puppet. I said I had no plasticine and so she said could she make a doll? I gave her some white sheeting and showed her how to make the body. Again I felt that if I could get her really interested she might settle for a greater length of time so I talked to her about the exciting possibilities of making a doll and dressing her. She has worked at the doll for two days and again I have noticed the satisfaction arising from having put herself into what she has been doing.

At least six girls have followed her example and Wendy went home and told her mother what she was doing and in the afternoon she brought a doll's face provided by her mother. One can see a real progression in the work with materials this week.

Tommy Bristol, Michael Swift, and two other boys have been making a fantastic ship with orange boxes and the actual work in it is much less crude than that in earlier models. They are very good-natured about individual children who join their group from time to time.

This morning Helen, who has done little work with material before, began to make a ship with boxes and she said it was to be a Christmas Ship. Tomorrow I shall stimulate her interest and effort further by providing lightly coloured and silver paper.

142 / ACTIVITY AND EXPERIENCE

After the first few days I found that when I said I was going into the hall for movement, most of the children wanted to come.

Dramatic movement work in the school hall

Experimenting with movement and music out of doors

Several stayed with Sheila — but curiously enough Garry Parker and Michael Swift (who were in the middle of a job and who were not invited, simply because they have always tried to dodge it before) stopped what they were doing and followed us into the hall and enjoyed the lesson thoroughly.

I have found it to work quite well if I cleared away at about 11:20 and took a class singing lesson for 20 minutes before assembly. The children have enjoyed singing together and I do not see how we could enjoy the pleasures of singing as a group otherwise. In the afternoon — the discussion has gone very well indeed, but there has been much more of the side-tracking type of discussion (described in detail later) than that in which the children have discussed the merits and faults and ideas of each other's models.

We have had several stories — The Sand Hoppers, Solomon Sammy and Perky Peter and a wealth of original story-telling by the children themselves.

Scripture and Hymns have taken place as usual.

My most superficial comments at the moment (and by "superficial" I mean *not* insincere, but those made before I have had an opportunity to analyse my own feelings and impressions) are these:

1. That I am much less tired at the end of this kind of day.
2. That I do much less nagging of individual children.
3. That I am much more aware of the effortless, timid and shy children.
4. That the 'reading' causes no anxiety at all and that even those children who apparently do very little seem to be improving rapidly.
5. That very few children choose number work but those who do, do it much more intelligently and with much more effort than before.
6. That very few children choose written news and in some cases there is an apparent retrogression in the written news.
7. That until we have more P.T. apparatus it is necessary to have a period for P.T. as the children are not getting enough of that kind of activity.
8. There is something quite different in the relationship between the class and myself and it is something which makes for a happier atmosphere.
9. One feels that there must be a regular 'taking stock' not only of what the children have done in work that can be measured but in the effect on the children themselves.

After a few more weeks it should be possible to say what is lacking and what one considers to be added advantages in this new way of life.

144 / ACTIVITY AND EXPERIENCE

Afternoon discussion time with the children

Penny

Early in the year I was concerned about Penny; she was petulant, disagreeable and obviously unhappy. She was excessive in her demands for my attention and she was resentful of any other child or adult who claimed my attention at any time (even of a stranger entering the room to speak to me). She would not (or could not) settle to any kind of activity other than sewing. She experimented with sewing materials in a creative way but even then she soon lost interest. She wanted to attempt anything she saw being done by other children but she soon flagged and her attempts at painting a picture or modelling with clay were soon abandoned. She had no interest in reading or working. She wanted to play a recorder but did not take hers to the music room and play on it as the others did frequently.

I tried to stimulate her interest in many ways but I did not feel that she could become absorbed.

I knew she was intelligent and in many ways mature and yet I realized she was not integrated nor was she applying herself in any way. I talked to her mother and I gathered that she was probably resentful about the home situation.

For a long time she had been the sole (and attractive) grandchild and niece of a number of admiring relations. At 1½ years she had a brother and at 3 years a sister and by this time there were also a number of cousins and Penny found that most of the attention which had been focussed on her was withdrawn. However her father, who had been in the forces, was beginning to think she had been spoiled and withdrew much of his attention and decided to be strict with her. I advised him against this course and at the same time I gave her rather more demonstrative affection myself whenever I could; but at the same time I would appeal to her to show me how sensible she could be, especially when I had a visitor. In this way she was gradually weaned from demanding attention in an overbearing way from me and she began to make conscious efforts to be controlled.

It seemed as if she knew that I was on her side, for almost immediately the tension became eased and she was much less resentful and petulant; she also began to develop poise. She brought her recorder to me one morning and began to play a number of tunes she had made up and it was actually through our apparent joy in her recorder playing and her ability to make tunes that good relationships were finally established. It was then that she began to settle and as soon as she did she began to grow in every way.

In a short time (a matter of a few weeks) she was reading fluently and without effort. She began to experiment with writing and to paint pictures. She would choose some difficult piece of work involving a problem — such as a shop with all kinds of calculations to be made — and she would settle down and work out the problems herself, concentrating and working with integrity of purpose for a whole morning.

It was interesting (I cannot say how much this was significant — or how far it was coincidence) to note that her first coherent and complete story was about her little sister Anne. It describes her attempts to come to school with Penny and other "baby" ways.

She had grumbled about Anne to me on many occasions but I felt this story showed a tolerance and understanding towards her. I laughed with her about Anne and I soon began to feel that Penny's problem was resolved.

She now seems happy and satisfied in herself and is developing into a clever girl with varied interests and obvious creative gifts — particularly in language — which she is able to express in different ways.

NOTTINGHAM COLLEGE OF EDUCATION
NOTES ON OBSERVING AND RECORDING

If the student is studying and observing her children in a positive way she will be ready to help and advise, to give a suggestion or a word of encouragement at the right moment and so prevent the child with little manual dexterity from becoming disheartened, and so losing confidence through too many unsuccessful attempts to control the material. When the children need or ask for her help, she should be ready to co-operate with them to see further possibilities which may give them greater satisfaction in their chosen activity. If she can do this without imposing her adult ideas then she can often stimulate further creative effort so that there will be a definite progression in the activity of the children at different stages of their development.

It will help the student in her study of the children, to keep a record bearing in mind the following points:

1. She should record any interesting piece of constructive work or imaginative play on the part of an individual child or a group of children.
2. She should notice the original ideas of the children, how these are stimulated, how they are carried out practically and what evidence there is of them in the class discussions and conversations between individuals.
3. She should make notes on the children who have original ideas but little ability to carry them out, and she should try to discover what helps them to improve.
4. She should keep a particularly careful watch on the children whose play always tends to be aggressive or destructive; on children who frequently say they do not know what to do or make and who seem to have an inability to play; on children who concentrate for short periods only; and on those who go from one activity to another without ever becoming really absorbed and leaving everything they begin to make unfinished.

    She should try to find out what are the difficulties of these groups of children. Careful observation of their play may help to reveal the nature of some of their problems and perhaps give some indication of how they can be relieved.

    When discoveries of this kind are made she can give the individual children concerned further opportunity for that kind of play which seems to help them most.

5. She should notice when specific interests in reading, writing, number and nature study arise. She should record how these interests are followed up, where they lead to and what ground is covered through the development of them.
6. In relation to the mathematical development of individual children she should notice and describe:
    (a) Situations in which children appeared to be forming number concepts through play.
    (b) Situations in which children used number knowledge in purposeful situations, and also those in which they needed to make calculations for their own purposes.
7. She should describe situations in which children linked one experience with another, using the knowledge gained through one experience to help them in solving problems met in a new situation.
8. And situations in which children showed evidence of constructive thought, reasoning, and also those situations in which they set certain standards for themselves.

Whenever it is relevant the student should record the content and nature of her own contribution to the children's experiences.

SOME POINTS TO REMEMBER ABOUT CREATIVE PLAY

1. There must be adequate provision of materials and they must be arranged in the room (and garden) before the children arrive; often the creative ability and imagination of a child is awakened and stimulated by the suggestiveness of the material.
2. Sometimes a child's play activity is stimulated by something he has seen or heard of, or by some event which has made an impression upon him. What may appear to us a trivial incident can often result in much thought, a wealth of imagination and much activity on the part of the child.
3. Children of all types show a need to express and relive their experiences through their activities. Some children play-act them; some will make a picture or a clay model of them but usually the very young children of Nursery age make themselves, in their play, into the actual object which has impressed them, e.g. a Nursery child who has visited a railway station will *be* the engine rather than make one.
4. A great deal of the children's play is based on fantasy and the chil-

148 / ACTIVITY AND EXPERIENCE

Sociable washing up out of doors

Discussing next steps in making a tower

One Teacher Reports / 149

Dramatic house play with real equipment and a friend or two

Working on the structural problem of fixing a mast onto their boat

Creative play outside on a pleasant day

dren use their imaginations in many different ways. They can make a brick or a piece of wood represent anything which they want it to be, from a doll to a hot water-bottle.

On other occasions they will play at being grown up and will use their imaginations to make the necessary furniture, household equipment and food. At other times they will invent highly imaginative dramatic games and will play-act stories with imaginative plots.

5. Children play out their fears and anxieties and situations in which they feel insecure, e.g., visits to dentists, hospitals and doctors, or fears of the imagination such as ghosts, burglars and other night terrors, and in this way they are able to face up to these fears.

They also find compensation in their play for certain feelings of insecurity and frustration, on such occasions as the birth of a baby sister and the temporary absence of their mother. Invariably the children express these anxieties in their play and their conversation with the dolls often reveals what they are feeling.

6. Children who find it difficult to concentrate must have opportunities for experimenting freely with a variety of materials. Once their interest is aroused they will be able to concentrate for longer periods.

Boys working separately but near each other in the early stages of constructing a cart

Sharing and discussing the finished product

7. The "effortless" children must receive constant stimulation from the material and need careful watching. They should receive endless encouragement in the use of material which has creative possibilities.
8. When children begin to work and play together during the activity period, we get the beginnings of real social development. When the children first come to schools their play is often individual: a child will play by himself or experiment with the material, alone. Some time later (the length of time depends on the individual child) he becomes interested in the activity of another child or in the material which the child is using, and through this interest or because of his desire to share the material or toy with him, he will start to play with him and in this way he establishes social relationships with others.
9. Children who have feelings of aggression can find a legitimate outlet in the scope for vigorous bodily activities with hammers, clay and bricks.

NUMBER EXPERIENCES IN AN INFANT SCHOOL

Many of us who are in infants schools believe that the life in our school should be based on the real needs and interests of the children and it was in trying to find out more about these needs and interests, that is the needs and interests of individual children, that we ourselves in the school in which I teach, discovered that we were building up an entirely new conception of what a school should be. As we became increasingly aware of the sense of living together, that is our living with the children and the children with each other rather than of us being there merely to instruct them, we realised that there was a noticeable growth of feeling in the community, and with this growth of feeling came new attitudes to learning. As we lived and shared the experience of the children we realised that each experience of an individual child was in itself something new and that as teachers we must deal with such an experience as it arose, making our contribution in the appropriate time. We felt we could sometimes add to the richness of such an experience by guiding the children towards natural progression, but we also felt from our own experience that we must guard against imposing our own adult conceptions. In the light of these observations we decided that it was no longer possible, or feasible, to plan a scheme of work beforehand. The activity of the children was not something we described in a weekly forecast and carried out according to a preconceived plan, and so, as our new conception of school began to take shape, we found that we had, of necessity, to cast aside many of our traditional ideas of planning, many of our former ways of working things out, and many of our former ways of recording progress. We realised, too, that we were gradually building up a new set of values, and this was particularly true in relation to our changing attitude to the Number work in our school. Formerly we had on our time tables periods described by the term "Number Activities." These were planned by us and based upon what we thought were the interests of the children. We provided a series of organised practical activities in which the children weighed and measured and shopped, but in a limited way according to instructions, and these activities were supplemented by a well known graded scheme, worked out in so called logical sequence. This scheme began by introducing pieces of apparatus for associating the number group with the symbol and continued through the various stages of addition, subtraction, composition, multiplication and division of these numbers with the aid of attractive and well-made counting apparatus. The child worked from a number of sum cards appropriate to each stage, and his progress was recorded as he completed each set of cards. Although there are a number of comments one could make about the different aspects of such a scheme planned at the time with considerable thought and good intention, there are, too, several observations one would wish to make about the various reasons which lead us to query the ultimate values of our number teaching as it was. Perhaps the most important of these is that our changing attitude, I think, was not a sudden thing, but a gradual process born out of a deepening awareness of the real needs of children. I know that as I myself became more aware I found that I was beginning to ask myself certain questions such as: "Does the teaching of number serve any purpose and if so what is the purpose? Of what use is number knowledge in everyday life and does the number teaching that I am attempting bear any relation to the day to day living of the children and, perhaps most important of all, does it mean anything to the children?" Through asking myself simple fundamental questions such as these and through thinking of the answers to them in terms of observations I had made on the children in my class I realised that much of my own well meant, well planned, number teaching was not only mis-directed, but often

Three different construction problems being worked on (double decker bus in foreground)

Collaboration on the difficult problem of fixing the wheels of a bus

divorced from the real life of the child. I had been thinking of Arithmetic or Number as a subject and unwittingly most of the emphasis had been laid on the teaching of the subject rather than on the integrated growth of the child or rather than on what it meant to the child and of what use and purpose it was to him. I think that many of us erred in a similar way over the teaching of reading and music. We often introduce the children to the technique of these subjects before they had any real interest in them. I know we may have achieved certain external results, but I think that the children gain little beyond a certain ability to work with numbers, words and notes. They may have had, or some of them may have had, rows of sums with ticks by them and nice books which we could enter into our note books so that we said the children can do this or do that just because they had completed a certain number of sum cards correctly with the help of the apparatus, but I don't think that this way of teaching helped them really to form clear concepts of numerical meanings and values any more than I think the kind of reading and music work that we did with them when we introduced them to the technique at too early a stage — any more than this kind of teaching helped them to read books for content and ideas or to love music and create melodies: and so it was that I began to put a different construction on the value of number experiences and think of them more in relation to the child's development as a whole person. I faced the fact that a child comes into contact with Number in a variety of natural situations. Throughout the day he gets up and sets off for school and has his meals and goes to bed at stated times and so the day is divided into periods of time. He eats a specific number of sweets, gives so many away and has so many remaining, and a child, even before he goes to school, soon knows how many sweets he has left if he is told to give so many away or if he gives so many away of his own accord. He sees his mother cut an apple into two parts, give one half to him and the other half to his sister and so he gets a concept of two halves making a whole. He goes shopping with his mother and hears her ask for 2 lbs. sugar or ½ lb. margarine. Sometimes he sees the grocer weigh these quantities. He sees a bottle of milk and hears it referred to as a pint of milk. Later he becomes aware of the number of times he can bounce his ball or skip without stopping. Most children from being quite tiny get into the habit of counting. Any good mother counts the stairs with her child as she takes him up and down, counts his beads on his cot, and so it becomes a natural thing to count and quite spontaneously he begins to count the number of bricks he needs to complete his tower and, even more important, he begins to estimate the number of bricks he will need for that purpose, or to judge the length of a piece of wood needed for the boat he is constructing. He begins to notice numbers on cars and houses and on buses and bus tickets: and these natural experiences of every child reappear in his play both at home and at school.

Discovering the need for measurement

THE INFANT SCHOOL AS IT MIGHT BE[1]

If one visualises the infant school as a happy and serene place in which the process of growth can be a continuous and integrated whole, it is not an easy task to describe the life within it in terms of "curriculum," "method" and organisation.

Those of us who believe that the upbringing and education of young children should be closely based on what we have learned of their psychological needs consider that our aims can best be served by the infant school in which there is "full scope for a sincere expression of feeling" and opportunity for "satisfying activity in a rich and stimulating environment."

We are well aware that as such phrases become part of our current educational jargon they are in danger of developing into familiar clichés which can be used far too glibly while conveying very little of the living and vital philosophy of the school or of the educational practice with which it is inseparably linked.

Therefore, in submitting this paper, I have decided that at all costs I must avoid what Professor Whitehead describes as "the airy path of brilliant generalisations"; this is my justification for trying to interpret "satisfying activity in a stimulating environment" in relation to the experiences

1. Evidence presented to the Plowden Committee. Reprinted by permission of the author.

One girl is making a guidebook for tourists to Britain

Making her own map of the British Isles and their coalfields

Pages from a boy's book on interesting places in Wales and near the Thames River

of living children and for illustrating the content of infant school education by actual examples of "the patient process of the mastery of details, minute by minute, hour by hour, day by day." (See Appendix A [page 163 herein].)[2]

If the aim is to provide the optimum environment for all-round growth then there must of necessity be a genuine acceptance of the concept of freedom which presupposes an understanding of the differences between licence and freedom in a school.

With the emphasis on meeting individual needs and the recognition that no two children learn in exactly the same way or at the same rate, we are faced with the task of finding the best way of planning the day to day life of the community.

The organisation of time needs to be very flexible, the general pattern following the idea of the "free day." This means that there will be long uninterrupted periods both in the morning and the afternoon when children, with the support and interest of adults, can work from their own choice indoors and out of doors as they wish.

They will have freedom to experiment with materials, freedom to move about and discuss their ideas and problems with others, freedom to make mistakes and begin afresh, and not least freedom to pause for thought and reflection without the fear of being hustled by an overanxious or overzealous teacher who fears that time is being wasted if children are not obviously "busy."

The Stimulating Environment *(See Appendix B, page 180)*

There will be provision for vigorous physical activity, for spontaneous dramatic and imaginative play (including mime and movement), for experiment, invention and construction with a variety of media which are both suggestive of possibility and satisfying to handle. With these they will be able to find their own creative level and to make and model from their own child-like images rather than the teacher's adult conception. There will be opportunity for children to experiment with sound, rhythm and melody through the use of simple instruments and the human voice; to make music and to listen to it; to use spoken and written language and to enjoy and use well written and well illustrated books both before and when they can read. There will also be the opportunity for witnessing at first hand the

2. To this paper. All appendices to the paper appear at the end of the chapter (Chapter 1, Part Two).

growth of living plants and animals, for observing physical phenomena and for making first hand discoveries about their own world through personal investigation.

If the environment is rich in stimulating material there will be no end to the self motivated activities in which children can become absorbed and through which they will acquire not only knowledge but "the art of the utilisation of knowledge."

The Free Day in Practice

The children will come to school many of them knowing beforehand what they intend to do when they arrive there. They will find the rooms and other parts of the school carefully prepared with materials and equipment invitingly displayed and ready to be used. Some will be eager to settle to work immediately; others will need to talk to their teacher or greet their friends first. A few will be undecided and their activity may be suggested by the stimulus of the environment, by an invitation to join with a group of established children, or by the suggestions of the teacher who will always be aware of her children as individual human beings and ready to help them to feel wanted and secure.

She will give practical assistance to those who, in the initial stages, find difficulty in the manipulation of tools or material; for there will always be some with little manual dexterity who would easily become discouraged by too many unsuccessful attempts to control the material. The skilful teacher will help such children to achieve success without doing the job for them. She will be ready to answer questions, discuss problems, and when her cooperation will add to the children's satisfaction and give added zest to their learning, she will participate in their activities. Whenever she sees possibilities for development she will facilitate a natural progression sometimes through providing opportunities for further discovery and sometimes by introducing questions, materials and books of a challenging nature. When occasions arise she will make the children aware of the mathematical aspects of their activities and in relation to these she will put them in the way of making mathematical calculations and solving problems for their own purposes. (See Appendix B [page 181].) Through her professional relationship with individual children as well as through the interesting and appropriate books and reading material she has provided, she will help children who are ready to become readers and to appreciate the uses of literacy.

The children will need to be assured of their teacher's interest as well as her willingness and capacity to teach them, but obviously they will not all require her help in the same measure at the same time. She will, therefore, give her fullest personal attention to individuals or to groups when it is most needed. Such tutoring may mean introducing a child to a new note on his recorder or helping another with his reading. John may need guidance in his "research" about volcanoes or cloud formation while Pat has to be put into the way of doubling the quantities in her baking recipe because she wants to make twice as many buns. Tony, who has just reached the stage of writing readiness and is excited about his original story, will dictate words and phrases to his teacher and ask her to write them for him to copy. In the same class we may find Joan and five of her friends wanting to be shown how to make decorative stitches on the garments they have made for their original play to be acted to the other children.

Obviously a child who is absorbed in painting his picture does not need his teacher by him all the time; nor do those who are enjoying their dramatic play or creating original dances and mimes. Similarly those children who reached the stage of reading readiness and have a genuine desire to read will spend long periods on their own with books asking for help from their teacher or another child only when they meet words not within their experience. But there will be times during the day (or week) when children need personal tutoring by their teacher, just as there are others when they need the opportunity to assimilate their learning and to try out and use newly acquired skills in their own way.

The children will work freely in this way until towards the end of the morning when on some days the older ones may gather together for a simple service which will not be compulsory. In the afternoon a similar arrangement will exist; again, on most days there may be times when groups of children (sometimes a whole class if the numbers are not too great) will gather together to listen to stories or poetry, to sing or to engage in ensemble work with instruments which, with the teacher's help, has developed as a progression from their individual experiments. There will also be opportunities for group and class discussions. Sometimes such occasions will arise spontaneously and at others the teacher will be aware of the need for such activity. Many of the children in the 6+ to 7+ range find the activity of discussing enthralling and it is in this field that the interested, mentally alert and creative teacher can see where the children's real interests lie and so direct them to further first hand discovery and to sources of information. This is one of the most sincere as well as the most

fruitful ways of basing the curriculum on the needs of the children.
Much thought and consideration has to be given to the role of the teacher in this newer conception of infant school life. It would be unrealistic as well as unsound to imagine that there could exist a single pattern but most of us who have tried to live and work in this way with children would agree that the teacher's contribution with its manifold facets is a vital one. She is the core of the "stimulating environment" and much of the children's learning will be dependent upon

1. the quality of her personal relationship with them
2. the quality of the material environment she provides
3. the skill with which she helps them to interact with their environment and to discover their own world.

She will make herself aware of her children's temperaments and special interests as well as their individual capacities and potentialities, she will know those who find it difficult to concentrate, those who make compulsive and excessive demands for her attention, and those she could easily overlook because they are so self-effacing. She will be aware of those who lack inner drive and make little or no spontaneous effort. She will try to discover the nature of the emotional difficulties which disturb some of her children, for until they gain some measure of relief they will be unable to become absorbed in any activity. They will find it difficult to co-operate and frequently disturb the serenity of the group. The teacher will be ready to give them sympathetic help and firm support; they must know that she is strong enough to protect them from their own uncontrolled feelings. Such knowledge will be the safeguard they need and through it they may gradually gain in confidence and control.

To the outstandingly gifted children she will also feel a special responsibility. She will make herself aware of their individual talents and frequently ask herself if the environment is sufficiently interesting and challenging to meet their needs. Whenever their own proposals are feasible she will make it possible for them to carry them forward; when they are not she will be ready to make suggestions in order to secure development in thought and practice. Amongst the highly intelligent she will also be aware of the children who seem unable to find a creative outlet as well as those whose gifts do not reveal themselves in an orthodox way.

In the rich environment of their infant school the children should have much to express. There will be pictures to be painted, models to be constructed, cakes to be baked, stories and poems to be written, books to be read and referred to, plays to be acted and songs, melodies and dances to be created.

During the last six months many of the children will develop an interest in some of the traditional "subjects" although these have not been approached in a traditional way. With their developing awareness of external reality and the world in which they live, their interests will extend beyond their immediate surroundings to the exploration of more distant situations or links with the past. Using their familiar experience as the point of departure they will become absorbed in certain aspects of History, Geography, Science, Biology, Music and Mathematics. Each child will pursue such interests in his own way, approaching them from an individual and personal starting point. At this stage they will often be absorbed for a whole morning in discovering, through first hand and second hand investigation, more about the wider environment outside the classroom. This kind of experience also provides for further opportunities for the normal expression of language and for learning and using reading, writing and mathematics in relation to the purpose they fulfill in daily living. Often such interests will be sustained over a period of weeks and will reveal the children's developing ability to work out an idea with integrity of purpose and to relate one experience to another. Those of us who have seen children actively participating in their own education in this way have been convinced that they were working with feeling and thinking creatively.

Greater Teaching Responsibilities

One realises that although we may have to cast aside some of our traditional ideas about curriculum and schemes of work and many of our former ways of assessing and recording progress, this will increase rather than diminish our teaching responsibilities , as well as involve a higher level of intelligent concern about them. Striving to develop the qualities which creative teaching encourages from the teacher's point of view, is itself a creative experience which can transform the taks and routines of teaching into creative opportunities in human development.

Some years ago Dorothy Sayers wrote: "Our worst trouble today is our feeble hold on creation. To sit down and let ourselves be spoonfed with the ready-made is to lose grip on our only true life and our only real selves. If we truly desired a creative life for ourselves and other people it is our task to rebuild the world along creative lines."

In facing up to some of the long term implications of creative teaching we may indeed assume that amongst other things it means involving one's self in this kind of forward looking attitude, which attributes not only to the actual process of teaching in the classroom but to its impacts on personalities and human relations.

Towards the end of their infant school life children will have acquired a vast store of knowledge which includes mathematical knowledge. In this field they should have had the opportunity to gain a wide and quantitative experience of daily life; their vocabulary should easily include the simple units of time, space and quantity and they should be able to make simple calculations for their own purposes. Many children will have begun to record their mathematical activities but in a variety of ways and it is from such recordings that eventually the abstract "sum" will develop. Ideally, except for some of the outstandingly gifted children, sound mental reckoning in a reasonable field (having regard to the individual's ability and experience) could take us to the limit of computation in the infant school.

Appendix A
Introduction

At the beginning of this paper I said that it would be difficult to describe the new conception of Infant School life in terms of curriculum, method and organisation. I think the real reason underlying our reluctance to describe exactly what our methods involve is that we find it impossible to describe in traditional language teaching that is no longer traditional in pattern; we cannot talk or write in precise and exact terms about a living and vital community in which teacher and child develop integrally. Nor can we give a clear cut picture of a typical day or week or even state in specific terms how we would teach certain "subjects." Not, I hasten to add, because we are haphazard and woolly headed in our thinking and planning but because such teaching techniques create new attitudes to learning. Each experience of an individual child is peculiar to him, and the way in which his teacher shares it with him, making her contribution to his development, is unique. For this reason we cannot tabulate what we are attempting to teach as we may have done in the past.

The content of the curriculum is not something we can include in a weekly forecast and carry out according to a preconceived plan based on past experience. The new technique involves dealing with each experience as it arises, adding to it and when possible enriching it; thus trying to ensure progression without conditioning children's thinking.

Perhaps the only way in which we can convey something of the "life" of the technique is to describe certain situations in schools where children are already actively participating in their own education. These will never be precisely similar to the situations in other schools, chiefly because different personalities are involved, but for those of you who have the time and patience to read the following records they may serve to show something of the basic principle in practice.

Appendix A, I

First let us look at *Michael* — a seven year old coming from a very drab home background. He was of average intelligence but inarticulate and had hitherto shown very little capacity for sustained interest. One morning he discovered a scrap-book made by other children containing pictures from obsolete Post Office Savings posters. These were arranged chronologically and showed the development of ships, aeroplanes, railway-engines, clothes; there was also a further series depicting the various invasions of Britain. Michael was particularly interested in the dates printed underneath each picture. He asked me "Why are those numbers there?" I explained their significance and then asked him if he knew the date of the current year, how old he was and if he could work out the date of his birth. He asked me several questions about the periods illustrated in the pictures and then said: "Have we any more books like this?" I directed him to the classroom library and told him to look for similar books; he selected "A History of Furniture," "A History of Transport, Trade and Travel" and "A History of Clocks." After browsing through them he came to ask for more but as our stock was exhausted, except for some encyclopaedias, I told him that I would bring him further books from home on the following day. Meanwhile he was so importunate that we decided to explore the possibilities of the encyclopaedias. Finding "History" in the index I made a note of all the pages containing historical information; the numbers of the pages were all in the thousands but working with Tony he found them all without my help.

As the two of them studied these pages they discovered a pictorial history of the Tower of London and the Tower Bridge. Michael said "We'll make the Tower Bridge." He gathered together a group of boys and with cardboard boxes and other waste material they constructed a working model of the Tower Bridge and a number of boats. Michael insisted that the boats should be of different periods and each one bore its own date. Most of these boys had little manual dexterity and Ronnie had hitherto found it almost impossible to work creatively with any kind of media. As a result of helping to make the bridge and then the boat he seemed to find the creative release he needed. On the following day he painted a picture and has done so from choice each day since; every day his enjoyment in painting and his sense of achievement has increased. Michael soon tired of working on the bridge and returned to his books. Next he made a book called "A History of Ships." Every ship had an original story and again each one carried its date.

His next request was that I should make him a list of all the kings and queens of England with the dates of their reigns; this I did, beginning with Egbert, 827 A.D. After poring over the list for some time he began to make a book about the English monarchs; then he set to work to calculate the length of each reign. I found pictures for him illustrating the life of the times and told him stories about some of the early kings and queens. His interest persisted throughout the term and any fresh information, picture or experience that came his way he related to his study and tried to fit it into a framework of time. For example: he discovered that his grandmother had an old picture of Queen Victoria — "When did she live?" Did I know she was eighty-one when she died? After hearing the story of the crucifixion at Sunday School he asked me "What king was reigning in our country at the time of the crucifixion?" Questions such as this led naturally to stories of Britain in the days of "tribes" and of the Roman invasions and occupations. Other children were interested in the stories, and as our own town was built on the site of a Roman camp, I was able to make this piece of history more real for them by taking them to visit the older parts of the town as well as the museum to see the remains. Several days after I told them about the history of our town David brought information he had discovered in the public library — that "Caster" meant "camp" and so Doncaster meant "camp on the River Don," and that all the towns ending in "caster" were where the Romans had their camps and those ending with "ton" and "ham" were where the Angles and Saxons had theirs. The other children were eager to tell us of the towns and cities they knew with these endings and were interested when we "flagged" them on a map.

Later four more children found books about the past in the Public Library.

I said: "What kind of books are these?"

Several children told me they were history books. I then asked them if they knew what "History" meant.

Susan said: "History tells you about people who lived at different times — some many many years ago."

Margaret said: "History tells you how things have changed."

So we decided we would make a list of things which had changed through the ages — and we discussed how they might have changed. The children suggested "Clothes," "Furniture," "Buildings," "Vehicles," and "Money." There was some animated discussion about what these things were like at different periods, each child contributing from his own experience.

Several had been to York Museum and could describe what they had seen there.

Margaret told us about Anne Hathaway's Cottage — and particularly about the fireplace.

Sarah's grandmother had an "old-fashioned bedstead with brass knobs on"; for the time being this was Sarah's most vivid link with the past.

Many of the children described pictures they had seen and recalled "the men wore wigs," and "the buses had no tops on" and "the beds had curtains."

Thus we accumulated a vast amount of varied information which needed to be sorted out and added to with the help of the teacher.

It may be argued that from the point of view of fact-finding and memorising none of this work goes very deep, but at least two important aspects emerge and are worth consideration.

First — coming back to Michael and his "dates" (and the many others like him who come from homes which can by no means be described as "literary"). Here we have a child dwelling on the past with absorbed concentration and singleness of purpose and with a real interest coming from within himself; he was obviously trying to get some grasp of time and to place incidents and happenings within a chronological framework.

The other point is that when children of this age are used to sharing in each other's activities their free and spontaneous discussions frequently stimulate an interest in the pursuits of their companions. They will ask questions and try to contribute helpful information and material so that often a general enthusiasm for a common topic may arise; a certain amount of communal discussion can thus be enjoyed – but we must always remember that individual children will follow up the discussion with further personal research only so far as their own interest and resources will take them.

Appendix A, II

David at seven years old was fascinated by a series of stories in his comic depicting life on an imaginary planet. For a time much of his conversation and dramatic play revolved round the super-human characters who inhabited that planet. I noticed, however, that although the characters and their adventures were highly fantastic, most of the astronomical language was correct. Thus such words as "asteroids" "sun spots" and "nebulae" became part of his vocabulary. When he related the adventures to me I listened to what he had to say and then at an appropriate time I talked to him about the solar system and planets which really existed. I showed him some charts and diagrams and produced illustrated books and encyclopaedias for him to study. I also took him and his three friends to a small homemade observatory of a young amateur astronomer. This young man, as well as letting them observe the moon through his powerful telescope, showed them some slides and explained their significance. After this, these four boys eagerly perused any reading material I provided as well as that which they themselves discovered in the library. Thus it soon became apparent that the interest sparked off by Superman and his companions was now a genuine one in Astronomy.

Although the boys continued to enjoy their "comic astronomy" and still made plans for exploring Mars when they were older, such plans now included considerations about scientific factors and they found great satisfaction in obtaining information from authentic sources. They discussed their findings with each other and with me and also compiled many note books and books of reference about the material they had collected.

The following extracts (with original spelling) are from one of David's books written at 7 years 3 months and show how much he has absorbed from his experience, discussion and reading.

A book about the Planets and the Sun and the Moon
Contents: The Sun, Mercury, Venus, Earth, Mars, Jupiter, Saturn, Neptune, Uranus, Pluto, The Moon

168 / ACTIVITY AND EXPERIENCE

> *The Sun* — Nobody has ever been to the sun as far as we can remember in history. It is 93,000,000 miles from the earth. It would take you 210 years to get there. You would only get about 80,000,000 miles before it burnt you up.
> *Mercury* — This is the smallest of the planets, but it is nearest to the parent body (the Sun). Life has not been found on it but red hot mountains are there.
> *Saturn* — This planet is different from all the others, it is very cold, but that is not the difference. The difference is that it has got couloured rings around it.
> *Neptune* — I know very little about this planet except it is freezzing.
> *Earth* — We nearly all know about our planet. Not red hot, and not freezzing. But medium. Nice gravity, nice air, nearly nice everything but one day we will collide with another heavenly body and we will perish. But we hope it will be a long time.

Similar descriptions are given of the other planets and at the end of this book there is a quiz of fourteen questions with their appropriate answers. On the final page there is a note which reads:

> Note: This is advice to everybody, it is about the sun when it burns out. If you are alive when it does it will send a very great drowsiness over you and somehow or other you feel you must get down and go to sleep. But you must *not* go to sleep. But keep working your arms and legs, until the cold catches you. You will feel nothing for it is a nice death. But once you are asleep you will never wake because you will die (conclusion).

About the same time he wrote a letter to his headmistress who was ill in hospital and sent her a big chart illustrating the solar system. Here is an extract from his letter:

> "John and I have made a paper with planets and stars on it to make you feel happier. We have put the extra planet in to remind you of Superman. Today Miss A. [his teacher] brought us a small paper for my astronomy gang and do you know they have discovered a star 50 million light years away."

The small paper he refers to was a scientific supplement to The Times and he and his friends read part of the Astronomy section with great interest and pleasure. A far cry from Superman and his comic, you may well observe! But this is how things can happen if we make it possible for children to have varied experiences.

Appendix A, III

 John, at seven and a half, had a great appreciation for poetry. As a younger child his father had read poems to him and they had enjoyed them together. Now he could read them himself and would often take an anthology from the book corner. One of his favourites at this time was:

> When you walk in a field, look down,
> Lest you tread on a daisy's crown.
> But in a city look always high
> And watch the beautiful clouds go by.

 He told me that as he was thinking of these words one day he suddenly decided that he "would watch the beautiful clouds go by" and as he looked at the clouds he saw all kinds of shapes. Quite spontaneously he made a little book called *Cloud Shapes* in which he drew fantastic shapes and wrote such comments as:

> Yesterday morning I looked at the clouds and I saw a wolf in cloud shapes. It had glaring teeth.
> Another cloud I saw was a man's head.
> Another one was a big brontosaurus.
> On Wednesday, April the fifth, I saw a big ghost!

 He was, of course, exercising his imagination as well as using his observation but it was clear to me that he was aware of the clouds and their variety. I gave him a book about the weather which contained many illustrations and photographic plates of the sky. He studied it with considerable interest and enthusiasm and quickly memorized the cloud names, taking a delight in rolling them round his tongue. Shortly afterwards he said:

> I am going to make my own weather book. It will be called: Clouds and the Weather, and its sub-title will be Weather Forecast.

 Each day he observed the sky, identified the clouds and then from memory, but often using encyclopaedic language, he wrote a description of them which was followed by an appropriate forecast in his own words. One extract reads:

June 21st.
Cirro-stratus: is the lowest type of cirrus cloud.

170 / ACTIVITY AND EXPERIENCE

> As we mentioned in cirrus they may be followed by signs of bad weather. Cirro-stratus are the clouds that follow cirrus in the event of bad weather coming. They cover the sky with a thick grey blanket through which the sun and moon can be seen. It was sunny a few minutes ago, but just now it has been pouring with rain.
> It was not raining hardly a minute and now the sun is trying his very best to make it dry again.

and another reads:

> *June 27th.* This is strange but I do not know the clouds today and the same thing happened yesterday. But the weather just now was rainy unexpectedly. Just now it is raining. Still on it is. Nothing but dark grey sky, and still cloudless. I am just going to wait until clouds appear. At last clouds are visible. Their names are cirronebula.

Appendix A, IV

Mark, another seven year old, after hearing a broadcast story, became interested in Charles the First and the happenings of his reign. He asked his parents many searching questions and both they and I, his teacher, provided him with illustrated books about the period.

One morning at school Mark painted a picture of Charles the First with a group of Royalist followers. He showed it to his class-mates and then he began to tell them about it. He said:

> I'd just like to tell you a little bit about my seventeenth century picture. During the reign of Charles the First there was a civil war. (In case you do not know what a civil war is I will explain.)
> During the last war England was at war with Germany. We were fighting people from other countries. But a civil war is when the people of one part of a country fight against those in another part of the same country and that is what happened in England in the seventeenth century.
> The civil war was between the Royalists and the Roundheads. Now the Roundheads were very strict puritans and a puritan is a strict protestant. They were led by Oliver Cromwell. The followers of the King (King Charles the first who you see in my picture) were called Royalists or Cavaliers and they usually had long curls and very rich clothes like those worn by the soldiers in my picture.

The other children listened eagerly to Mark's description and asked him a number of questions which he answered very ably. For the next few days much of their dramatic play in the playground, organized by Mark, was concerned with the activities of the Royalists and Roundheads. As a number of children seemed genuinely interested in the historical facts, I supplemented a little the information given by Mark; but as his interest went so much deeper than theirs I provided him with a number of books to which he could refer if he wished. He seemed to steep himself in the period and then began to write a story about Charles the First. He referred to this in a letter he wrote to me when I was away for a day.

> Just a few lines to tell you what my next story will be called and what it will be about: *"King Charles the First and Parliament."* I am going to have nearly all the people who took part in that reign such as Oliver Cromwell, John Hampden, Thomas Wentworth or Lord Strafford, William Laud or Archbishop of Canterbury and many other Roundheads and Cavaliers. It is John's birthday today and I have sent him two cards with dogs on. He is 15, and I, my John, my own cousin, will have happy times after his birthday.

When he was writing his story his books were never by him and although parts of the text he reproduced from memory, he also added many comments and descriptions of his own. He would sometimes put his own words into the mouths of these historical characters and it would seem as if he imagined himself living in the period.

About this time I had occasion to visit London and I told the children about the State Opening of Parliament and referred to the decorations and flower boxes in Whitehall.

Mark, who had never been to London, said, "Whitehall is very old, isn't it?" and remembering his interest I told him that I saw Charles' palace and the place where he was executed. He quickly commented "Designed by Inigo Jones wasn't it? I wish I'd been with you to see it." He was quietly thoughtful for a moment and then, smiling at me in a knowing way, he began to quote:

> He nothing common did or mean
> Upon that memorable scene,
> But with his keener eye
> The axe's edge did try

and added "That is what I would have thought of if I had been with you."

172 / ACTIVITY AND EXPERIENCE

Once again I have described in some detail the activity of one child for I feel that it is important for us to understand the many facets of a child's development towards "an appreciation of the uses of literacy." Only by such examples can I show the full implications of learning to read with understanding.

Appendix A, V
Angela and Christine (aged 8½) working for the whole of the morning made a complete puppet show. The puppets were merely lumps of clay stuck on to sticks and the stage an old margarine box with a hastily sewn curtain. The handwork was crude, but the activity was satisfying and the children were absorbed for over an hour. Their handling of the puppets and their dialogue was spontaneous and dynamic. They invited me to watch their show and several other children gathered round. As soon as they played to an audience Angela and Christine realized the limitations of their puppets and stage but in the afternoon Gerald brought them two handsome puppets made by his ten year old brother. Christine said "We really need six good puppets like these." I told her that if they were prepared to take time and trouble I could show them how to make similar puppets. They were eager to do this so I provided the necessary materials and showed them how to make puppet heads with plasticine and layers of papier maché. Angela and Christine gathered together a small group of children who had been interested in their original play and organized them into making and dressing puppets for a new play which they invented spontaneously as they made the puppets. They found obvious satisfaction in this natural progression from their original activity.

Appendix A, VI
The following "situation" is in an active class of forty-nine children (age range six to seven plus). It is particularly concerned with *John* (six and a half) and the impact of his "activity." For an hour he had been painting a picture of mountains; when it was finished he said "How I'd like to make a book about volcanoes. I've been thinking a lot about volcanoes as I painted my mountain picture." I gave him a book (several sheets of blank paper stapled together) and after illustrating the cover he said "I'll make it into a book about mountains as well as volcanoes; Mount Etna is a volcano so I'll do about that first." Graham said: "I'll help you to find out about mountains and volcanoes — how do we begin?"

John fetched a set of old Geographical magazines from which they selected pictures and information. As John did not know the names of any other volcanoes I told him of Vesuvius and shewed him photographs, pieces of lava, ammonia and sulphur which had been sent from there. Later in the day I heard him explaining to a group of nine children what I had already told him.

On the following morning I produced the encyclopaedia, with the pages of reference marked on a slip of paper. From this he was able to look up information about the size of craters, the location of volcanoes, the names of the most spectacular and descriptions of their various eruptions. He studied the pages with great interest and selected certain items for his own book. He was particularly impressed by two facts and said to me "Did you know that there were more than a hundred volcanoes in Iceland and that many volcanoes are under the sea?"

Sometime later he and Gerald worked with a mass of clay making a model of Vesuvius with a large crater. As they worked they discussed their ideas about how a volcano erupted. It seemed as if they were trying to externalise their thoughts in an attempt to understand the nature of a volcano.

As I helped John to find his way about the encyclopaedia, Martin, who was making a study of animals, came to ask how to spell "OKAPI." Teasing him I said "I don't believe such a creature exists." He immediately replied "Yes, it does: it is a member of the giraffe family. I'll draw you a picture of one." He quickly made a sketch to prove his point and then I said "We'll borrow this book from John and look it up. Accordingly we traced "OKAPI" in the encyclopaedia and discovered an illustration very similar to Martin's sketch. As he handled the encyclopaedia Martin was fascinated to see many sketches of extinct animals in its pages. He said: "When John has finished with it may I borrow the book to find out all about the animals I have never heard of?"

Meanwhile John discovered that the moon, as well as volcanoes, had craters. He now began to look for further information about the moon. He drew some pictures and then I saw him shew these to Christine and Pat and explain that the moon was not so big as the sun.

Pat said: "The moon is made of cheese."

John replied: "No, Pat, it isn't, that is just a fairy tale. The moon is made of rock and stone and it has big craters."

Christine said: "It is very cold on the moon, isn't it John?"

Then John tried to explain to the two girls some of the features of the moon but as they had no conception of what he was trying to describe he found it difficult. I joined in their discussion and produced pictures, pointing out the features I thought they could understand. The girls became interested and John was gratified and relieved to have his own knowledge elucidated and confirmed.

After I had given him the pieces of rock and lava he developed an interest in other natural phenomena. One day he brought a fossil and a bone to me and asked if he could make a museum. Again Graham helped him and we reorganised the classroom so that it would house a museum. John and Graham explained its purpose to the rest of the class who responded immediately by bringing a variety of exhibits from the past and present. John and Graham carefully labelled all the exhibits and, after discussions with their owners and me, wrote explanatory notes describing when and where they had been found. Their next suggestion was to place maps on the table so that the children could locate the places where the exhibits had been found.

In the scope of a short account it is not possible to describe the detailed development of this activity, but I hope that it will be seen how it could (and did) spread into different areas of the curriculum and included many children who were stimulated by it to follow their own interests.

Appendix A, VII
(This account describes the ways in which the children approached the study of living things).

A Nature Study Environment in the Classroom. First there was the Nature Corner which included a table, bookshelves and display wall. The children were encouraged to bring flowers and twigs and I tried to provide evidence of the changing seasons from further afield than their own garden. From time to time they had rabbits, mice, guinea pigs, hamsters and pigeons to care for. I made books with pictures of birds, animals, trees, flowers and insects and simple reading matter describing them; there were also attractively illustrated books, pamphlets and postcards.

Most of the children shewed a daily interest, browsing amongst the books and pictures, asking questions and making comments. Many were particularly interested in animals, familiar and unknown, and spent considerable time in looking for information about them. Several children began to make books in which they drew and labelled pictures of animals and then asked how to write about their habits and habitat. In this way a number of them became interested in reading and were soon reading the script fluently, recognising unknown words from the context.

Exploring the School Garden. At the beginning of November a genuine interest in plant and insect life began when Martin and Ann were looking at the pictures to see how many of the plants they could identify. They asked if they could go into the garden to "hunt for some of the things." The ground was hard and the trees bare, but this did not deter them. They were joined by Paul, Ronnie and Diane and later returned excitedly with the worms, wood lice and other creeping insects as well as twigs from evergreen shrubs. Because they were so enthusiastic I produced a glass tank and shewed them how to set up a wormery.

They made labels for all their "discoveries" and Martin wrote an account of their search. Diane painted a lovely picture of the five children searching the borders.

Following Up a Natural Interest. Before the end of the morning many other children had become interested in their exploits, so I suggested that

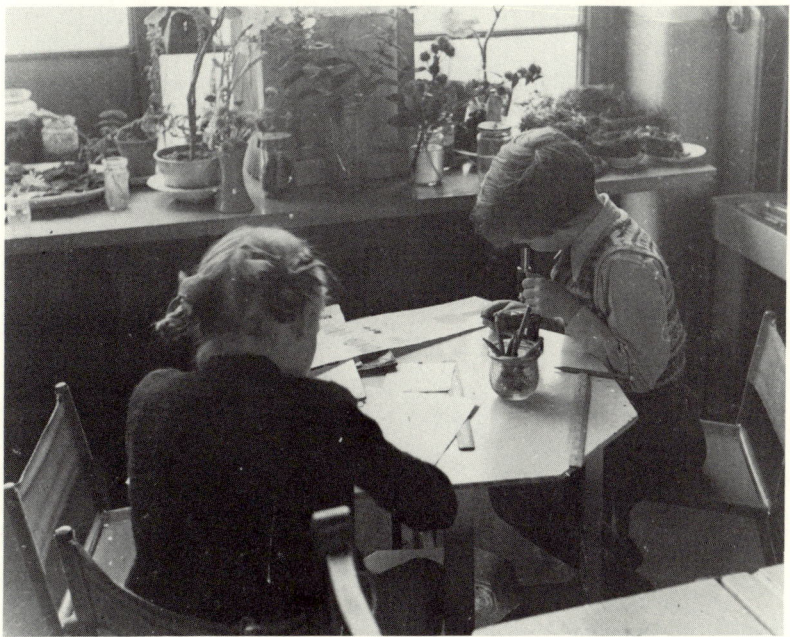

Two children at work on nature study

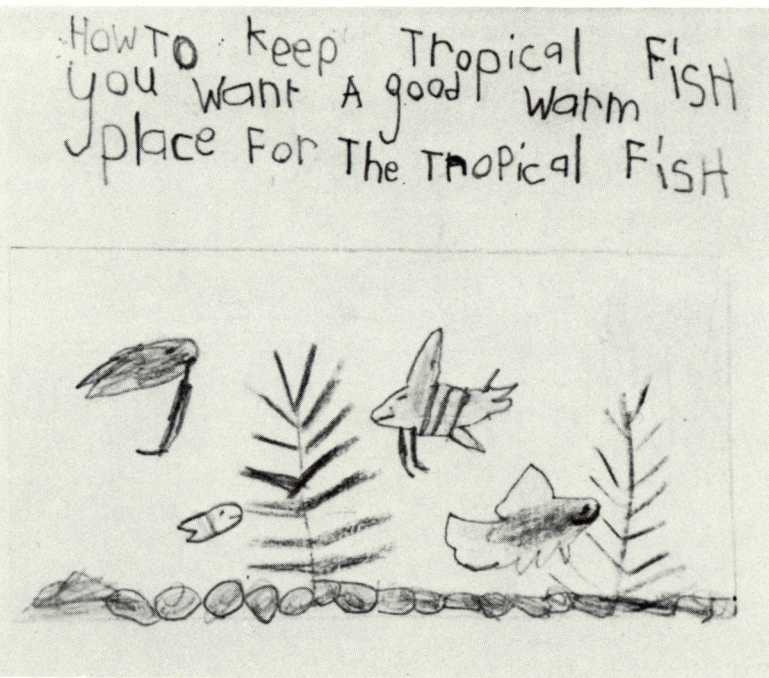

Pages from one child's own book

they gather round to examine what had been found. As we looked at the specimens the children commented on the usefulness of a Nature Table saying that it enabled you to look at things more closely than you could in their natural surroundings. I then produced a magnifying glass and small microscope and shewed the children how to use them.

Ann had found some moss so I suggested that she should plant it, water it, and examine it daily through the magnifying glass. I told her that last year when Bryan had done this he found a pretty blue flower growing in it. John said: "I expect a bird has dropped a seed in Bryan's moss." This comment led to a discussion about methods of seed dispersal in which I asked the children to name familiar seeds. They mentioned fruit "pips" and nut kernels and later planted some. I provided peas and beans which several children planted and then watched them germinate; I suggested several experiments such as planting them upside down or leaving them in the dark to see what happened. Ronnie and Paul planted cress seeds, watched them grow to maturity, then cut the leaves and made sandwiches. They recorded the stages of growth, the final illustrated entry reading "Tea for Two." David planted an onion and at regular intervals measured the roots and shoots; one morning a group of children were questioning him and their interest led me to talk to them about "food storage."

Other children brought bulbs and geranium plants and even weeds so that they would have something to "grow"; every day, contributions for the Nature Table were brought and identified.

Meanwhile Martin and Ann began to organize a Nature library, selecting suitable books, magazines and even pages from comics. They told the children how the material was arranged shewing them where to look for information. Their leadership was accepted by the others who used the library intelligently; many began to make their own "nature books." I encouraged them to shew these to each other and the ensuing questions led to talks about such topics as migration, hibernation and protective colouring.

Their interest continued through the winter months; the nature table was usually full, sometimes untidy but always vital and a result of their own spontaneous efforts. I could not help reflecting that my own well-ordered Nature Tables of the past had never been a source of such lively interest.

The Development of "Research Attitudes." With the coming of Spring everyone's interest was intensified. Ann and Martin were still the undisputed "authorities" in the Nature corner and spent some part of each day tidying, watering and re-labelling. In the meantime many children, including Martin, had become interested in some "Geographical Magazines." Martin said: "I am going to look through them to see if I can find anything about nature study." In a short time he had interested twelve children in the idea of cutting out appropriate pictures to make books for the library. Their work was purposeful and thorough; as they looked through the magazines they discussed different aspects of their activity. On certain pages they discovered maps; one child suggested that they should find out which animals and birds were natives of the countries represented by the maps; then another suggested finding out all the birds, animals and fish coming from one specific country. They compiled over thirty illustrated books of reference and in doing so discovered much new knowledge (such as whether polar bears hibernate — and what can be made from the llama's wool), which they eagerly shared with others in the class.

Exploring Further Afield. As the weather improved it became a delight to take them for regular walks to fields, woods and ponds. They were keen-eyed and searched with enthusiasm. Aquaria, stick insects and silk worms were now introduced to the Corner. Questions were asked both at home and at school and I told children and parents about the broadcast talks on the natural phenomena of the previous month.

Thus, their study continued both indoors and out, Martin and Ann quietly stimulating the interests of more children so that they had real delight in finding and recognising plants, pond-life and animals in different places. More often than not they would go to Martin, rather than me, for verification.

It is impossible to relate all that was said and done by the children and by me, but each week I was more aware that here was a *real* interest in a *real* environment and not merely in a subject. It was part of their lives and shewed itself in the eager anticipation with which they waited for the appearance of the earliest snowdrop, aconite, crocus, and catkin, and the birth of the first lambs. These arrivals were announced by the observers and acclaimed by the others with genuine feeling and personal satisfaction, and perhaps their whole attitude is most aptly summed up by Angela's remark as she was about to go home one winter afternoon, "I must hurry home before it gets dark because as soon as I get home

I am going to get into my old coat and Wellingtons and then I'm going out into the field to look for Nature."

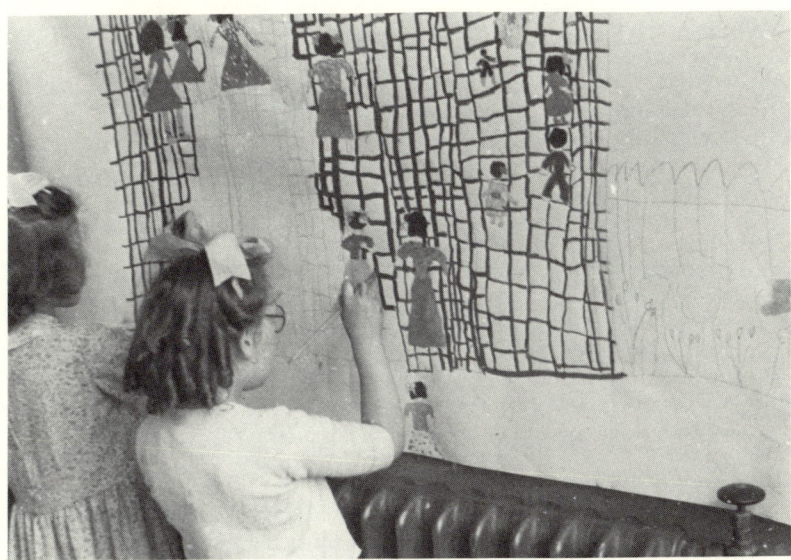
Large pieces of paper

Modeling figures

Appendix B

Suggested Materials and Equipment to Be Used in Infants' Schools

1. **Woodwork**
   Hammers, saws, nails, sandpaper, pieces of wood or wooden boxes, cheap paint when available for painting wooden things.
2. **Brick Building**
   Wooden blocks (varying sizes and shapes), ladders, steps, boxes, planks for construction and imaginative and dramatic play.
3. **Modelling**
   Large lumps of clay, boards, protection for table, aprons.
4. **Painting**
   Large sheets of paper, bright coloured paints (blue, red, green, and yellow), large brushes and for those children who have reached a stage when they like to draw first, pieces of charcoal or soft crayons.
5. **Cut Paper Work and Collage Pictures**
   Pieces of plain paper for background, poster paper in bright colours, a variety of fabrics and other materials, scissors and paste. Children cut out or tear from coloured paper and make pictures by sticking on to background.
6. **Construction from Waste Materials**
   Cardboard boxes, cartons, corks, cotton bobbins, spools from films, cardboard rolls, corrugated cardboard, wire string, old batteries, old wheels, pipe cleaners, crepe paper, etc. Do not tell the children what to do with these waste materials, but leave them free to investigate and experiment as they wish.
7. **Water Play**
   Baths, bowls, jugs, trough, rubber tubing, funnels, bottles, jars, spoons, rubber aprons and mats.
8. **Sand Play**
   Sand tray with sand, tins, pails, vessels of different sizes and pails, tin with holes in, spoons, water.
9. **The Wendy House**
   Where there is no house, try to screen off a corner of the room. Dolls, dolls' clothes, furniture, tea-set, cooking set, prams, cradles, beds and bedclothes.
10. **Dramatic Play**
    A box of dressing up clothes (these should be simple, but effective). Some of these should be for the children when they are playing at being grown up, others suggestive of imaginative and dramatic play, (e.g. hats, crowns, feathers, cloaks, aprons).
11. **Domestic Activities**
    Sweeping, polishing, dusting, scrubbing, brushing, cleaning shoes.
12. **Equipment for—**
    Bathing dolls, washing clothes, shopping, baskets, purses.

13. **Nature Corner and Interests**
    Children arrange flowers, water plants, set seeds. Children care for and feed such pets as rabbits, kittens, guinea pigs, pigeons. Aquarium.
14. **Garden**
    Wherever possible, the children should have the opportunity to dig, weed, hoe and plant and care for seeds and plants.
15. **Other Activities for Nurseries Include**
    Bright coloured chalks and blackboard, bead threading, attractive jigsaw puzzles, hammer peg toys and posting boxes.
16. **Large Pushing and Pulling, Climbing and Clambering Apparatus**
    Trucks, carts, wheelbarrows, trolleys, bicycles, swing boats, climbing frame, rope ladders, balance plans, big logs for stepping stones, balls, hoops, bean bags, skipping ropes.
17. **Quiet Corner for Picture Books and Story Books**
    Home-made books. These should be bright and strongly made. Attractive published books including stories, poems and books of reference.
18. **Sewing and Making and Dressing Dolls or Puppets**
    A box of brightly coloured materials — pieces left over from garments or old frocks cut up, braids, trimmings, needles, wools, cottons, fur, lace, net, beads.
19. **Writing Activities**
    Pencils, crayons, paper and little books for children wishing to write stories, poems, plays, prayers, and letters, books about personal interests.
20. **Musical Instruments**
    Record-player, bells, dulcimers, harps, chime-bars, percussion instruments, recorders and improvised instruments. Children experiment and compose tunes and make up words to tunes.
21. **Scientific Investigation**
    Equipment to stimulate an interest in "how things are made and how they work." Parts of old watches, clocks, gramophones, and other mechanical works. Insides of torches, magnets, iron and steel and brass filings. Small screw drivers. Equipment for simple experiments with air, gas, water, etc.

The above is a brief synopsis of some of the materials and equipment which we should aim at providing for the children. Many of these materials are cheaply and easily obtainable and the most important of all are the crude materials. With these the children find their own creative level at each stage of their development.

Some Mathematical Opportunities Arising Through Experiences Provided in the Classroom

In the Wendy House
1. Laying the table — matching groups to people — sharing biscuits, parting a cake, etc.

2. Playing with dolls – proportion – matching sizes – making doll's clothes – weigh and measure dolls (record by block graph).
3. Baking – purchasing ingredients – weighing and measuring same – temperature of even-timing cakes – selling produce.
4. Making curtains and furniture.
5. Working in a confined space – arranging furniture – sizes of equipment, fitting equipment into storage spaces.
6. Telephone – telephone numbers – distances – price of calls – keeping account book.
7. Seaside "Wendy House" – hotels – bookings.
8. Milk bar – bottles in crates – square numbers and triangular numbers.
9. Household accounts.

Bricks
1. Putting in order of sizes – counting – grouping – calculating (e.g. length of wall, number of bricks needed).
2. Building to measurement – area – capacity. Ground plans.
3. Shapes of bricks – fitting shapes – fitting into a box.
4. Principles of building – Tower Bridge – ramp – platform – walls of house – plumbline – spirit level.
5. Purchasing new bricks from catalogue.

Sand and Water
1. Behaviour – e.g. when poured – principles of cone.
2. Conservation – takes shape of vessel used – comparing shapes filled by same quantity.
3. Making a fountain.
4. Using a hose pipe – jet and spray – shape of course taken by water.

Making Pictures in varied media – paint, collage
1. Composition – arranging shapes in limited area.
2. Perspective – proportion.

Woodwork
1. Size and shape of pieces of wood – graded sizes of nails and screws.
2. Shape of tools and their purpose.
3. Measuring materials used.
4. Angles – purpose of right angle – principles of strength.
5. Solid shapes – constructing solid shapes from flat pieces.

Making Books
1. Calculating size of book, number of pages – half and quarter sheets – size of covers.
2. Counting and numbering pages.

Modelling
1. The discipline of materials used – e.g. clay – changing shape of lump.
2. From waste materials – measuring and estimating – length of wire, string, elastic.
3. Sizes of dowelling rods, clips and fasteners.
4. Cutting with economy from sheets of felt, tinfoil, paper, etc.

Sound Corner
1. Making a bottle organ — 8 bottles — amounts measured and level maintained.
2. Speed of sound — 1 mile in 5 seconds — calculate distance of cliff from school (sound and echo — double journey of sound). Distance of storm — crack of thunder (noise of flash of lightning) heard after flash is seen, e.g. 5 seconds after = 1 mile away.
3. Stretched rubber bands — length and sound.
4. Vibrations of piano string — e.g. frequency of tone "C" — 256 per sec. same sound at different levels — ½ length twice as fast "C" also — 512. Scale = ladder of tones: 256, 288, 324, 342, 384, 432, 486, 512.

Measuring
NB. Use equipment in real situations, e.g.
1. Measure height of each other — of shadows — of dolls and teddy bears — of own jump — make graphs. Ditto weight.
2. Weigh milk in bottle and bottle empty. How much? Stones and boulders.
3. Capacity, e.g. How much milk do we drink in a week, a year?
4. Timing, e.g. How long does it take?

Shopping — Using Real Money
1. Buying biscuits, nuts, fruit. Keep accounts and records of sales.
2. Buying paint for new book case, classroom equipment, etc.
3. Ordering food for a party, entertaining mothers on open days, etc.
4. Making doll's clothes, skirts and pinafores for self.

Junk Play and P.E. Apparatus
1. Balls in boxes — half dozen, dozen — ditto all small apparatus.
2. Bouncing balls — height — counting — throwing = parabola.
3. Skipping — timing — counting.
4. Games and scoring — length of pitches — surveyor's tape — chain.
5. Construction with junk — principles of lever, ramp, pulley.
6. How many children can crowd into a cubic yard?

Natural Investigation
1. Recording the weather — thermometer — indoor and outdoor — temperature graphs. Calendar. Rain gauge — milk bottle graph. Strength of wind — direction. Sun — hours of sunshine — rise and set. Barometer.
2. Growing plants — rate of growth — length of shoot — size and weight of bulbs — calendar and season.
3. The sky — cloud shapes — phase of moon (draw shape each night) — path of sun — stars and planets (distances and sizes).
4. Shells — shape and pattern — spiral.
5. Pattern in growth — Fibonacci sequence — sunflower head — petals.

Investigation Table
1. Magnets — how many nails? Weight of nails? Distance from magnet?
2. Magnifying glass — multiplication — microscope.
3. How does it work? Locks, hinges, doorknobs, taps, padlock.
4. Wheels of all sizes — relationship between diameter and circumference.

184 / ACTIVITY AND EXPERIENCE

5. Electrical equipment.
6. Machines and motors to dismantle — clocks — syringes — scent sprays — squeeze bottles.

Dramatic Play

Whole range of mathematical problems in everyday living. Children can be encouraged to talk about mathematical experiences and develop a mathematical vocabulary. They can be helped too to see the mathematics in any situation.

Appendix C
Experimental Work in Music

Consider the following points in relation to experiments in sound, rhythm and other musical experience of the children.

1. The development of musical growth in children.
2. The enrichment of children's lives through music.
3. Look for examples of happiness and satisfaction experienced by individual children through music work at school.
4. Look for examples of absorption and concentration through interest in musical experiment.
5. Note how the satisfaction gained through creating music stimulates the desire for further experience in creating music.
6. Make a note of which children are intuitively musical and pick out

Discussion about correct musical notation

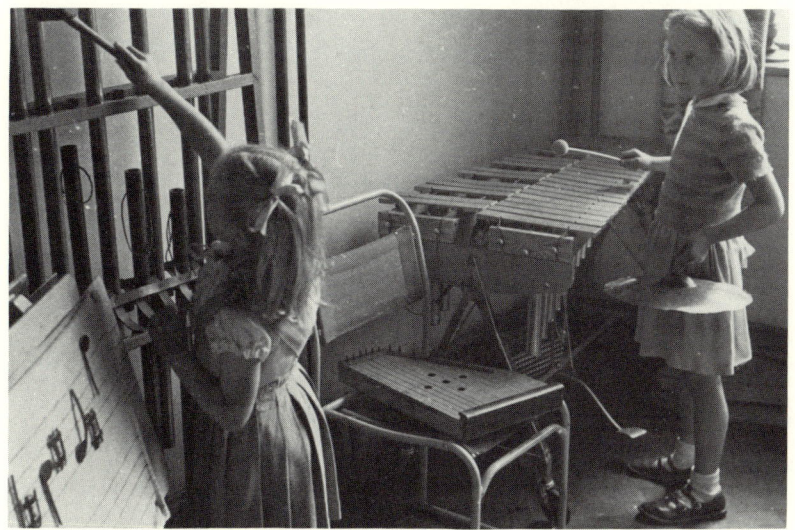

Trying out ways of playing the melody

Finished pages from a child's book

tunes in an apparently effortless way. Give these children many opportunities for musical experience.

7. Record examples of children's original tunes.

186 / ACTIVITY AND EXPERIENCE

Finished pages from a child's book

8. Notice which children continue to create tunes and songs with their voices after the fifth year. What is the effect of encouragement by the teacher?
9. Note the varying approaches to creating tunes on the different instruments, e.g.,
    (a) children who create tunes intuitively.
    (b) children who think out tunes.
    (c) children who know ("in their heads") what they want to play and try to find the tune.
10. Note the instruments in the environment, how they are used, especially the development and progression in their use. Consider the ways and means of stimulating development and progression, e.g.,
    (a) encouraging the children to think in phrases.
    (b) questions and answers in phrases (without reflection)
    (c) phrases to rhythms, to rhymes, to poems.
    (d) working in one key; starting from and returning home.
    (e) realising for themselves the necessary accidentals with a change of key.
    (f) picking out known tunes (playing by ear).
11. The development of musical memory. Look for examples of outstanding musical memory.
12. The writing of tunes. How does this develop? Note the tunes created by individual children and written down.
13. In what other ways has creative music work developed? How can it be used with other instruments?
    Can percussion work and other instrumental work with larger groups develop from individual work and the experiment of small groups?
14. What opportunities have the children for listening to music? What is their response?
15. How has the music work affected the life of the child?

Chapter 2
SOME FURTHER DOCUMENTS

This chapter contains three other original documents. One concerns some early work in art in Yorkshire and how a development was brought about. One describes what movement means in a child's growth. And the third is a chapter from a longer book, carefully analyzing what active inquiry means for children as they grow and develop. Each is written by an acknowledged expert in the field, and each deals with areas not often given much attention in the United States.

YORKSHIRE ART WORK

by *Ruth Scrivener Mock*

In the spring term of 1947 I was asked by the headmaster, Mr. James, to visit his junior middle school because a boy, Terry, aged I think 9, had won a local painting competition and his parents wanted to know if he should have special art teaching. The boy's work was skilful, but as far as I can remember it consisted chiefly of copying cartoons and advertisements from magazines, and so I told Mr. James that on this evidence it was impossible to judge whether the boy had any genuine talent, and also that at such an age he should be having enough practice in art and craft in his normal school curriculum.

I asked to see the art throughout the school, and my general impression remains of numerous small water-colour paintings, usually copies of drawings made by the teachers on the blackboard, all of which were in the how-to-do-it-book style and tradition. I remember particularly the trees done in Mr. Wright's class and his tree on the blackboard, and I said that I did not think that this was the best way to teach children either to appreciate the individual characteristics and beauty of a tree or to record in their own way their particular impression of it. Mr. Wright disagreed most vehemently, and in the subsequent break all the staff attacked me on my belief that drawing, painting and craftwork are creative activities which must be based on personal observation and sensibility, and experience in the use of different media. They did not seem to be willing to consider any method of teaching art other than that of copying and obeying certain inflexible rules, and so I left believing that it would be useless for me to visit the school again.

Mr. James came to the Bingley Vacation Course in the summer of 1947 and he was in my group. I think I devoted four sessions to drawing and painting (there were others in which we did modelling) and I took as topics: (1) the practical organisation of the media and equipment and of the room to be used for the art class; (2) the various media which are likely to be helpful and inspiring to a child and the possibilities in the use of them; (3) subjects which will extend a child's visual curiosity and appreciation both of the natural world and of the materials at his disposal, and finally (4) the quality of development and improvement which the teacher can justifiably expect and look for in a child's work and how he can assess it.

I chose these topics because I wanted to give the teachers as much practical help as possible at a time when materials were still in short supply and most schools were ill-equipped for creative work. I also wanted to emphasise the importance of the quality of the medium in drawing and painting and that each child must develop his own control of it if his work is to have any significance as a personal expression of his visual experience. I discussed subjects at some length to show how a wise choice of subject helps a child to realise through his own interest, and therefore most profoundly, some new aspect both of the visual world and of the media he is using. Finally, I hoped that the teachers would learn to enjoy and appreciate a child's natural, and considerable, achievement in drawing and painting, to realise how he develops at his own time and his own way, and to understand that while one never can, or should, anticipate the results of an art class — for every picture should be a surprise as the original expression of an individual experience — there are certain efforts which we must encourage, particularly in concentration and control.

During the course Mr. James sat at the back of the room with several other teachers from his district and they were very lively, but I did not know if they were getting any real help from any of the sessions. However, later in the following term Mr. James asked me to visit his school again and I found the transformation in the art work which is now well-known. Mr. James told me at that time that it was the discussions on the use and control of media which had helped him most on the Bingley Course and afterwards in presenting a different approach to art teaching to his staff. Incidentally, the work of the small boy Terry developed very well indeed.

THE IMPORTANCE OF MOVEMENT IN THE DEVELOPMENT OF CHILDREN AT THE PRIMARY STAGE[3]
by *Ruth Foster*

1. The discharge of energy in the form of apparently superfluous action is a characteristic of childhood. This is a stage when children run rather than walk, bounce up and down instead of standing, wriggle rather than sit still. Their joints are still flexible so that, anatomically speaking, they are highly mobile, and physiologically they "burn" (their metabolic rate is higher than that of adults) more fiercely than they will when they are older. Motion and emotion are linked conspicuously.

This stage seems to last right through the primary school, though it begins to fade in some girls towards the end of their last year. It may not be a "critical period," but where children are unable to enjoy it to the top of their bent it may well be that something has been lost forever, especially the capacity to explore, and to achieve the "impossible."

The restrictions of urban life, especially, perhaps, of suburban life, and those imposed by school may well have a quenching effect on this characteristic mode of childhood, though some schools, especially infant schools, may afford opportunities that are missing at home. It often appears that the more sedentary and sedate the regime in school, the more children seem given to surreptitious "mean" behaviour in the classroom, and to barbarous action outside. In such schools timetabled periods of movement must have as a first purpose the release of pent up energy, and it may be difficult to pursue other aims such as the development of skill.

2. Perception of weight, distance and size are gained through action; it is in traversing space that we realise it. It is true that a child's perception of weight and distance alters as he grows in strength and in length of limb, and that it will be set against his experience of actual measurement, but insight comes, in the first place, through action.

[3]. Reprinted by permission of the author.

3. A child's sense of identity, of himself as a whole, is built up in various ways, but kinaesthetic experience is a crucial factor in the process. Movement also plays an important part in a child's development of his image of himself, of his weakness, his power, his weightiness, lightness, strength, swiftness, skill or clumsiness. He extends this image by climbing high, by swinging and leaping through the air, by sliding, floating and swimming, and by his acts of identification with others. It is probably a process of identification, rather than of imitation, that leads him to take on characteristic modes of movement of his father and other adults.

4. Movement is one of the main, and perhaps the most immediate, means of expression, not merely in everyday communication, but also in those phases of exuberance referred to previously, and in the process of identification with both everyday and imagined characters and situations. The exuberant mode of movement leads to acts of agility (including running, jumping, "tumbling" and games) and towards dance; the process of identification develops in the direction of drama. It is usually agreed that in drama children come to terms with everyday situations, and that they also extend experience by exploring beyond them. It is not always understood that girls probably need to play masculine as well as feminine roles (a girl can be accepted by a mixed class as Perseus, Moses or even Bottom), and that boys should be able to be gentle and compassionate, as well as strong and vigorous.

April, 1964

WHAT ACTIVE ENQUIRY MEANS FOR THE CHILD[4]

by *Nathan Isaacs*

I

We have seen in earlier chapters [of Isaacs' book] the questions which children of the Primary School ages ask, the interests they express and the capacity they can display for following these through. We have watched them pursue far-reaching explorations with great zest and enjoyment and end up with the most worthwhile achievements.

The keynote of this volume has been that all the main activities required for both the pursuit and the appreciation of science are spontaneous

---

4. A chapter from *Approaches to Science in the Primary School* (1960) edited by E. Lawrence and N. Isaacs. Reprinted by permission of Mrs. Isaacs.

natural interests in most normal children. The present chapter aims at showing how we can go a vital step further. We can say that not only are these interests commonly present, but where at all marked, they represent important *needs* for the child's inward poise and happy growth. Thus in helping these interests to thrive to the utmost of each individual's capacity, teachers are not merely achieving invaluable educational ends, but also strengthening some of the main stabilising forces within the child.

From such an angle, however, we must look afresh at the five year olds who enter our Primary Schools, and what these schools can do for them. Naturally if all we want is to drill somehow into large numbers of them certain elementary skills and information, we hardly need to concern ourselves with them as persons. We know that they all differ in character and temperament, but our very aim is to get them as similar as possible, at least to the extent of this basic equipment. Anything more is not really our affair.

But once we do think of each child as a person and aim at getting him really interested and carrying him with us, we have to give a new attention to what everything we are trying to do for him means to him. And if we are to start from his own interests and to help him to advance educationally through the most constructive use of these, the need to understand how things look and feel from inside his mind becomes paramount.

We are of course still faced with individual differences of capacity and temperament which we have to accept. But we must now attempt to grasp at any rate the background needs and problems which most of our children are likely to share; that is, which as a normal result of their history during infancy and early childhood, they are likely to bring with them as they enter the Primary School.

In the course of the last decades, we have in effect greatly deepened our understanding of their first eventful years. We have therefore a far fuller and truer picture of what things signify for him, what he needs and why, and what can best serve his further growth. Above all, we have learned to appreciate, as never before, how the story of every child is one and indivisible from birth; how closely feeling and acting and learning, real inward learning, are intertwined in this story and depend on one another; and how impossible therefore it is to understand any one of these aspects of children's mental life without taking into account the interacting history of them all.

II

This story cannot be considered in any detail here; all we can do is to pick out a few main points that seem most important for real sympathetic grasp of the typical mental phase and outlook reached by the ordinary Primary School child.

(a) In the first few months an infant's life must mainly consist of alternating feeling states, with only the barest rudiments of the outer world entering in. These feeling states would seem to be already capable of great intensity: eagerness-joy-bliss-contentment-craving-distress-pain-disappointment-rage-fear are all strongly manifested in turn. But one thread that tends to run right through is the infant's state of almost complete helplessness and dependence which can get linked even with his bliss, that may be *withdrawn,* or his satisfactions, that may be *withdrawn,* to say nothing of the distresses, fears or pains that may be suddenly *thrust* on him. Yet over against this there are also the first faint beginnings of the future answer to helplessness: the first active turnings towards stimuli in the outer world, the first absorbed and following attention to what goes on there and even the first exercises of the infant's powers of *action.* Within a few months indeed these achieve their first great triumph: the hand learning to grasp what the eye perceives ushers in a new world of achievement. There is now really something to set off against the earliest all but complete helplessness; and the infant, as we know, makes the very most of this new *sense* of power.

(b) As the first year progresses and the second unfolds, the same sort of alternation of feeling-states continues, but in addition there are also thrown up particular protracted crises; for many infants that of weaning, for all the drawn-out process of teething. Again, these come on him helplessly and painfully. At the same time, however, he is making the most exciting and prodigious progress in what *he* can now do and achieve in the outer world. He learns to stand, to walk, to accomplish a variety of successful and satisfactory actions, to recognise more and more persons, things and situations and to foresee what is going to happen next. All this supports him and buoys him up against those other states of helpless dependence. Yet these become in a way more acute too; for as his scope and powers in the outside world grow, so does his awareness of it and with this his sense of all the things he cannot do, and above all of everything which he is restrained or prevented from doing. Indeed, as we know but he does not, the more his powers grow, the more does he need, in those early days, to be kept in check in his own interest. Moreover, his resentful but impotent chafings against such restraints become just one element more in a deep conflict of feelings inside himself, in which he is peculiarly helpless. From perhaps the latter part of the first year onward, as his sense of the main persons round him grows more and more distinct, they become for him the focus of directly opposite emotions and impulses; his mother means everything to him, yet also very often denies and thwarts and constrains him; his father, besides playing a similar alternating role, provokes his special hostility by frequently drawing the mother away from him. With these warring feelings, whenever they lay hold on him, the infant has no means at all of coping; but comes nearest to getting away from them as he exercises and further expands his rapidly growing powers in the outward role.

(c) In the course of the second year, these powers gain the further accession of the vast new one of language and communication. This quickly multiplies a hundredfold all his capacities for real achievement and all but creates for him a new capacity for phantasying and imagining, thus opening up for him a kingdom of make-believe might and accomplishment stretching immensely beyond everything — however much — he is now really able to do.

However, here once more there is an equivocal side to his advance. With his new powers come new lessons in dependence and impotence. He suffers a daily training in submission to an order of things constantly growing more unlike that of his "feather-bedded" first year. He must accept his mother's going about her own business, adapt to rules and routines, and learn to subordinate his will to other and superior ones. In particular he has to learn one great adaptation which often comes anything but naturally to him. From a very early stage he has taken the most absorbed interest in all parts of his own body and all that happens to them, not least among them his eliminatory functions, which readily get charged with specially strong feelings for him. These are of course for him experiences like any others, since he knows nothing yet of our taboos. However there comes a time when he becomes aware of ever heavier pressures on him to change his ways altogether about just these functions. He is expected to learn to behave quite differently and even to feel differently, and though presently he learns to do so, this happens rarely without some struggles and often only after a long and severe battle of wills.

This struggle is an important part of his inward history and indeed may well bring home to him in the most pointed way how powerless he still is. How reluctant his submission is apt to be and how superficial, may too frequently be evidenced by subsequent relapses. But he may be tried even more severely, especially should he be a first child, if during his first few years, a baby brother or sister comes on the scene, and he finds himself, virtually overnight, turned out of the place which has so long seemed all his own. It is not difficult, if one really tries to relive the whole experience with him, to grasp the catastrophic difference — all the losses and all the fears — which this sudden dramatic dislodgment *must* mean to him.

This succession of dramatic experiences, in all of which his mother is so centrally involved, add their own further complexities and tensions to the tangle of contradictory feelings in which the child is already caught up. They discharge themselves to some extent through his phantasies and make-believe play, but can also all too easily manifest themselves through every sort of arrest or disturbance in the tenor of the child's life: temper tantrums or night terrors, feeding difficulties or stubbornnesses or hostilities and aggressions, shynesses or phobias, or obsessional habits. In a large proportion of cases these, if not too severe, are happily left behind in the ordinary course of growth. But an essential part of this growth consists precisely in the child's sustained orientation to the world outside him and steady ever-increasing advance within it. From two to five he progresses by giant strides. Through his physical play he continually develops his powers of co-ordination and control and acquires new manual skills; at the same time with boundless curiosity and interest he explores, experiments, takes to pieces, puts questions, tries build up and construct and mold and fashion, compares and sorts and arranges, seeks new experiences and new worlds to know and conquer.

These are the very processes by which psychologically he grows and they constitute a natural hygiene to which he constantly turns. In this fashion he can break away from conflicts and oppressions and fears within himself and expand freely in a limitless larger world. But to understand all that this world means for him we must also be able to put ourselves back in his place, go through all the vicissitudes and drama of his early years with him, relive ourselves imaginatively his first utter helplessnesses and dependence, his slow struggles out of this, the plunges back into it which he suffers and the incessant outwardly directed activity by which he alone can make good his eventual emancipation. This sort of attempted view from within is what the present thumbnail sketch has tried to indicate.

By the age of five to six, if he has come through reasonably easily and successfully so far, his worst crises may well be over. He has normally established a tolerably settled relation to the world around him, both human and physical, and this would go with a fairly stable balance in his feeling life and a large measure of security and confidence both in people and in the scheme of things. To the extent of his habitual surroundings, he would have a reasonable notion of that scheme and would know generally what to expect of it and also what was demanded from him. We should see him as a typical five year old, running and playing, talking and asking questions, dramatising and pretending, eager to be taken around and shown things, but also to find them out himself, to do things, to construct, and so on. But the familiarity of this picture should not lead us to take it for granted and should not mask from us the fact that our apparently carefree five year old has behind him a long history, on the one hand of inner storms and stresses and on the other of intellectual growth and advance, in which he has accomplished a vast miracle of learning. This miracle we need to understand if we are to contribute anything towards continuing it. The attitudes of mind, the interests and the activities which have enabled the child to achieve the miracle, largely for himself, drawing whatever help he could from those around him but not class-educated or even tutored by them into it: these are assets still available to us. Ought we not therefore, by full understanding and co-operation, to make the utmost possible use of them?

III

If now, in the above broad sketch of the child's background history, we go back to the question of what the outer world means to him, we can sum up its value to him somewhat as follows:

(a) This world, as the child advances in it, proves to be one which is mainly stable and solid and bright and open, and to which he can turn with security and confidence. Things for the most part remain constant in it and he can rely on them and look ahead and act accordingly. In addition he can always go on exploring further and further; there is more to find out in every direction. Moreover his new gains very generally join up with what he has already discovered in such a way that his sense of understanding and of security is both consolidated and further extended. And all the time his activities secure him a double reward. First there is the excitement and satisfaction of each success achieved; secondly, there is the opening out of the field for more activity of the same kind, with the renewed sense of stimulus and forward-looking interest which this can bring.

(b) To these two rewards there is added the great further one of the child's expanding power of actually *doing* things. The "finding out" process itself leads him to acquire all sorts of new skills and abilities each of which carries with it new pleasure and a fresh zest. Any one such conquest moreover often serves as a bridge to others, so that the child's range and level of reward-bringing activities are constantly stimulated to advance in an ever-widening field.

(c) Moreover as part of the same cycle of processes he is always coming up against difficulties, obstacles and problems which act as a challenge but which – often with no more than a hint or a simple question from the co-operating adult – he can himself learn to resolve. This again can be a great exhilaration and triumph and at the same time a renewed spur and encouragement to go on.

(d) These trains of activity, in which one thing leads to another and the child can so readily become completely absorbed, have in exceptional degree the power of "taking one out of oneself." They are thus among the most effective means of breaking away from inner tensions and stresses and a means which the child's teachers can help him to put to the fullest use.

(e) There is also a less apparent way in which many of his "finding out" activities can render large aid to the constructive progress of his mental life. We know only too well that in most of us, children and adults, there is pent up a mass of disruptive and destructive impulses (strongly nourished, if not produced, by our early emotional vicissitudes) which present us with a most difficult problem of control. We recognise the importance of finding directions where they can be given their head so that they may as far as possible be diverted from disastrous channels. Now the one direction which most clearly stands out for its positive value is that of scientific knowledge. To advance this we must break things up to see what they are made of; we must take them to pieces to find out how they work; we must in fact practise the most varied forms of destruction and even keep learning new ways of destroying, precisely in order to learn. To serve its scientific purpose, it has of course to be a strictly controlled and carefully limited destruction (which, in the case of children, we should not allow at all to be applied to living things), but this fact itself can enhance its psychological value. For in most of us the very impulses to destroy are themselves deeply linked with strong impulses of remorse and contrition — impulses to repair and rebuild and make whole again. And the peculiar worth of destruction for the sake of learning and understanding is that we can so justly feel that it is being done for a positive and constructive cause. Scientific knowledge enables us to put right what has gone wrong, to relieve and cure ills, to synthesise and build and create in a thousand different ways.

All this of course need not be present to the minds of those who find special satisfaction in the more forceful ways of inquiring into things; but it is not difficult to see evidences of the processes at work, particularly in children. In them we can readily follow through all the transitions from just destroying to doing so *in order* to find out and then often *only* for this purpose, together with an increasing desire to use the "finding out" in order to restore, to set right, to construct and build. This kind of transition can then be encouraged and fostered, to the enduring benefit of the child's mental well-being as well as his educational progress.

(f) Finally — and here we may well have a particularly valuable bridge between the child and the community around him — the activities by which he enlarges his knowledge and understanding are usually "combined operations." At home there are most often co-operating adults; at school we have group or team enterprises led by a teacher. These operations give the child all the satisfactions of "doing things together," a continual sense of harmony and unison and an enhancement of power. And this is strongly nourished by the actual productiveness of such "finding out" missions and the manifold rewards which, as already described, they bring. Moreover as the team form develops, there is the feeling not only of working in co-operation, but of being carried along in a great enterprise. In this one is indeed playing one's own active part — so that all the time one is a member, it is what "we" are doing, but one is also sharing in something far bigger than one could oneself accomplish. Here, therefore, is a reassuring contrast to all the forces, within and without the child, that are so apt to draw him into rivalry and strife, and a living model, in which the child himself participates, of the satisfactions which harmonious co-operation can give and the great things which it can accomplish.

IV

These then are the values which the child's exploratory and allied activities in the outer world can signify for him. But how far they will in fact do so becomes now the teacher's problem — a problem partly, as we have seen, of restrictive conditions, but partly also of psychological understanding and patience and resource. The problem of understanding has here been our main concern; but even where this and all other needs are met, the Primary School teacher's task is no light one. The resources of young children are still very limited; their attention is quickly fatigued; they are easily distracted and diverted; and they are only very imperfectly masters in their own minds. Their mood may change, or a fit of obstinacy or defiance or quarrelsomeness may come over them suddenly. Thus the way may be blocked to the very kind of activity that might relieve and help them. These are the inevitable hazards of any teaching methods that seek to work *with* the child rather than to stamp a set pattern *on* him.

Yet a teacher who understands what he needs to do can through his steadfast support of the positive, constructive side of the child, make all the difference. He can get his children mostly so eager and absorbed that attention does not flag and is not distracted or blocked. His secret will be always to tempt them on, to keep them engaged, and to make them go on feeling that this is *their* adventure, *their* enterprise, *their* set of discoveries and *their* achievement. He will indeed also know when to stop; that is, when real unavoidable flagging and fatigue sets in. Yet he will throughout enjoy the sense that he is not only aiding children to learn, in the most real and lasting way, but also strengthening the forces of future growth in them. In one direction after another, he will be extending their power of setting their own further goals, finding their own way forward, keeping their own educational progress going. For every one of their roads of exploring, ordering and constructing, imagining and testing in the real world does in fact lead on endlessly. The great number of future non-scientists can thus be borne forward to the appreciation and enjoyment of science, and the smaller number of future scientists straight to its dedicated pursuit.

V

This is obviously still in many ways a simplified picture. It aims at making clear a point of view which seems both important and valid, but there are qualifications which must be recognised along with it. Thus:

(a) As was emphasised from the outset, children differ, in capacity and temperament and personal bent, so that there can be no one rule for them all. Apart from sheer native limitations which nothing can touch, there are variations of need which must be understood and met. The ways that lead broadly into the "scientific" world are for a good many children not their most helpful roads to inward balance or security or happy growth. Their road may be that of music or craftsmanship or modelling or writing or trying to excel in some bodily skill or game, or even the pure abstractions of mathematics. In a number of these children the exploring and allied interests may indeed also be strong, and if so, everything which encourages and enriches them may still have much inward feeling-value over and above its educational one. In other instances, however, there may be little such interest or response, and this fact needs equally to be accepted. Throughout, the teacher can only give his most valuable help by co-operating with whatever marked personal interests there are, as faithfully as he does with the would-be scientific ones.

In general the teacher can only go by what he finds — but can only find by sympathetically and patiently *looking*. In some children the "exploring" motive springs will be found so vigorous that all that needs to be done is to open ways for them. In other cases, though present they may be fitful, hesitant or self-unsure; here the teacher may need to coax them on or to infuse confidence. Even where various soundings have elicited little or no interest, the teacher may need to think of the possibility that it may merely be blocked in those directions. By dint of patient trying he may discover ways through which he *can* unlock new gates for real and fruitful growth in the child. The possible directions of growth are after all as manifold as our world itself. The material in this book shows that these are no impracticable counsels of perfection, but roads that may well be open for most teachers with most children and there is usually no lack of response and counter-encouragement from the children themselves as they go along.

(b) It must be recognised that education which seeks to take these forms establishes a new relation between the school and the children's homes. If they are not only to learn by their own active enquiries, but also to derive inward support and help from doing so, the efforts of the school may well be defeated unless the climate of the home marches reasonably with them. Otherwise the child may merely be involved in new emotional difficulties and conflicts. A girl of nine, whose mother held views diametrically opposite to those of her favourite teacher, was cruelly teased by her older brother about this clash. "Whom do you believe," he asked, "mother or teacher?" The little girl replied at once, "I believe teacher." But then, overcome with confusion and a sense of betrayal, she rushed to her mother and added, "But I love mommy." This situation may not always be avoidable, though it need not be thus wantonly brought to a head. However, it illustrates how important it may be for teachers to explain to parents what they are trying to do and why, and to draw them, if at all possible, into active interest and co-operation. This, though increasingly accepted in principle, is still too largely the exception rather than the rule. Yet clearly the kind of education that seeks to get inside the mind of the child and to help him in every way to grow from within will only finally prosper if parents can be induced to play their part no less than teachers. They must somehow come to see their own vital share in this enterprise. Instead of taking "schooling" for granted, rather like other municipal services and thinking of it as just the drilling of some needed gimmicks into their children's minds, parents must view it as an essential part of their children's *lives* and thus in every sense also *their* affair. They must be persuaded into sympathetic and lively participation in what the teacher and school are trying to do; and they must give their own encouragement and best help to their children who are seeking to grow by questioning and inquiry, exploration and experiment. It would be this kind of co-operative and harmonious effort that would bear the fullest fruit.

VI

The further chapter which follows* presents the actual case of a child who has *not* been able to find his way into the outer world. It is a first hand account by psycho-therapist of a boy for whom that way became blocked at a very early age, and who thus became gravely ill and utterly incapable of normal growth. The therapist, however, found the means of helping him through her psycho-analytic insight into his terror of the real world and her grasp of the vicious circle in which he thus became self-imprisoned. Her study shows how liberation was achieved and how the process of growth was allowed to make a fresh start. It will be seen how the whole problem was pivoted on the attainment of that confident and active reaching out into the world which we tend to take so much for granted in our normal children. But by the same token we may realise how much can

*Not included in this excerpt.

turn on the success with which our schools are able to nourish that sense of confidence and carry it further. It is a major trust placed in the teacher's hands and we can see again how greatly he can contribute towards making it into a true instrument of continuing growth.

BIBLIOGRAPHY

While I was in England, since I was traveling most of the time, meeting and talking with people, I was unable to read as much as I might have during a longer stay. Thus I made no effort to read *everything,* as anyone expert in the field will soon see. Instead, I concentrated on searching out source material which was directly relevant to my work. I read the two major periodicals from the early years of this century; some books of theory, both philosophical and psychological, which pioneer teachers told me had been helpful to them in their teaching; as many of their personal accounts as I could find, both anecdotal reports on work in their schools, and manuals for teaching in child-centered ways; the important government publications which presented an official point of view; historical works about English innovative education; and some recent books about English education which are not widely known in the United States.

For a more general listing of books on informal education and British infant schools, the reader might do well to turn to Lillian Weber's *The English Infant School and Informal Education* (Englewood Cliffs, N. J.: Prentice-Hall, 1971) or to Roland Barth's *Open Education and the American School* (New York: Agathon Press, 1972). Both contain extensive bibliographies which are worth consulting. Also, since their publication, an important set of books has come out which the reader would find useful, namely, a group of twenty-three small volumes dealing in specific and practical terms with many aspects of the work in good British primary schools today. The Anglo-American Primary School Project was funded by the Ford Foundation in the United States and by the Schools Council in England; under the editorship of Joseph Featherstone (who is also the author of the introductory volume) the results were published simultaneously in both countries as *Informal Schools in Britain Today* (New York:

Citation Press, 1972). Readers interested in the theory and practice of British informal schools should consult these references. I do not intend to duplicate them, although a little overlapping is inevitable.

Periodicals

The two leading periodicals in the period between the world wars were, clearly, *Education for the New Era* and *The Bulletin of the National Froebel Foundation* (later called simply *The Froebel Journal*). *The New Era,* as its title implies, was the voice of the progressives who had formed the New Education Fellowship, which was later expanded to become the World Education Fellowship. Beginning in the 1920's, their journal published articles about many aspects of progressive education, especially those descriptions of theory or practice which were in line with their belief in education as the fundamental method of building a better world. Thus, Dewey appeared early in their pages, and others familiar to Americans, such as Kilpatrick, A. S. Neill, Rugg, and Montessori, as well as early notices of the work of Piaget, Susan Isaacs, Decroly, Cizek, Viola, Adler, and many others. There were also first-hand accounts of successful schools, written by obscure teachers with great charm and simplicity, and having a decidedly modern ring. There was regular interest in education in other countries — often a whole issue would be devoted to the work of one particular nation, such as Poland or Denmark. And especially before World War II, there were many articles about education as mankind's last, best hope for democracy in a world where such a hope was growing dimmer.

The Froebel Journal shared *The New Era*'s basic attitudes toward what made for a sound education for the world's children, and therefore the two periodicals had some authors and concerns in common. Yet *The New Era* was somewhat more political and social in its tone, and *The Froebel Journal* more psychological and philosophical. Neither of them, however, published any articles on the administrative details of operating a school, presumably because their editors assumed that a sound philosophy of education would produce equally sound practices as a matter of administrative course. One is reminded again that head teachers in England are exactly that and that in the United States the profession of school administration has moved far from the classroom and developed a language and expertise of its own.

In particular, *The Froebel Journal* is noteworthy for its early and continued emphasis on the importance of studying child development, in all its aspects, and its reprints are still widely sold and read. Again, there was early discussion of Freud, as well as of the publications of Anna Freud and Melanie Klein, as they appeared, usually reviewed and commented upon by Susan Isaacs. And Piaget was read with great care beginning in the 1930's with the early translations of his work. Thus, study of the emotional and cognitive growth of children was a regular feature of the journal, as well as ongoing work in schools which seemed to promote such growth.

One or two articles might be mentioned among the many worth attention. In the issue for April, 1948, M. Langdon's "Active Methods of Learning for Large Classes in the Junior School" appeared. It was a study of practical and gradual ways of bringing about change in the junior school based on the long experience of the author. This article shows, again, that at least some people were thinking about moving "infant school methods" upward toward the junior schools quite early on. Another article of historical interest is a pair of short pieces appearing in the issue for October, 1969: "Dorothy Simpson, M.B.E.," and "The Park Infant School." The former is one of several articles dealing with the life and work of major teachers and heads of informal schools; the latter is written by Mrs. Glynn, Miss Simpson's associate at the Park School (whose work is described in considerable detail there and in Part II of this book), work which had been underway and well-known since 1935.

One other article was of particular interest to me: Nathan Isaacs' essay, "Piaget's Work and Progressive Education," published in 1955 as part of a group of essays called *Some Aspects of Piaget's Work,* which went through eight editions up to 1965 and is still available. This article is an especially lucid account of the connections between Piaget's work on child development and the goals of the progressive wing of educational thought, particularly the Froebelian strand of it in England.

Other important pamphlets or reprints still published by the National Froebel Foundation are as follows:

The Junior School Today, by B. Ash and B. Rapaport.
Activity and Experience in the Infant School, by E. H. Walters.
Activity and Experience in the Junior School, by E. H. Walters.
Piaget: Some Answers to Teachers' Questions, by Nathan Isaacs.
What is Required of the Nursery-Infant Teacher in This Country Today?, by Nathan Isaacs.
Designing Primary Schools.
Children Learning Through Scientific Interests.

Learning Through Creative Work, by B. F. Mann.
Scientific Interests in the Primary School, by G. Allen and others.
Froebel and English Education, by E. Lawrence.
Early Scientific Trends in Children, by Nathan Isaacs.
Practical Nature Study in Town Schools, by M.M. Hutchinson.
Mathematics in the Primary School, by M. Ironside and S. Roberts.
Discovering Man's Habitat, by I. Doncaster.
The Place of Play in an Infant and Junior School, by G. E. Cooper.
The Growth of Understanding in the Young Child, by Nathan Isaacs.
New Light on Children's Ideas of Number, by Nathan Isaacs.

One other article came my way that might escape notice otherwise; it is Ruth Foster's "The Analysis of Movement — A Current Conception and the Reasons for It," published in a special issue of *The Advancement of Science,* No. 64 (March, 1960), entitled "Physical Education." Miss Foster's article deals with the analysis of movement that stems chiefly from the work of Rudolf Laban, who came to England in 1936, and with the significance of that work as it has spread and developed in English schools, much to the benefit of the children. For the American reader, it expands and deepens the understanding of this uniquely English school activity.

A final note about the publications of these periodicals: the great majority of the authors are women. The English custom of using only first initials masks the fact that often the "B." stands for "Barbara," the "E." for "Evelyn," and so on. There is no question that many of the leading authors, and therefore the leading thinkers and writers in the progressive school of educational thought, were women.

Educational Theory

A few books of educational theory should be mentioned aside from Sir Percy Nunn's book, dealt with at length in Part I, Chapter 4. There were many others, each with its own viewpoint, and often the teachers whom I met would have a particular favorite which they shared with me. John Dewey's books were widely read, perhaps more so in England than in his own country: *School and Society,* published in 1899, *The Child and the Curriculum,* in 1902, as well as other works later on. Bertrand Russell wrote *On Education* in 1926, which went through nineteen editions up to 1971 and is still available.

The philosophy of Friedrich Froebel has been a very important part of English educational thinking since the mid-nineteenth century. His

Mother's Songs, Games, and Stories came out in England in 1885, *The Education of Man* in 1887, and *Pedagogics of the Kindergarten* in 1900. In 1896, Kate Douglas Wiggin published a three-volume examination of Froebel's thought entitled *The Republic of Childhood*. Volume I was entitled *Froebel's Gifts,* Volume II *Froebel's Occupations,* and Volume III *Kindergarten Principles and Practice*. Although these books were written in a style not much used today, they are helpful explanations and attempts to modernize Froebelian ideas in an English setting.

Other books concerned with child development and the psychology of sound growth date from a similar period. In 1901, Margaret McMillan's *Early Childhood* came out, a moving description of the work and thinking behind the McMillan sisters' extraordinary teaching of very young children. This was followed by *The Nursery Years* in 1919. Dr. Maria Montessori came to England and was widely acclaimed there and ran a series of training courses for teachers between 1919 and 1938. The Froebelian tradition, however, meant that English educators felt that her contribution was limited to her pioneering medical description of child development and to her willingness to free the child for individual work with materials and furniture and equipment planned especially for him. However, many of her works were and still are read with interest, such as *The Montessori Method* (1912). Alfred Adler's *The Education of Children* appeared in 1939, presenting a psycho-analytic (though not Freudian) point of view about children's emotional development. In 1931 came Kathryn Bridges' *Social and Emotional Development of the Pre-School Child,* and in 1935 appeared both Ruth Griffiths' *A Study of Imagination in Early Childhood* and Charlotte Bühler's *From Birth to Maturity*.

Later on, the work of Arnold Gesell and his colleagues in the United States attracted a good deal of attention in England; although it is now considered oversimple, nonetheless it did provide an easily understood way of looking at growing children which coincided with the experiences of many teachers. Undoubtedly the greatest impact, however, in the area of psychological theory came from the two streams of work by Freud and by Piaget. In the 1920's, Susan Isaacs and others were studying Freud's writings and publishing reviews and explanations of it in periodicals. In 1935, Anna Freud's book *Psychoanalysis for Teachers and Parents* was published, soon followed by the work of Melanie Klein. Dr. Isaacs' own contributions to the growing literature on child development were *Intellectual Growth in Young Children* (1930) and *Social Development in Young Children* (1933).

These were based on her pioneering experiment with children at the Malting House School in Cambridge, which she directed from 1924 to 1927, and on her analysis of the ways in which children develop naturally when given the freedom to do so. For many years thereafter, she lectured and wrote of her findings, often using active teachers to give a practical dimension to her theoretical framework. *The Children We Teach* dates from 1937, as does *The First Two Years*. In 1948 came *Children and Parents: Their Problems and Difficulties* and also *Childhood and After*. Then in 1942, Miss D. E. M. Gardner succeeded Dr. Isaacs at the Department of Child Development of the University of London Institute of Education. Miss Gardner had published *The Children's Play Center* in 1937, and *Education Under Eight* came out in 1949. In 1942 she published an attempt to trace the results of progressive work in infant schools, *Testing Results in the Infant School;* this work was later expanded upon in 1966 and republished as *Experiment and Tradition in Primary Schools,* a controlled and objective study of the results of two kinds of schools, experimental and traditional. Surprisingly, this last-mentioned work remains nearly the only careful comparative study of the actual results of British primary schools. In 1965 she and Joan Cass brought out *The Role of the Teacher in the Infant and Nursery School,* and, finally, in 1969 she wrote a biography of her cherished friend and mentor: *Susan Isaacs: The First Biography.*

This does not exhaust the books one could mention in the field of child psychology, but my intention was to speak of the early and influential ones and then to trace the specific publications of two important figures in the field.

Books by Practicing Teachers

Another group of books I found especially interesting were the accounts written by practicing teachers; some were descriptions of the work in a particular school, and some were practical handbooks for younger teachers who needed help in moving from traditional ways to methods based on children's activity and experience. Some of these are as follows:

> Vicars Bell, *The Dodo* (n.d.).
> E. R. Boyce, *Play in the Infants' School* (1938).
> E. R. Boyce, *Infant School Activities* (1940).
> E. R. Boyce, *The First Year in School* (1953).
> Nancy Catty, *Learning and Teaching in the Junior School* (1954).

Homer Lane, *Talks to Parents and Teachers* (1928). (See also E. Baseley's *Homer Lane and the Little Commonwealth,* (1969.)
Lillian DeLissa, *Life in the Nursery School and in Early Baby Hood* (1949).
Sybil Marshall, *An Experiment in Education* (written in 1963 about work in a school just after World War II).
Edna Mellor, *Education Through Experience in the Infant School Years* (1950).
A. S. Neill, *Summerhill: A Radical Approach to Child Rearing* (1960, but published earlier as well about work in the 1930's).
Dorothy Simpson and Dorothy Alderson, *Creative Play in the Infants' School* (1950, about the Park School, founded in 1935).
Elizabeth Taylor, *Experiments with a Backward Class* (1946).
Frances Tustin, *A Group of Juniors* (1951).
Edith Warr, *The New Era in the Junior School* (1937).
Edith Warr, *Social Experience in the Junior School* (1950).

There are by now many accounts of current work being done in the British primary schools, most of which appear in the two bibliographies already mentioned. The above list is given with dates to show that earlier accounts did exist, both before and just following World War II, and all describing teaching which had been going on long before it. Again, the reader will note how many women authors are represented (E. R. Boyce is Mrs. Francis Coleman), since it was mainly women who were teachers in these years.

Government Publications

There is also a distinguished group of government publications which must be mentioned, since they represent an official point of view at the time each was written. There were, to begin with, the famous reports of the committee chaired by Sir Henry Hadow: in 1926 came the first one, a report on education for adolescents, in 1931 one on primary schools, and in 1933 one on infant and nursery schools. The last two, in particular, "were not descriptions of a dream but statements based on experience," writes one of the witnesses for that committee (29) whom I met. He goes on, "The experience was well founded, but it was limited to a small fraction of the schools of this country;" clearly the importance of the Hadow reports is that they did notice, describe, and thereby encourage the good work going on in that small fraction of English schools. And as I noted already it is to the Hadow Report of 1931 that we owe the now-famous statement — many times quoted to me — "The curriculum is to be thought of in terms of activity and experience rather than of knowledge to be acquired and facts to be stored." To some extent, at least, this was an official position within education circles in the government, and it gave fresh heart to HMI's, head teachers, and teachers whose instincts were congenial to that point of view.

There were also the Handbooks of Suggestions for Teachers, the first of which appeared in 1905 and later ones in 1918, 1937, and 1944, and finally *Primary Education,* which appeared in 1959 and which updates and summarizes the earlier ones (see Part I, Chapter 4). It is noteworthy that these handbooks were subtitled "Suggestions for the consideration of teachers and others concerned . . .," and their intent was not to impose a set of dicta from on high but merely to present descriptions and discussions of good practices as observed in actual schools.

Part I, Chapter 4, also deals at length with the famous *Story of a School,* published in 1949, which was also a government publication. In 1952 there appeared *Moving and Growing: Physical Education in the Primary School.* It is listed as Education Pamphlet No. 24 in Her Majesty's Stationer's Office and gives both pictures and narrative to explain the importance of teaching movement. Although by English custom the author's name is not given, this book and its second volume were written by Ruth Foster (11). John Blackie's *Inside the Primary School* was written in 1967. It is now available in the United States through Schocken Books; it remains one of the clearest and most thorough accounts of the informal British primary schools. In 1967 also came the famous 2-volume Plowden Report, *Children and Their Primary Schools,* of which Volume I is perhaps the most useful to the general reader, as Volume II contains a good deal of statistics.

Historical Works

No such project as mine could have been carried out without some historical reading, and I list below those books which were of especial use and interest to me. Their titles give the reader a fair idea of the contents, so that further comment seems unnecessary:

W.H.G. Armytage, *Four Hundred Years of English Education* (Cambridge: Cambridge University Press. 1964).

G. W. Bassett, *Innovation in Primary Education* (London and New York: Wiley, 1970).

H. A. T. Child, *The Independent Progressive School* (London: Hutchinson, 1962).
Elizabeth Lawrence, *The Origins and Growth of Modern Education* (Baltimore: Penguin, 1970).
Irene Lilley, ed., *Friedrich Froebel: A Selection From His Writings* (Cambridge: Cambridge University Press, 1967).
G. A. N. Lowndes, *The Silent Social Revolution: An Account of the Expansion of Public Education in England and Wales, 1895-1965* (Oxford: Oxford University Press, 1969).
W. J. McAllister, *The Growth of Freedom in Education* (London, 1931).
O. Barbara Priestman, *Froebel Education Today*, 2nd ed. (London: University of London Press, 1952).
W. Kenneth Richmond, *Education in England* (Harmondsworth: Penguin, 1945).
R. R. Rusk, *Doctrines of the Great Educators* (London and New York: Macmillan, 1965).
R. J. W. Selleck, *English Primary Education and the Progressives, 1914-1939* (London: Routledge and Kegan Paul, 1972).
W. A. C. Stewart and W. P. McCann, *The Educational Innovators*, 2 vols. (London: Macmillan, 1967).
William Van der Eyken and Barry Turner, *Adventures in Education*, (Harmondsworth: Penguin, 1969). Chapter 1 deals with the Malting House School; Chapter 3 is entitled "Art and Craft: Marion Richardson and Robin Tanner."
Nanette Whitbread, *The Evolution of the Nursery-Infant School* (London: Routledge and Kegan Paul, 1972).

Other Books of Interest

It remains only to mention a group of more recent books, now in print in England. Some are psychological, some are descriptive, some are analyses of current practices. But in general, unlike the many books describing the British infant school, these have received little attention in the United States.

Lady Allen of Hurtwood, *Planning for Play* (London: Thames and Hudson, n.d.). This book describes the author's work in establishing "adventure playgrounds."
M. Ash, ed., *Who Are the Progressives Now?* (London: Routledge and Kegan Paul, 1969).
John Blackie, *Inspecting and the Inspectorate* (London: Routledge and Kegan Paul, 1970).
E. B. Castle, *The Teacher* (Oxford: Oxford University Press, 1970).
M. Brearley, ed., *Fundamentals in the First School* (Oxford: Basil

Blackwell, 1969). Now published in the United States by Schocken Books under the title *The Teaching of Young Children*

E.B. Castle, *The Teacher* (Oxford: Oxford University Press, 1970).

Sir Alec Clegg, ed., *The Changing Primary School: Its Problems and Priorities. A Statement by Teachers* (London: Chatto and Windus, 1972. New York: Schocken Books, 1972).

Philip Gammage, *Teacher and Pupil* (London: Routledge and Kegan Paul, 1971).

G. M. Goldsworthy, *Why Nursery Schools?* (Letchworth, Herts.: Garden City Press, 1971).

S. C. Mason, ed., *In Our Experience: The Changing Schools of Leicestershire* (London: Longman Group, 1970).

S. C. Mason, ed., *The Leicestershire Experiment* (London: Councils and Education Press, 1957).

Susanna Millar, *The Psychology of Play* (Baltimore: Penguin, 1968).

E. H. Walters and E. B. Castle, *Principles of Education* (London: Allen and Unwin, 1967).

Finally, there are two books which present the opposing point of view: one is R. S. Peters' *Perspectives on Plowden* (London: Routledge and Kegan Paul, 1969), and the other is the collection done by Cox and Dyson of the celebrated *Black Papers* (London: Davis-Poynter, Ltd. 1971).

RESPONDENTS

The following thirty-nine people were kind enough to answer my questions, and, in most cases, to record their ideas and recollections on tape. Although I met many more than thirty-nine people, and the Acknowledgments are intended to express my thanks to them all, these were the source people from whose words chapters 2 and 3 of Part I are derived. Some of the 39 have not been quoted directly, but their recollections have been most helpful in formulating my own thinking. The number preceding each name is used after the quotations which belong to each person, for purposes of identification if desired. I did not put the name after each quotation because I felt that doing so would distract the reader from the overall, general impact of their words taken as a whole. But this list is intended for those who know the people in the field and wish to find out who said what.

It is also intended to show the caliber of people whom I contacted. I was extremely fortunate in being passed from one major figure in the educational world to another, and although I did not meet everyone who would have been helpful or worthwhile to talk with, I feel that I did meet a large proportion of the people who were able to speak with authority on my topic. Further, the reader will note that I talked not just with early teachers and/or HMI's, but rather with a wider variety of people than that. And in my visits and travels, I met and talked with an even greater variety of people, whose names, again, appear in the Acknowledgments section. Thus in three months I cast my net as widely as time and distances would permit, and I feel fortunate that I was able to reach so many people and hear so many points of view in that brief time.

It should also be understood that every one of the thirty-nine people on this list has been offered the chance to read and edit Chapters 2 and 3 of Part I, in which their words appear. I wrote to each, asking for written permission to use their remarks and offering to send those two chapters for them to check over. Many availed themselves of this opportunity, and I

214 / ACTIVITY AND EXPERIENCE

must acknowledge with thanks the careful editing job done by several. In one or two cases, indeed, the material was almost wholly rewritten, and the results of such care mean that my text is much more accurate and vivid. Also, a few of these people have kindly gone over the entire manuscript, and I have benefited very much from their corrections and comments.

Following is the list, then, alphabetically arranged and with at least some biographical data of interest supplied by each person.

1. **Lady Allen of Hurtwood, FILA**
   Inventor and founder of the "Adventure Playgrounds"
   Hon. Vice Pres., Institute of Landscape Architects
   Vice Pres., Nursery School Assn. of Great Britain
   Founder and President, World Organisation for Early Childhood Education (OMEP)
   Publications: *The New Small Garden; Design for Play; New Playgrounds; Play Parks;* and *Adventure Playgrounds*

2. **John Blackie**, M.A. (Cambridge University)
   Taught at Lawrenceville School, N. J., USA, and Bradford College, Cambridge
   Her Majesty's Inspector of Schools (1933-1966)
   Chief Inspector (1952-1966)
   Assessor to Plowden Council (1963-1966)
   Part-time Lecturer, Homerton College of Education, Cambridge (1966-1970)
   Senior Counsellor, Open University (1970-1973)
   Senior Tutor, National Extension College (1973)
   Companion of the Order of the Bath
   Publications: *Inspecting and the Inspectorate* (1970); *Good Enough for the Children?* (1963); *Inside the Primary School* (1967); and *Changing the Primary School* (1974)
   (16, 20, 32, 38, 42, 48, 61, 70, 77, 79, 81, 84, 122)*

3. **E. R. Boyce** (Mrs. F. Coleman)
   Head teacher, Raleigh School, Stepney, London (1932-1936)
   Her Majesty's Inspector of Schools (1936-1939)
   External examiner of education in training colleges:
   Universities of London, Durham, Leeds, Wales, etc. (1946-1956)
   Contributor to *Child Education, Nursery World, Education, Teachers World*, etc.; Author of *Play in the Infant School* (1938); *Infant School Activities* (1939); *First Year in School* (1953); *Today and*

---

*These are the page numbers on which direct quotes appear. Where a quotation runs on more than one page, the number given is that of the page on which it begins.

Tomorrow (1962); *Gayway Series of Reading Books and Materials* for Macmillan (1955); and *Individual Materials for Use in the Teaching of Reading* (1956)
(21, 39, 40, 46, 50, 69, 71, 73, 74, 82, 123)

4. **Miss M. H. Bradley** (deceased)
Formerly head, Bedford Froebel Training College
Later connected with the Institute of Education, Cambridge University
(24, 25, 32, 67, 69, 77, 79)

5. **Molly Brearley**
Formerly Principal, Froebel Institute
Educator, writer on education, teacher of children aged 3-18, as well as college and university students.
Publications: Edited *Fundamentals in the First School* (U.S. title, *The Teaching of Young Children*) (1969); with Elizabeth Hitchfield, *A Guide to Reading Piaget* (1966)
(19, 27, 28, 33, 38, 80, 81, 107)

6. **Kate C. Brown**
Teacher at a private school near Manchester (1905-1906) and at Froebel Practising School (1909-1911) and at a school near Glasgow (1911-1918)
On staff of Education Dept. of Froebel Institute, Roehampton (1923-1952)
In charge of Grove House School, Froebel Institute
(28, 46)

7. **Sir Alec Clegg**, M.A., L.L.D., D.Lit (York and Clare College, Cambridge)
Teacher of languages, St. Clement Danes Grammar School, London
Educational administration in Worcestershire, Cheshire, Birmingham
Chief Education Officer, West Riding, Yorkshire (1945-1973)
Member: Furniture Development Council, Council of Industrial Design, Schools Broadcasting Council, National Advisory Committee on the Training and Supply of Teachers, Central Advisory Committee for Crowther and Newsom Reports, University Grants Committee, Ass'n. of Chief Education Officers (President, 1965), Social Science Research Council, ITA Educational Advisory Council, Governing Council of the Open University, and governor of two independent schools
Publications: *The Excitement of Writing* (1963); *The Changing Primary School* (1972); *Revolution in the British Primary Schools* (1971); *Enjoying Writing* (1973); and *Children in Distress*, with B. Megson (1968)
(17, 18, 20, 22, 23, 38, 53, 67, 76, 80)

8. **Edith Cranitch** (deceased)
Head of Pasture Road School, Goole, Yorkshire, into the 1950's
(20, 23, 40, 45, 52, 53, 63, 74, 123)

216 / ACTIVITY AND EXPERIENCE

9. **Emilie Davies**
   Teacher in urban schools, as assistant head and head teacher, for 18 years, mainly at primary level
   His Majesty's Inspector (1942-1965) at primary level
   Other work: direction of National Primary Courses, service on central committees, chairman of divisional committees, primary adviser to colleagues and schools. Since retirement: in-service training of teachers in England and overseas
   Contributions to publications of the Inspectorate
   (16, 20, 24, 39, 63, 66, 67, 68, 73, 85, 107)
10. **Miss S. M. C. Duncan**
    Her Majesty's Inspector (1945-1971)
    Seconded to Plowden Committee (1963-1966)
    Staff Inspector, primary and middle schools (1966-1971)
    Contributions to Ministry of Education and Dept. of Education and Science, to the Plowden Report, and to research
11. **Ruth Foster**
    Many teaching and advisory posts, especially in movement
    Her Majesty's Inspector
    Vice-principal and head of Dance and Drama, Dartington College of Arts (1965-1971)
    (23, 25, 36, 41, 54, 55, 59, 61, 68, 110)
12. **Mrs. Dorothy M. Glynn** (formerly Dorothy M. Alderson)
    Assistant, then Deputy Head Teacher, Park School, Doncaster, Yorks. (1935-1952)
    Lecturer at University of London, Manchester, Sheffield, Exeter, Reading, Leeds, Oxford, Southampton, Nottingham
    Tutor and co-lecturer with Dorothy Gardner, University of London
    Tutor to National Nursery Examination Board Certificate Course
    Governor of National Froebel Foundation
    Principal Lecturer in Education, Clifton College, Nottingham
    Publications: two papers for Plowden committee; articles for *Froebel Journal, New Era, Child Education,* etc.; *Creative Play in the Infant School* (1950), with D. Simpson; *Teach Your Child to Read* (1963); and *The Dominoes* (1972)
    (25, 35, 40, 41, 44, 56, 63, 66, 67, 70, 109, 112)
13. **Mrs. G. M. Goldsworthy**
    Teacher at Bedales School (1923-1925)
    Staff of Gipsy Hill Training College, heading their demonstration school (1925-1939)
    Superintendent of three war-time nursery schools
    Organiser and then Inspector of Nursery Schools in London
    Fellow of the Royal Society of Arts
    Publications: numerous articles and lectures on nursery education;

Part-Time Nursery Education (1963); and *Why Nursery Schools?* (1971)
(19, 21, 25, 26, 46, 58)

14. **Mrs. Evelyn Lawrence Isaacs**, B.Sc.Econ., Ph.D.
    Teacher in London schools, (1913-1926)
    Assistant to Susan Isaacs, Malting House School, Cambridge (1927-1929)
    Chief Social Worker, London Child Guidance Clinic (1929-1930)
    Lecturer in Education, National Training College of Domestic Subjects (1930-1943)
    Director, National Froebel Foundation (1943-1963)
    Married Nathan Isaacs (1950)
    Publications: *Intelligence and Inheritance* (1930); edited *Friedrich Froebel and English Education* (1952)
    (20, 21, 29, 50)

15. **Eglantyne M. Jebb**, C.B.E.
    Lecturer in Education, Birmingham University
    Principal of Froebel Institute (1937-1945)
    Author of papers in educational journals over the years
    (62, 63, 109, 118)

16. **Mr. G. C. Mabbutt**
    Student at Emergency Training College (1946-1947)
    Teacher in London primary schools (1947-1959)
    Headmaster, Hotham Primary School, Putney, London (1959-1966)
    Lecturer/Senior Lecturer, Furzedown College of Education, London
    Publications: *Religious Education,* with J. Holm (1964-1965); Series of six books for primary schools; *Topic Books, Laws, Books 1 & 2* (1971)

17. **Miss J. Mack**
    Her Majesty's Inspector of Schools, infants level
    Lecturer in Education, Leeds
    (21, 38, 59, 61, 62, 64, 70, 82, 83)

18. **Sybil Marshall**, M.A.
    Unqualified assistant teacher, South Woodham Primary School, Essex (1937-1940), then at Huntingdon School
    Head teacher, Kingston County Primary School, Cambridgeshire, (1942-1960)
    Lecturer in Primary Education, Institute of Education, University of Sheffield (1962-1967)
    Reader in Primary Education, University of Sussex (1967–)
    Educational adviser to Granada Television for "Picture Box"
    Consultant and in-service workshops in the United States (1966, 1971, 1972, 1973)

218 / ACTIVITY AND EXPERIENCE

    Publications: *Experiment in Education* (1963); *Fenland Chronicle* (1966); *Adventure in Creative Education* (1967); *Aspects of Art (5-9)* (1968); *Creative Writing* (1973); and *Expression,* books 1-6 (37, 45, 50, 66, 67, 68, 82)

19. **Stewart C. Mason,** C.B.E., M.A., Hon.D.Sc., Hon. ARCA
    Asst. Master, Harrow School
    His Majesty's Inspector of Schools (1937-1939, 1944-1947)
    Director of Education for Leicestershire (1947-1971)
    Curator, Institute of Contemporary Prints (1972—)
    Other work: National Advisory Council on Art and Design, National Council for Diplomas in Art & Design, Trustee of Tate Gallery, Trustee of National Gallery, Member of Victoria and Albert Advisory, Standing Commission on Museums and Galleries
    (70, 84)

20. **Mrs. Ellen C. Mee,** C.B.E., M.A.
    Lecturer in education and English, Bristol University and Goldsmiths' College (1921-1929)
    His Majesty's Inspector of Schools (1929)
    Staff Inspector for Training of Teachers (1945)
    Advisory Committee on Education in the Colonies (1938-1952)
    Assistant Secretary, McNair Committee on Training of Teachers, (1942-1944)
    Chief Inspector, Ministry of Education (1952-1958)
    Consultant, Schools Broadcasting Council, since 1963
    (27, 36, 37, 39, 59, 64, 68, 72, 78, 79)

21. **Margaret Metcalfe-Smith**
    Some years teaching children under 12
    Training students for infant, nursery, junior schools, at Fishponds College, Bristol, Whitelands College, London, and City of Leeds College (1934-1939)
    Lecturer in Primary Education, University of Leeds (1950-1969)
    In charge of Advanced Diploma in Primary Education of experienced teachers, University of Leeds
    Student and associate of Susan Isaacs
    (76)

22. **Rae Milne**
    Teacher and lecturer in college of education
    Area Adviser, West Riding of Yorkshire, since 1958
    (13, 17, 25, 51)

23. **B. H. Montgomery**
    Teacher and then Headmaster, King Alfred School (1944-1962)

24. **Edith Moorhouse,** O.B.E.
    Head Teacher

Training College Lecturer
Senior Adviser for Primary Education, for Oxfordshire County Council (1946-1968)
Author of various articles in educational press.
Chapter I of *Teaching in the British Primary School,* edited by Rogers
(16, 26, 30, 37, 41, 43, 54, 57, 67, 69, 72, 75, 79)

25. **Lady Plowden**
Chairman, Central Advisory Council (England) (1963-1966)

26. **Olga Barbara Priestman**
Teacher of English in several girls' high schools and in the Froebel Institute of Education
Headmistress for 23 years of Froebel Demonstration School, including evacuation years
Teacher of English and teacher training work for ten years in Jamaica, B.W.I.
(16, 26, 34, 39, 53, 57, 58, 59, 64, 67, 68)

27. **Barbara Rapaport**
Principal Lecturer in Education, and responsible for junior students, Froebel Institute, College of Education
Publications: *Creative Work in the Junior School* (1957), with B. Ash; and *Skills in the Junior School* (1960)

28. **Mrs. Lorna Ridgway**, M.B.E.
Teacher and headmistress of primary schools, inner London area, for 29 years
Lecturer, Stockwell College of Education, Bromley, Kent; now Senior Lecturer, since 1963
Teacher, University of London, Institute of Education
Publications: Co-Author of *Family Grouping in the Primary School* (1965) and *Education and Social Work* (1967)
Director of educational films: *Children Are People* (1970) and *Task of the Teacher* (1973)
(21, 29, 37, 62, 69, 73)

29. **Christian Schiller**, C.B.E., M.C., M.A.Cantab.
His Majesty's Inspector of Schools (1924-1955)
Senior Lecturer, University of London, Institute of Education (1955-1963)
(12, 18, 52, 62, 65, 69, 70, 72, 83, 85, 86, 122)

30. **Dorothy Simpson**, M.B.E.
Head teacher in Doncaster, Yorkshire, (1924-1935)
Head teacher of Park School, Doncaster, (1935-1953)
Author of *Creative Play in the Infants School* (1950), with D. Alderson
(13)

31. **Thyra Smith,** O.B.E.
    Various industrial and teaching positions
    His Majesty's Inspector of Schools (1928-1950)
    Author of *Stories of Measurement* and *Story of Number*
32. **Lisl Steiner**
    Teacher in nursery and infant schools in London
    First warden of Childrens Centre, University of Leeds (1954-1961)
    Principal Lecturer in Education, and Head of Department of Nursery Education, University of London, Goldsmiths' College (1961–)
    Other work: consultant to UNESCO committee on pre-school education in Hamburg, Germany, member of Consultative Committee of Schools Council (U.K.), Research on Pre-school Education, Chairman of Consultative Committee of Schools Council, Research on Early Language Development
    Author of "Back to the Drawing Board in Early Childhood Education," *Ideas* (October, 1973)
33. **A. L. Stone**
    Teacher of boys aged 13-14 for 7 years
    Teacher in a Borstal Institution for 2 years
    Head teacher of two junior schools
    Drama Adviser for Worcestershire for 2 years
    County Council Inspector (Yorkshire) for 18 years
    Part time lecturer in College of Education since 1963
    National Courses for Primary School Teachers, Ministry of Education (1947-1965)
    (19, 29, 53, 77, 85)
34. **Robin Tanner,** R.E.
    Art teacher in London and Wiltshire until 1935
    His Majesty's Inspector of Schools, (1935-1964) specialising in art and primary education
    Publications: Author of *Children's Work in Block-Printing* (1930's) and *Lettering for Children* (1930's). Illustrator of *Wiltshire Village* by H. Tanner (1939) and *Flowers of the Meadow* by G. Grigson (1950)
    Many original etchings now in Boston Public Library, and in Ashmolean Museum, Oxford
    (15, 21, 22, 39, 52, 61, 70, 72, 122)
35. **Miss Beatrice Vint,** M.B.E.
    Asst. teacher of children 3-8 years old in Leeds (1909-1922)
    Head mistress (1922-1949), including being Head of Blenheim Demonstration School, Leeds College of Education, for 14 years.
    Lecturer and tutor for summer schools organised by local Education Authorities, Nursery School Association, and Froebel Foundation
    (23, 43, 51, 71, 74, 81)

36. **Elsa Hopkins Walters**, Ph.D., D.Litt.
    Teacher of primary grades for 14 years
    Senior Lecturer at two training colleges for teachers
    University of West Indies, training primary school teachers for ten years
    Deputy Director of Institute of Education, B.W.I.
    (16, 26, 34, 39, 53, 57, 58, 59, 64, 67, 68)

37. **Edith B. Warr**
    Headmistress of High March School, Beaconsfield, (1925-1948)
    Senior Lecturer in Education, Offley Training College, Herts. (1950-1961)
    Tutor, Primary Department, Cambridge Institute of Education (1961-1967)
    Part-time tutor, Royal College of Nursing, Dept. of Education (1963-1969)
    Examiner in Teaching for National Froebel Foundation (1932–)
    Extra-mural examiner, University of London (1966-1969)
    Organiser of Education Course for Physiotherapy Students from Overseas, in conjunction with WHO and International Physiotherapy
    Publications: *The New Era in the Junior School* (1937); *Social Experience in the Junior School* (1950); and various articles in educational journals
    (14, 19, 26, 28, 57, 62)

38. **Monica M. Withers**
    Teacher (1923-1938)
    His Majesty's Inspector of Schools (1939-1961)
    (14, 21, 29, 33, 34, 42, 47, 49, 59, 71, 84, 123)

39. **Charles H. Zoeftig**
    Teacher of children aged 4-18, especially 5-12 group
    Head teacher of two schools in London
    Senior Lecturer in Education, Avery Hill College of Education and Battersea College of Education
    Tutor to New York University students (1960-1965) on "Education in Europe" annual tour
    Contributor to various educational publications
    40 years' service with the London Education Authority
    (21, 29, 44, 47, 61)